W9-ACD-811

WITHDRAWN

Gramley Library
Salem College
Winston-Salem, NC 27108

WALT WHITMAN

THE CENTENNIAL ESSAYS

WALT WHITMAN

Edited by Ed Folsom   Drawings by Guido Villa

UNIVERSITY OF IOWA PRESS   IOWA CITY

Gramley Library
Salem College
Winston-Salem, NC 27108

University of Iowa Press, Iowa City 52242
Copyright © 1994 by the University of Iowa Press
All rights reserved
Printed in the United States of America

No part of this book may be reproduced or used in any form or by any
means, electronic or mechanical, including photocopying and recording,
without permission in writing from the publisher.

Printed on acid-free paper

01 00 99 98 97 96 95 94 C 5 4 3 2 1
01 00 99 98 97 96 95 94 P 5 4 3 2 1

Library of Congress Cataloging-in-Publication Data
Walt Whitman: the Centennial essays / edited by Ed Folsom; drawings
   by Guido Villa.
         p.   cm.
   Includes bibliographical references and index.
   ISBN 0-87745-459-0 (cloth), ISBN 0-87745-462-0 (paper)
   1. Whitman, Walt, 1819–1892—Criticism and interpretation.
   I. Folsom, Ed, 1947–   .
   PS3238.W369   1994   93-40838
   811'.3—dc20   CIP

TO GAY WILSON ALLEN
Dean of Whitman Scholars

Contents

viii CONTENTS

Acknowledgments

"WALT WHITMAN: The Centennial Conference," held March 26–29, 1992, in Iowa City, Iowa, was made possible by grants from the National Endowment for the Humanities and the Iowa Humanities Board. A generous gift from Esco Obermann allowed scholars and translators from outside the United States to gather in Iowa City for a seminar at the University of Iowa Center for Advanced Studies immediately following the conference. Jay Semel, director of the Center for Advanced Studies, and Lorna Olson, administrative assistant, provided extraordinary support.

For help too vast and various to specify, I thank Victoria Brehm, my administrative assistant, who worked her organizational magic to make it all happen. Vicki negotiated with travel agents, reservation clerks, internationally famous poets and scholars, chefs, talented musicians, television crews, designers, and artists and managed not only to keep her own sanity but to preserve mine. Nina Metzner, assistant editor of the *Walt Whitman Quarterly Review*, provided invaluable assistance, and my research assistant, Dan Lewis, developed Whitman software and was instrumental in the editing of this volume of essays.

Pat and Ben uncomplainingly did without the usual family spring-training trip so that this remarkable gathering of talent could occur, and I thank them, as always, for their love and support.

Abbreviations

AP   Horace Traubel, ed., *An American Primer* (1904; rpt., Stevens Point, Wis.: Holy Cow! Press, 1987).

BB   Arthur Golden, ed., *Walt Whitman's Blue Book* (New York: New York Public Library, 1968), 2 vols.

CORR   Edwin Haviland Miller, ed., *Walt Whitman: The Correspondence* (New York: New York University Press, 1961–1977), 6 vols.

DN   William White, ed., *Daybooks and Notebooks* (New York: New York University Press, 1978), 3 vols.

DT   F. DeWolfe Miller, ed., *Drum-Taps (1865) and Sequel to Drum-Taps (1865–66): A Facsimile Reproduction* (Gainesville, Fla.: Scholars' Facsimiles and Reprints, 1959).

EPF   Thomas L. Brasher, ed., *Early Poetry and Fiction* (New York: New York University Press, 1963).

HT   Horace Traubel, *With Walt Whitman in Camden*. Vols. 1–3 (1905–1914; rpt., New York: Rowman and Littlefield, 1961). Vol. 4 (Philadelphia: University of Pennsylvania Press, 1953). Vols. 5–7 (Carbondale: Southern Illinois Press, 1964, 1982, 1992).

LG   Sculley Bradley and Harold W. Blodgett, eds., *Leaves of Grass: Comprehensive Reader's Edition* (New York: New York University Press, 1965).

LG55   Malcolm Cowley, ed., *Leaves of Grass: The First (1855) Edition* (New York: Viking, 1959).

LG60 Roy Harvey Pearce, ed., *Leaves of Grass, 1860 Facsimile Text* (Ithaca: Cornell University Press, 1961).

MLG Fredson Bowers, ed., *Whitman's Manuscripts, Leaves of Grass (1860): A Parallel Text* (Chicago: University of Chicago Press, 1955).

NF Richard Maurice Bucke, ed., *Notes and Fragments* (Ontario, Canada: A. Talbot, 1899).

NUP Edward F. Grier, ed., *Notebooks and Unpublished Prose Manuscripts* (New York: New York University Press, 1984), 6 vols.

PW Floyd Stovall, ed., *Prose Works, 1892* (New York: New York University Press, 1963–1964), 2 vols.

SL Edwin Haviland Miller, ed., *Selected Letters of Walt Whitman* (Iowa City: University of Iowa Press, 1990).

TV Sculley Bradley, Harold W. Blodgett, Arthur Golden, William White, eds., *Leaves of Grass: A Textual Variorum of the Printed Poems* (New York: New York University Press, 1980), 3 vols.

UPP Emory Holloway, ed., *The Uncollected Poetry and Prose of Walt Whitman* (Garden City, N.Y.: Doubleday, Page, 1921), 2 vols.

Introduction

"Generations Hence"

Others will see the islands large and small;
Fifty years hence, others will see them as they cross, the sun half an hour high,
A hundred years hence, or ever so many hundred years hence, others will see them,
Will enjoy the sunset, the pouring-in of the flood-tide, the falling-back to the sea
of the ebb-tide.

. . .

I am with you, you men and women of a generation, or ever so many generations hence.

("Crossing Brooklyn Ferry," LG, 160)

IN 1987, five years before the hundredth anniversary of Walt Whitman's
death and less than a year before his own death, Charles Feinberg, the
great collector of Whitman materials, called me and said it was time to
start thinking about the Whitman Centennial. He had already been thinking
about it quite a bit, and at the time of that phone call he was devastated about
a letter he had received from a prominent librarian at the Library of Congress,
where Charlie had donated his monumental collection of Whitman books,
manuscripts, and materials. The librarian, in response to Charlie's request that
the Library of Congress organize an appropriate Centennial exhibition and
program, had stated flatly that there would be no special recognition for
Whitman in 1992 because "1992 would be Columbus's year." The nation's library, it seems, had decided on a Columbus-only celebration, and the officials
wanted nothing to dilute what seemed at that time destined to be a year of joy
dedicated to the commemoration of the Genoese mariner's great voyage of
discovery. The Whitman Centennial, said the librarian, would not be a no-
table event; perhaps, if they got around to it, they would display the manuscripts of Whitman's "Columbus" poems in some corner of the opulent
Columbus exhibit.

What a difference five years makes! Nineteen ninety-two turned out to be
something of a bust for Columbus admirers, who endured a year of seeing
their hero denigrated as a representative of imperialistic European hegemony
in the New World. There were Columbus conferences, to be sure, but they
ended up interrogating his voyages of discovery more than celebrating them.

While the Library of Congress stuck to its guns and refused to acknowledge the Whitman Centennial in any meaningful way, other groups and organizations around the country and around the world turned their attention to the good g(r)ay democratic poet. In 1992, Whitman was honored in major programs and conferences from Philadelphia to Fresno, from Miami to Los Angeles—and in Italy and Spain and Germany and England and Portugal and Argentina. New York City put on a series of exhibitions and symposia lasting two months. The premiere performance of a new symphony based on *Leaves of Grass* took place in Tokyo; a feature film on Whitman appeared in Canada; and major journals in France, South America, and the United States devoted entire issues to Whitman.

But the major international gathering of Whitman scholars took place in Iowa City, Iowa. "Walt Whitman: The Centennial Conference" opened on March 26, 1992, one hundred years to the day after Whitman's death. Over 150 Whitman scholars attended and heard papers by twenty of the world's most eminent critics of Whitman. There were sessions on Whitman and Biography, Whitman and Language, Whitman and Sexuality, Whitman and Politics, Whitman's Influence on American Poetry, and Whitman's International Influence. After each session, participants divided into seminars and carried on discussions with the presenters. These lively exchanges, sometimes lasting a couple of hours, often extended to dinner conversations and colloquies long into the night. Following the main conference events, Whitman translators and scholars from ten different countries held a two-day seminar at the University of Iowa Center for Advanced Studies; they discussed the problematics of translating Whitman's poetry and investigated his absorption into the literary traditions of other cultures. During the Centennial Conference, Whitman lived again not only in the circulating energy of talk about him but also in a remarkable series of events surrounding the conference, events that brought him alive in music, poetry, photographs, and even in a recording of his voice.

The opening night's session was covered by a crew from CBS's "Sunday Morning" and was also featured on National Public Radio's "Morning Edition," as well as in feature articles in the *New York Times* and other newspapers across the country. That night, exactly a hundred years after it was silenced by death, Whitman's voice filled the room once again. Thomas Edison in 1889 had written that he wanted to make a recording of Whitman, and a copy of what appeared to be the long-lost wax-cylinder recording of Whitman reading four lines from his 1888 poem "America" resurfaced just months before the conference. The recording was reengineered to remove background noise and improve sound quality, and Whitman's newly refurbished voice sounded out once again, clearer than ever. Listeners across the nation were able to debate the authenticity for themselves, as that opening night event was televised by CBS and the recording played on NBC Radio, CBS Radio, and NPR. That night I also showed wall-sized projections of all 130 photographs of Whitman, the earliest taken when he was in his twenties, the last taken just months before his death. Many of those in attendance commented on the eerie sense of a restored presence as Whitman's voice and visual image were once again embraced by the ears and eyes of the present. The poet who, more than any other American writer of the nineteenth century, celebrated technology turns out to have been better preserved by technology than any of his contemporaries—he is the most photographed American writer who died in the nineteenth century and the only one to have his voice preserved.

On the second night of the conference, Whitman came alive in song, as David Gompper (with mezzo-soprano Katherine Eberle and bass-baritone David P. Meyer) presented a retrospective of vocal music inspired by Whitman's poetry, including the earliest Whitman song (Frederick Louis Ritter's setting of "Dirge for Two Veterans" [1880]), the seldom-performed setting of "Ethiopia Saluting the Colors" (1915) by the black composer H. T. Burleigh (a song greatly admired by Langston Hughes, among others), and more familiar pieces by Ned Rorem, Ralph Vaughan Williams, and Kurt Weill. On the third night, Whitman lived in the voices of four prominent "Poets to Come." James Galvin melded his own Whitman-inspired poems with Whitman's poetry; Jorie Graham gave a stunning reading of "Crossing Brooklyn Ferry" that made the poem sing in a different key than anyone had heard it in before; Gerald Stern chanted Whitman with his inimitable passionate affirmation; and Galway Kinnell read from his favorite Whitman poems, then read his own rewriting of Whitman's compost themes in a poem on "Shit." On the final afternoon of the conference, participants witnessed the "battle of the Whitmans," as the two best-known Whitman performers—Bruce Noll and Carrol Peterson—put on their Whitman shows one after the other. Noll's younger, lean and energetic Whitman, poetry in motion, complemented Peterson's genial, portly, conversational older Whitman, who reminisced about his life and answered questions, often furtive as an old hen. "Homage to Walt Whitman," a major exhibition of Whitman paintings and drawings by the Italian artist Guido Villa, was open throughout the conference, and Villa himself was there to answer questions about his powerful visual reconstructions of Whitman. The illustrations in this book reproduce several of Villa's works that were on display during those days.

But the heart of "Walt Whitman: The Centennial Conference" was the series of original essays presented by some of the most innovative and important scholars working in the field of American literature. My goal, when I first talked to Charlie Feinberg about this conference, was to bring together three generations of Whitman scholars and create a forum where the generations could talk back and forth to each other. This dream became a reality when the most eminent senior Whitman scholars—Gay Wilson Allen, Roger Asselineau, C. Carroll Hollis, and James E. Miller, Jr.—all agreed to prepare new papers. These four scholars were honored at the conference as "Centennial Scholars"; they all published their first essays on Whitman at least thirty-five years ago. The middle generation of Whitman scholars—those who had been students of the senior group—includes Harold Aspiz, V. K. Chari, Arthur Golden, Jerome Loving, Robert K. Martin, Joel Myerson, and Alan Trachtenberg; they began publishing on Whitman in the 1960s or early 1970s. The emerging new generation of Whitman scholars—Betsy Erkkila, Walter Grünzweig, George B. Hutchinson, M. Jimmie Killingsworth, Vivian Pollak, Kenneth Price, M. Wynn Thomas, and James Perrin Warren—have made their major contributions within the past fifteen years, and some quite recently.

It is appropriate that this collection of Centennial essays begins with Gay Wilson Allen's overview of Whitman biography. Allen's first publication on Whitman appeared sixty years ago, only forty years after Whitman's death. His work on Whitman—from his *Walt Whitman Handbook* to his definitive biography, *The Solitary Singer*, to his general editorship of the *Collected Writings of Walt Whitman*—has made him the towering presence in Whitman scholarship. In a very real way, commentary on Whitman over the past four decades has been an ongoing extended footnote to Allen's work. In this new overview of Whitman biography, Allen raises the key issues that occupy the other distinguished scholars whose works make up this volume: the problematic significance of Whitman's sexuality; his attitude toward the developing structures of socialism and labor; the intriguing way he was embraced by socialist and communist thinkers; his interrelationships with other cultures; his remarkable lexicon that fused the mystical, the divine, and the physical; and the recent turns in Whitman studies toward issues of language, politics, and sexuality. In tracing the difficulties that Whitman biography had in getting started (the very first generation of Whitman scholars had only hagiography, much of it composed by Whitman, to depend on), Allen ends by suggesting that his own kind of biography "may have gone about as far as it can" but that there is still room for some creative new approaches to biographical issues.

The next several essays in the volume indicate what some of those new approaches might be. Jerome Loving suggests that one direction Whitman biography might move in would be the writing of biographies of the poet's early biographers, for only then would we come to know the motives behind the originating biographical constructions of Whitman, constructions that became the foundation for our own troubled understanding of the poet's life. In his essay, Loving offers original research on the life of Henry Bryan Binns, Whitman's first "objective biographer." In the story Loving tells, we gain insight into Binns's portrayal of Whitman's sexuality, and we see some of the power struggles involved in Binns's attempt to gain authority for his representation of the poet. Following Loving's essay, Joel Myerson proposes that one of the most neglected aspects of Whitman's biography has been innovative work with bibliography, and he suggests some surprising ways that analytical bibliography can clarify key aspects of the poet's life: Whitman's life may have shaped his books, but no more than the publication of his books shaped his life. In the final essay in this group, Vivian R. Pollak demonstrates a psychobiographical approach, arguing that "When Lilacs Last in the Dooryard Bloom'd" is Whitman's "last major poetic perturbation," after which he had "nothing left to obscure." Her account exposes a dark undercurrent in Whitman's long history of antipresidential sentiment and his ambivalent attitudes toward Lincoln before the assassination. Pollak traces in Whitman an antipathy—emerging from his troubled relations with his father—that may have united him at some subterranean level with John Wilkes Booth, attacker of a tyrannical father figure. "Lilacs" becomes, then, an "ambiguous emotional project" which not only attempts to transcend the poet's grief over the loss of Lincoln but also tries to obscure the poet's complicity in the aggressive act. Pollak's evocation of Whitman's antebellum attitudes toward the South and his views about the perpetuation of slavery sets the stage for Arthur Golden's, Alan Trachtenberg's, and M. Wynn Thomas's essays, which also deal with these issues.

The second section of this book is concerned with the origins and the stylistic impulses of Whitman's work. Roger Asselineau offers a lively overview of the European roots of *Leaves of Grass*, reminding us that Whitman was not quite the naive nativist that he made himself out to be; Asselineau catalogs the wide array of influences that Whitman the autodidact absorbed through translations. C. Carroll Hollis, developing his longstanding fascination with the oratorical underpinnings of *Leaves*, examines the 1860 edition of Whitman's book and discovers a plethora of "discourse markers," particular words that, as linguists have demonstrated, are signals of conversational discourse, oral exchange. By employing a strikingly large number of such oral cues, Hollis suggests, Whitman created a written poetry designed to strike the reader as speech, thus strengthening the illusion of textual intimacy. Developing this notion of textual intimacy, M. Jimmie Killingsworth looks at Whitman's "physical eloquence," the way that the poet intensifies his rhetoric by insisting on sexual intimacy as his trope for the acts of reading and writing. If such acts generally demand prudence and withdrawal from normal physical activity, Killingsworth observes, Whitman's sexual metaphors can nonetheless direct readers toward physical experience, "creating a desire without satisfying it." Killingsworth reminds us of some mid-nineteenth-century moments on the U.S. Senate floor when sexual figures of speech led quite directly to physical assault. James Perrin Warren, also interested in how Whitman constructs his "voice," analyzes the poet's "reconstructive strategies" and points to some surprising continuities between his early and late styles, including his carefully constructed "figure of an audience," his creation of readers who would respond positively to his "figure of eloquence." Warren looks at the multiple connotations of Whitman's use of the word *reconstruction*, noting that reconstruction is as much a textual strategy for him—a way to pull together disparate passages of writing—as it is a political strategy for reuniting the divided nation. Warren's focus is on *Democratic Vistas*, Whitman's postbellum tough-minded assessment of America's future, but a piece that Warren demonstrates had its roots in Whitman's antebellum writing. Arthur Golden, too, is interested in *Democratic Vistas*, as he investigates the distance between Whitman's idealizing poetic voice, which celebrated the American common people, and his condemnatory prose voice, which found fault with them. Whitman's poetry, Golden argues, includes blacks in the definition of America, but his prose excludes them. In Golden's reading, Whitman finally was unable "to justify his fabled 'divine average' as a vital factor in day-to-day living in a viable democratic society."

The third section of this book probes Whitman's politics and his sexuality—the politics of his body, the politics of his poetry, the politics of his identity (as well as the identity of his politics). The issues that Golden raises in textual terms, Harold Aspiz develops in political terms. Like Golden, Aspiz is intrigued by the unresolved contradictions between Whitman's awareness of the corruption of the American masses and his stubborn faith in the "grand, common stock" that would create a heroic populace. Aspiz tracks how Whitman appropriated the commonplace body politic metaphor and transformed it into a strikingly physical trope, creating a nation that consumed, digested, excreted, metastasized, copulated, received blood transfusions, turned disease to nutriment, grew, and evolved. Turning from the politics of the body to the politics of labor, Alan Trachtenberg identifies a specific site where labor occurs for Whitman: it is at the place where the poet works to convert "democracy" into "America." The performance of that conversion is what makes the poet's work political work, what renders a poem the figure that labor makes. Trachtenberg offers a compelling reading of "A Song for Occupations," demonstrating how labor provides a model for Whitman's own work, how Whitman employs the word *work* as both verb and noun—process of labor and product of labor. Whitman's work is the labor of retrieving "occupations" from the cold type of dead classifications and returning them to living praxis; Trachtenberg shows how the poet accomplishes this, but not before he takes a hard look at Whitman's disturbing racialist equation of freedom with white labor. M. Wynn Thomas is also concerned about Whitman's faith in free white labor as the basis for his condemnation of slavery, and he proceeds to demonstrate the ways in which the dreams and realities of the nineteenth-century world of labor crucially shaped Whitman's reading of American political affairs. Thomas rehistoricizes and resurrects the radical nature of some of Whitman's 1860 poetry that has come to sound safe and predictable to our ears. He shows how Whitman's intentional vagueness of verb tense and pronoun referent allows him to sidestep dangerous political divisions and to offer instead a usefully indeterminate future. This "rhetoric of conciliation" and "pragmatics of the present" serve to soften Whitman's revolutionary discourse and to offer instead an evolutionary gradualism that is more palatable to the South and thus more conservative of the Union. Thomas concludes with a poignant look at Whitman's pathetic failure to confront the nation's severe labor problems during the last two decades of his life.

The politics of labor is a key factor in the structure of Whitman's poetry, and it shades imperceptibly into the politics of sexuality. One of the most volatile areas of Whitman criticism has come to be the terrain where his "radical" sexuality—his Calamus love—meets his "conservative" politics—his idealistic faith in the secure future of American democracy. This unstable terrain is the subject of Betsy Erkkila's essay on Whitman's "Homosexual Republic." She begins with Malcolm Cowley's memorable observation that Whitman made a "strange amalgam . . . between cocksucking and democracy." Erkkila shows the amalgam is not so strange after all, as she explores the ways that Whitman's language of democracy (comradeship, brotherhood, equality) intersects with the sociolect, with all kinds of discourses—temperance, sexual reform, spirituality, heterosexual love. She argues that the perceived dichotomies of Whitman's poetry—between the sexual and the mystical, for example—are in fact not dichotomies at all but instead are radical lexical conflations intended to move language into articulations of experience for which there were yet no words (such as *homosexuality*). What gives Whitman's poetry its sustaining power, Erkkila argues, is precisely Whitman's refusal to separate his expressions of democratic ideals from his expressions of same-sex love; he speaks of same-sex love in and through the conventional language of brotherly love and of male-female love, and so his diction works to make the boundaries between private and public, male and female, heterosexual and homosexual, more permeable. Erkkila concludes with a revisionist reading of Whitman's infamous letter to John Addington Symonds, in which the poet asserts that he had fathered six children. Robert K. Martin, too, works creatively with this letter in which Whitman seems to deny that his poetry celebrated physical love between men. Martin shows that Whitman had good (and surprising) reasons to distance himself from Symonds's equivocating, clinical, upper-class, "transcendentalized" notions of male-male sexuality, and he analyzes a "trip-tych" of "Calamus" poems that trace out the construction of a particular gay identity. As do several of the writers in this volume, Martin uses the occasion of the Centennial Conference to update and realign aspects of his earlier work on Whitman.

The final section of the book deals with Whitman's influence. The opening essay of this section, by James E. Miller, Jr., weaves together a number of is-sues that other contributors explore. Like Erkkila and Killingsworth, Miller warns against the dangers of failing to comprehend just how inextricably inter-related politics and sexuality and spirituality are in Whitman's work, a meld-ing that Miller names the "omnisexual theme." Miller comments on the many writers who have had strangely ambiguous or ambivalent responses to Whit-man, and he deals with the ways various writers have incorporated Whitman's omnisexual theme. He concludes with a discussion of Whitman's powerful in-fluence on women writers like Anne Gilchrist, Kate Chopin, and Muriel Rukeyser, who "turn to Whitman for the very element that the male writers [like Emerson, Thoreau, Lanier, and Swinburne] would suppress." George B. Hutchinson shows how Whitman's legacy worked among writers of the Harlem Renaissance, how these African American authors "embraced him with an intimacy that defies the codes typical of interracial relations in the United States and exceeds that of most 'white' American modernists." Hutchinson argues that Whitman's work "contributed crucially to some of the most fruitful developments in black writing of the twentieth century," and he looks particularly at Alain Locke, James Weldon Johnson, and Jean Toomer. An important aspect of Hutchinson's argument is his insistence that it is vital to study the *effects* of Whitman's work apart from the intent or the inherent ideology of his work: the effect of his work was to nurture emerging black tra-ditions even while the work itself may have been "complicit with white American hegemony." Kenneth M. Price, who is investigating the ways that Whitman has influenced American fiction, takes as his subject the case of John Dos Passos, examining Dos Passos's "career-long engagement with

Whitman" and tracing how he was able to make Whitman accompany him from communism to Goldwater Republicanism. Walter Grünzweig examines an important but little-known phenomenon—the tradition of German poets responding to Whitman in poems. Grünzweig traces this revealing series of poems, from Arthur Drey's 1911 "Walt Whitman," an expressionist poetic response, through Johannes Becher's construction of Whitman as "a fighter against bourgeois decadence," on up to Jürgen Wellbrock's "Dein Selbst kann ich nicht singen," a 1976 leftist attack on Whitman. Finally, V. K. Chari, who wrote the definitive study of Whitman's relation to Vedantic mysticism, here turns his attention to the Indian "theory of poetic emotions" called *Rasa*, and he offers a polemical response to recent schools of Whitman criticism, arguing that it is time to turn away from politics and biography and sexuality and to turn our attention instead back to the "emotional tone" that Whitman's poems provide their readers.

This collection gathers the current state of Whitman scholarship from the most influential Whitman critics working over the past half century. Some of the essays are retrospective, others prospective. They all speak across generations, to each other, back to Whitman, and forward to the critics to come, who for the next hundred years will continue the important work of understanding ourselves through Whitman. Whether critics interrogate or celebrate his poetry, it is now clear that no American poet has had the impact on succeeding generations that Whitman has had, and no American writer has more fully helped us clarify the elements that compose this culture. Just prior to Whitman's death, George William Curtis in *Harper's Monthly* wrote, "There is no critic living who can foretell whether a hundred years hence our good friend Walt Whitman will be accepted as a great poet or have fallen into the limbo where the vast throng of Kettell's poets lie." On the centennial of his death, at least we have the answer to Curtis's query, an answer so affirmative that it is even possible to begin imagining "Walt Whitman: The Bicentennial Conference" and to begin wondering just what kind of a curiosity the scholars at that conference will find this volume.

THE LIFE

When I read the book, the biography famous,
And is this then (said I) what the author calls a man's life?
And so will some one when I am dead and gone write my life?
(As if any man really knew aught of my life,
Why even I myself I often think know little or nothing of my real life,
Only a few hints, a few diffused faint clews and indirections
I seek for my own use to trace out here.)

("When I Read the Book," LG, 8)

Whitman Biography in 1992

O NE HUNDRED years ago (March 26, 1892) Walt Whitman died at 6:40 on a rainy evening in Camden, New Jersey, just in time to make the Sunday morning headlines in the New York and Phila-delphia newspapers. The timing was perfect. Within a few hours reporters were swarming into the poet's shabby frame house at 328 Mickle Street. Though the literary establishment had never accepted Whitman, his reputation for unconventional dress, manners, unrhymed verse, and daring sex poems made him good copy for the journalists.

As a printer, editor, and journalist himself, Whitman had acquired friends in the newspaper world. Now his death was important news. The *New York Times* gave him nearly two-and-a-half columns, with a triple-decker headline; the *World* three columns; and the *Herald* and the *Tribune* were about equally generous with space and praise. A Reuters reporter cabled the news to the *London Chronicle*, which printed two-and-a-quarter columns in the Monday morning edition. Newspapers on the European continent and even in Russia picked up the story of Whitman's death. He had always appreciated publicity, and it is a shame he could not have been around to read his obituaries.

All these newspaper accounts had to rely on the biographies of John Burroughs and Dr. Richard M. Bucke for details of the poet's life (as did critics for over a decade after Whitman's death), and we know that Walt himself partly wrote and thoroughly edited both books. In these and numerous prefaces and self-written interviews, Whitman had done his best to control interpretations of his poems. Through Burroughs he fostered the idea that " 'Leaves of Grass' is an utterance out of the depths of primordial, original human nature. It embodies and exploits a character not rendered anaemic by civilization. . . . Whitman was indebted to culture only as a means to escape culture."[1] Books, that is, were less important than the outdoors.

In his 1855 Preface to *Leaves of Grass*, Whitman had declared that the American poet must "incarnate" the natural life and geography of his country. In imaginative flights he did that in "Song of Myself," and to make it all seem authentic he misled Burroughs into thinking that he had extended his five-month-long trip to New Orleans to two years of travel around the country. Even in a manuscript dated 1890, only two years before his death, and probably intended for newspaper publication, Whitman elaborated this myth: ". . . went off for two years on a working and journeying tour through nearly every one of the Middle, Southern and Western States, and to Louisiana and Texas (during the Mexican War of 1848 and '9)" (NUP, 1:41).

Whitman's insistence through such assertions that *Leaves* was autobiographical misled critics and thwarted truthful biography for many years. William Douglas O'Connor tried to create another myth of Whitman as a modern Christ. In a short story, he had the poet performing what seemed like a miracle on Christmas Eve, and this seemed to give biographical sanction to the passages in "Song of Myself" where the "I" plays a messianic role.

Bliss Perry in his 1906 biography of Whitman excoriated the "hot little prophets" for their hagiography, and he tried to write a truthful account, but at that time many of the key documents were not available. In fact, it was not until 1941 that Katherine Molinoff in *Some Notes on Whitman's Family* was able to make a full revelation of the sordidness of the poet's background.[2] Molinoff's main source was Louisa Van Velsor Whitman's letters to her son Walt, in which she detailed her troubles—and her troubles were numerous. Her oldest son became insane and had to be committed to an asylum. Her youngest son had a mental disability and needed constant care. An infant died before being named. Another son died of cancer of the throat, and his wife became a beggar. Of Louisa's nine children, only three—Walt, George, and Thomas Jefferson (Jeff)—did not experience these kinds of problems. Her husband, Walter Sr., a failure as a farmer and carpenter, was soured and embittered; Walt described him in "There Was a Child Went Forth":

> The father, strong, self-sufficient, manly, mean, anger'd, unjust,
> The blow, the quick loud word, the tight bargain, the crafty lure. (LG, 365)

He became so crippled by arthritis that he could not work, and Walt had to take over support of the family.

In spite of Walt's devotion to his mother, Jean Catel may have been right in suggesting that in his youth Whitman found escape from his family in the streets and city crowds.[3] He led an urban, not a pastoral, life. His sentimental juvenile stories and graveyard poems were the product of a miserable, discontented youth. The recently discovered letters that he wrote to Abraham Paul Leech in 1840 and 1841 reveal a bored, dissatisfied country school teacher who detested his loutish students and their uncouth parents (SL, 5–13). His complaints may have been justified, but these letters give no intimation of the future compassionate poet of *Leaves of Grass*.

Fortunately, journalism allowed Whitman to escape country school teaching. After various ventures, he edited an important metropolitan newspaper, the *Brooklyn Eagle*, for two years and later the *Brooklyn Daily Times*. Some biographers say he was a failure in journalism, but actually journalism failed him. Because he stood for principles he passionately believed in (such as the rights of labor and the evils of slavery), when the New York State Democratic party compromised with the southern faction, the *Eagle* (a Democratic paper) had no further use for Whitman. After returning from New Orleans he tried to start a Free Soil newspaper, but his office was burned by a mob, and he failed to get financial backing for a new start. He became a carpenter and contractor because journalism, highly partisan at the time, was closed to him. His brother George thought he could have prospered in building houses if he had not lost interest in financial success.[4]

For reasons still only partly understood, Whitman in the early 1850s became convinced that he could accomplish in poetry what he could not in journalism. His notes of this period sound as if he had experienced a religious rebirth, to use the Protestant evangelical term, but he did not attend any church and had a low opinion of denominational religion. Yet somehow he attained a new kind of "wisdom" which changed his life, as we can see in this note:

> The ignorant man is demented with the madness of owning things. . . .
> But the wisest soul knows that no object can really be owned by one man
> or woman any more than another. . . . He cannot share his friend or his
> wife because of them he is no owner, except by their love, and if any one
> gets that away from him, it is best not to curse, but quietly call the offal
> cart to his door and let physical wife or friend go, the tail with the hide.
> (UPP, 1:67–68)

Although Whitman knew the New Testament well, this language does not sound at all like it. But time and again he used the word *soul*. In many notes and later in "Song of Myself," he insists that body and soul are not only equal but are in fact one and the same. This is not a Christian concept, but it does strongly resemble some Hindu concepts which he seems to have encountered in his reading at this time, probably in the public library on 14th Street in New York. This, of course, contradicts his and Burroughs's claims that he owed nothing to books. However, four years before his death he stated in "A Backward Glance O'er Travel'd Roads" that he had read "the ancient Hindoo poems" in preparation for writing *Leaves*, and there are good reasons for believing him (PW, 2:722). As early as 1866 Viscount Strangford and Moncure Conway suggested these sources, and over the years others have confirmed them, like the recent Indian scholar, Sudhir Kumar, who says Whitman's sense of the words *soul* and *spirit* closely parallels their meaning in the *Bhagavad Gita*, the *Vedas*, and the *Puranas*.[5]

Dr. Bucke claimed Whitman as a mystic who possessed "Cosmic Consciousness." And a number of biographers and critics believe that he had at least one mystical experience, as described in Section 5 of "Song of Myself":

> I believe in you my soul, the other I am must not abase itself to you,
> And you must not be abased to the other. . . .
> I mind how once we lay such a transparent summer morning,
> How you settled your head athwart my hips and gently turn'd over upon me,
> And parted the shirt from my bosom-bone, and plunged your tongue to my
>   bare-stript heart,
> And reach'd till you felt my beard, and reach'd till you held my feet.
>
> Swiftly arose and spread around me the peace and knowledge that
>   pass all the argument of the earth. (LG, 32–33)

It is true that the effects of this experience (whether it was imaginary or real) closely parallel William James's definition of such events in *Varieties of Religious Experience*.[6] Of course, some recent critics have also seen in this passage evidence of Whitman's awakening homosexuality—though it sounds to me more like autoeroticism. What is unmistakable is that Whitman's sexual emotions were so strong that he made them a part of his poetic program and would protest all his life against prudish suppression of sex in literature. This desire to promote sexual liberation had, I believe, two sources: his personal life and his discovery of the importance of sex in the literature of India and in the ancient religions, like the Egyptian.[7]

That Whitman was homosexual is now recognized by nearly everyone who writes about him. But in his lifetime most Americans and British regarded homosexuality as unnatural, immoral, and even criminal. Whitman was fully aware of this fact, and so his first reaction was to prove that his sexual emotions were "natural" and "healthy." Then, in a moral crisis at the time of writing the "Calamus" poems, he vacillated between shame and aggressive defense. It is highly significant that at this time he felt isolated and was hungry for affection. If the "Calamus" poems can be read autobiographically, then we can conclude that for a brief time he found a male lover who made him happy but who was jealous of Whitman's role as the lover of the nation. So Whitman announced in a "Calamus" poem:

Take notice, [America] . . .
For I can be your singer of songs no longer—One who loves me is jealous of
    me, and withdraws me from all but love, . . .

.   .   .

. . . I will go with him I love,
It is to be enough for each of us that we are together—
We never separate again. (MLG, 80–83)

But evidently they did separate, and then, after a severe emotional depression, Whitman recovered his literary ambitions when a Boston publisher offered to print a new edition of *Leaves*. In this new edition, he reprinted the "Calamus" poems, but from this time on he insisted on interpreting them as poems of comradeship.

The communists liked his term "camerado" so much that, after the Russian Revolution, they adopted "comrade" as a patriotic salutation. For them it had no sexual connotation. In fact, communists in all countries bitterly objected if anyone called Whitman a homosexual. Gilbert Frey in Brazil called him a bisexual and said that his poems overflowed with "a personalistic and fraternal sense of life and community, a sense so vibrant as to seem at times homosexualism gone mad, whereas it probably was bisexualism sublimated into fraternalism."[8]

A French communist, Paul Jamati, in his Introduction to a translation of selected poems from *Leaves*, accused all those who called Whitman a homosexual of deliberately creating *"une contre-légend."*[9] Instead of attacking democracy directly, Jamati believed, they would attack the most famous poet of democracy. The Russian biographer of Whitman, Maurice Mendelson, also objected to the "bourgeoise" misinterpretation of Whitman's "love" and "comradeship": "Whitman's depiction of joyful full-bodied life based on a community of equal and free individuals was an expression of his active protest against social injustice."[10]

In retrospect, now that communism has collapsed, it may seem odd that Whitman the great individualist should have had such great influence in the Soviet Union. But it was no accident. Even before the Bolshevik Revolution the Futurists were attracted to him because they thought he anticipated their dream of a utopian society where humans were completely transformed.

Kornei Chukovsky, Whitman's main translator in Russia, who in his youth was attracted to the Futurists, saw in Whitman's poems the model for an ideal community.

So far as I know, Whitman never read Karl Marx, but there are similarities in their social ideals: Whitman's Jeffersonian-Jacksonian democracy and Marx's proletarian society. By the time Whitman wrote *Democratic Vistas* (late 1860s), he knew that his own so-called democratic nation had become shamefully corrupt. But he clung to the hope that it could be reformed, arguing that political democracy in America, "with all its threatening evils, supplies a training-school for making first class men" (PW, 2:385). A book that throws new light on Whitman's stubborn hope for an egalitarian government of artisans is M. Wynn Thomas's *The Lunar Light of Whitman's Poetry* (1987). The visionary who wrote *Leaves of Grass*, says Thomas, "produced his own distinctly American view of what Marx, at virtually the same time, with tragic splendor, was calling the simultaneous 'rise and decline' of the individual."[11]

Whitman believed that only a new appreciation of the self could stop this decline. He wrote "Song of Myself" to show the divine origin of the self and the happiness and pleasures it was capable of achieving in individual lives, including sensual gratifications of the body. The failure of most of his fellow Americans to respond to this teaching was the great disappointment of his life. Of course, a few did respond, and in old age he found consolation in his growing reputation abroad as the "poet of democracy." And as this Centennial gathering of scholars from various countries demonstrates, Whitman's worldwide influence has never been stronger.

Biography of the kind that Roger Asselineau and I wrote nearly half a century ago may have gone about as far as it can, though with few new facts but an original point of view, Justin Kaplan managed a few years ago to write an interesting biographical narrative. Carroll Hollis has predicted that "the wave (and the way) of the future" of Whitman scholarship will be linguistic and interpretive studies, and he cites Mark Bauerlein's recent *Whitman and the American Idiom* as an example.[12] Bauerlein has some interesting insights, but I have difficulty believing that Whitman's emotional depression between 1858 and 1860 really was the result of his loss of faith in a theory of language. There were plenty of devastating biographical causes (erotic, financial, and social) that more convincingly account for his discouragement and loss of confidence. Biography is not dead yet; it will continue to supplement semiotics and linguistic studies as we go on reconstructing Walt Whitman.

NOTES

1. John Burroughs, *Walt Whitman: A Study* (Boston: Houghton Mifflin, 1896), 76.

2. Katherine Molinoff, *Some Notes on Whitman's Family* (Brooklyn: privately printed, 1941).

3. Jean Catel, *Walt Whitman: La Naissance du Poète* (Paris: Les Editions Rieder, 1929), 34.

4. Horace Traubel, Richard Maurice Bucke, and Thomas B. Harned, eds., *In Re Walt Whitman* (Philadelphia: David McKay, 1893), 33–34.

5. Sudhir Kumar, "The *Gita* and Walt Whitman's Mysticism," in Abhai Maurya, ed., *India and World Literature* (New Delhi: Indian Council for Cultural Relations, 1990), 524–534. See also R. K. DasGupta, "Indian Response to Walt Whitman," *Revue de Littérature Comparée* 47 (1973): 58–70.

6. William James, *Varieties of Religious Experience* (New York: Longman Green, 1902), 370.

7. Gay Wilson Allen, *The Solitary Singer* (New York: New York University Press, 1957), 121–123.

8. Gilbert Frey, quoted in Gay Wilson Allen, ed., *Walt Whitman Abroad* (Syracuse: Syracuse University Press, 1955), 229.

9. Paul Jamati, *Walt Whitman: Une Étude, un Choix de Poèmes* (Paris: Pierre Seghers, 1948).

10. Maurice Mendelson, *Life and Work of Walt Whitman* (Moscow: Progress Publishers, 1976), 321.

11. M. Wynn Thomas, *The Lunar Light of Whitman's Poetry* (Cambridge: Harvard University Press, 1987), 1.

12. Mark Bauerlein, *Walt Whitman and the American Idiom* (Baton Rouge: Louisiana State University Press, 1991). Hollis's comments appear on the book jacket.

The Binns Biography

T HE RESULTS of my research into the life of Henry Bryan Binns and his 1905 biography of Walt Whitman can only be described as incomplete as we observe the poet's centennial. Binns's *A Life of Walt Whitman* has been authoritatively described by Gay Wilson Allen as "one of the most reliable accounts of Walt Whitman's life."[1] It brought together on the fiftieth anniversary of the first publication of *Leaves of Grass* most of the known facts about the poet's life in a lively, readable narrative that links Whitman's life and work with the emerging international stature of the United States.

Published in England by Methuen and written by an Englishman whose only visible connection to Whitman and the United States was the possibility that his mother was an American, this biography appeared to be the first account that was not distorted by the zeal of the poet's disciples, those folks we now refer to as the Whitmaniacs who surrounded Whitman in his final years, some of whom divided up his literary and personal papers after his death and organized the Whitman Fellowship meetings and publications which lasted into the 1920s. Despite the fact that Binns has been hailed as the first "objective" biographer, little is known about his personal life, except for a brief biographical sketch and what can be gleaned from his many publications, which include an essay on Edward Carpenter in 1895, a biography of Lincoln in 1907, and an abbreviated version of his Whitman biography in 1915.[2]

Binns was born in Ulverston, Lancashire, in 1873, and he died in Devon on February 23, 1923. He published at regular intervals between 1902 (when his

Moods and Outdoor Verses appeared under the pseudonym of Richard Askham) and 1921, the year his book of poems entitled *Hill-Tops* appeared. The only other direct evidence of his literary existence, besides his hard-to-find books (mostly chapbooks of poetry, short editions on obscure subjects) and their listings in the National Union Catalog, comes from a single entry in the 1906–1934 volume of Who Was Who in Literature, which places his general address in Sussex, south of London. We suspect that his mother was born in America from the dedication in the Whitman biography: "To My Mother and Her Mother, The Republic."

As Sculley Bradley first suspected, Binns came to the United States at least once—during the writing of his Whitman biography.[3] Upon visiting Timber Creek, now a New Jersey suburb of Philadelphia near where the family of Harry Stafford lived and where Whitman found in his final years his version of Walden Pond, Bradley praised the accuracy of Binns's description of the place and how it became the basis of descriptions in subsequent biographies. I have learned from Binns's letters to Horace Traubel in the Library of Congress that Binns visited Timber Creek in 1904 and took several photographs of the retreat which appear in his biography. He also visited West Hills, Fire Island Beach, Boston, Belmont, Cambridge, and Camden or Philadelphia, where he met Traubel. In his first letter to Traubel, announcing that he had been "commissioned" to write the Whitman biography, Binns revealed that he was a Quaker who hoped this background would grant him special access to "any *living Quaker* in Philadelphia, Camden or Long Island, who was at any time intimate with Whitman."[4]

Binns enjoyed another connection with Whitman, however. On April 2, 1891, at the tender age of eighteen, he wrote the bard what can only be termed a "Master" letter, greeting Whitman at the *end* not only of his "great career" but, of course, his life. From Reigate in Surrey, Binns took the enfeebled poet at his former word that it was "just as lucky to die" as it was to be born when he concluded his epistle with the hope that "when the hour of separation comes we can trust you best in His Hand, whom we believe to be the clue & reason of creation. . . ." There is no allusion in Traubel's *With Walt Whitman in Camden* (either the published or yet-to-be-published volumes) to this rather impolitic letter from one of Whitman's future biographers, but we can guess that the poet dismissed the letter—as he does others in Traubel's accounts—as the work of a fanatic and a foolhardy romantic. This impression may have also accounted for part of Traubel's reticence in cooperating with Binns thirteen years later when Binns was researching his biography.

For the record here and for the basis of my assessment of the Binns biography, however, I think it is helpful to quote a good part of Binns's 1891 letter, part of

Gramley Library
Salem College
Winston-Salem NC 27100

which is already available in Edwin Haviland Miller's *Walt Whitman: The Correspondence*. Opening with the salutation of "My dear Master," Binns wrote:

> I plead no other excuse in writing to you but my great wish to thank for making yourself known to me in your books and in your portraits. There is no other link between us—between you who are near the end of the race, already being crowned, and I, who am but now beginning,—than the world-circling bond of universal brotherhood, by which I claim the privilege of doing the nearest thing to shaking your hand, telling you how much I desire to do so. . . .
>
> For, as it has doubtless been with many before me, in your books I have found myself [freshly?] defined—I have found, through them, new latent possibilities & affinities, new tendencies, new hopes, new faith. You have been "the Answerer" to many inarticulate questionings. And so, further, I want to thank you for being an honest modern man,—true to your inmost self,—true to your age, & true to the eternity of progress—, gothic,—stalwart,—one with men & one with nature; for being the prophet & voice of Americanism, as progress & comradeship, and, withal, a true poet . . . an original, deep-thinking, religious, working, *man*, with faith in present as well as future. . . .
>
> The peoples of the world will arise some day & acknowledge you as their pioneer,—their leader, their spokesman, ever in their own front rank, their poet, expressing for them in song, free & simple, their unknown, blind longings—Not only of America, but here in England, in Europe, in the whole world.
>
> As you stand now on the shore of the Unknown Ocean, I long to send to you a message of love & of greeting across our little sea to cheer you, maybe upon your journey, though I know that you are ever of good cheer. Before the greatness of eternity & space untravelled, the little distances of earth vanish away and it seems almost that I can reach your hand across the Atlantic drawing me on amid other influences to higher & still higher things. With you I believe, that the after-ages will enshrine your memory & your words—your life—as their prophet-poet, that the future is for you where men (even "the great masters") will come to learn of you—or rather that you are for the future. . . .
>
> The world owes you a debt never to be repaid by it, perhaps not realized as yet. As a poet you will be ours forever, and as a man may the Father of our universal Brotherhood see fit to spare your strong presence to be with us yet a little longer.[5]

This letter suggests someone influenced by both the romantic individualism of the nineteenth century and the budding socialism of the twentieth, a commingling of two democratic systems that *Leaves of Grass* itself embodies. Binns's political asides in the biography reject socialistic theories in favor of individual responsibility in their interpretations of Whitman's political philosophy;[6] yet such phrases as "world-circling bond of universal brotherhood," "progress & comradeship," and calling Whitman the future "spokesman" of social progressiveness seem to align him with the emerging idea of Fabianism, begun in 1887, which rejected capitalism in favor of a vague socialism but also rejected Marx's theories of economics and class struggle and his political methods and organizational forms. Following Binns's meeting and epistolary exchanges with Traubel, he appears to have drifted more in the direction of socialism but never as far as Leon Bazalgette, a noted French socialist who published his biography of Whitman in 1908. A year after Binns's biography had appeared and he was complaining about the lack of money, he responded to Traubel's quasi-socialistic rhetoric in the June 1906 issue of the *Conservator* by saying, "It is the message we want. I am trying to learn to give it, too. So here, again, is my hand comrade."[7] Binns's initial democratic leanings, however, were not those of the political activist (or actually even of the Fabians, as that group split away in the 1880s from the Fellowship of the New Life) but were linked instead to the idealistic and romantic Christian socialist organizations that envisioned utopian retreats away from the corruption of the city. "Of the period and of the communion to which Binns belonged," writes Christopher Charlton in 1985, ". . . socialism was a cult, with affiliations in directions now quite disowned, stressing theosophy, arts and crafts, vegetarianism, and 'the simple life.'"[8]

The eldest son of Elizabeth (Bryan) and Richard Binns (self-described as a "manure manufacturer"), Binns was educated in schools at Christchurch and Hitchin, and by 1894 he had taken up fruit growing.[9] In an essay on the "New Fellowship" in a magazine called *Seed-Time*, he wrote:

> The difficulties, the chances, the care and toil of farming . . . point me with logical accuracy either to cooperation or to that pleasant portal of the workhouse, whereunder men's emasculated lives are charitably murdered in pauperism. Nor will I work my days into weariness for food and fire and shelter, and tax privilege of society. Here in this craft, I am learning, are unsurpassed possibilities for true worship of the Divine.[10]

Henry Binns sounds like Henry Thoreau, but he soon left his rural Eden (in 1897) to marry Katharine Ellis of Leicester, a woman six years his senior with a comfortable income derived from her father's interests in stone quarries, lime, and coal. Since he later complained several times to Traubel of lacking funds, it is possible that this source of income may not have endured long past the turn of the century.[11] At any rate, Binns and his bride removed to York, where Binns joined John Wilhelm Rountree in editing the multi-volume *Present-Day Papers* and founding the utopian program it advocated—the Adult School Movement. Unlike the Fabians, these reformers made a distinction between capitalism and its abuses. Poverty, the movement argued, was largely the result of the abuse of privilege in a free-market society: high rents, low wages, and exploitation by employers. "For Rountree and Binns," Charlton writes, "the regeneration of society would [have to] depend upon the arousal of a sense of personal responsibility and social duty." A Quaker-inspired program, the Adult School Movement sought to "conduct investigations for local reform and, by house to house visits, analyse the causes of poverty on a parish level."[12] Results of their inquiries were published in *Present-Day Papers*, and Binns's contributions carried such titles as "Essays on Self Realisation," "The Indwelling Christ," and—under his pseudonym of Richard Askham—"Poverty." By the time he had published his Whitman biography, Binns had also helped to found with his wife and others the rural dream village of Garden City in Letchworth. It included the Letchworth Adult School, which continued until 1934.

Charlton's biographical sketch of Binns barely mentions the Whitman biography, except to say that Binns was known for his books on Whitman and Lincoln. In fact, the sketch is almost apologetic about Binns, emphasizing his frail health and withdrawn demeanor. Charlton quotes an obituary in the *Friend* of April 1923 in which Joseph Wickstead, who knew Binns well, remarked that "when I think of the days I spent with Henry Binns, . . . it is sometimes only by effort that I can remember that he was there."[13] This reminiscence squares with Binns's modest disclaimer in his Whitman biography that it made "no attempt to fill the place of either a critical study or a definitive biography."[14] Yet Binns did indeed produce the first "definitive" biography, and in doing so he was his own person—in terms of avoiding Whitman discipleship if not altogether romantic ideology about the poet.

The most memorable of his arguments for Whitman was the explanation of the New Orleans period. Binns was the first biographer to make indirect use of Whitman's 1891 letter to John Addington Symonds in which the now-famous phantom children and grandson were announced. Carpenter first published the letter in *Days with Walt Whitman* in 1906 and as a mentor of Binns probably shared the letter's contents with him. Binns's conclusion that Whitman had experienced heterosexual relations was logical, given the poet's declaration of paternity, but Binns also may have been trying to counter the emerging theory of the poet's homosexuality, which Carpenter had been mulling over and at least hinted at the possibility of in his book. Whitman's "sex pathology" was first argued by the German critic Eduard Bertz in *Der Yankee-Heiland* in 1905, and later that year Binns said in a letter to Johannes Schlaf, another German critic and Traubel's equal as a Whitmaniac, that he was happy Schlaf was resisting Bertz's assertions: "The question you raise about Calamus & [Peter] Doyle is one of the most difficult of all. I have said little about it [in my biography]." In another letter, he thanked Schlaf "for the Bertz book," saying that "evil though it may be!" he would pass it on to Carpenter.[15] Binns argues in his biography that Whitman experienced a literary awakening as the result of "an intimate relationship with some woman of higher social rank—a lady of the South where rank is of the first consideration." As the result of this "experience of sex-love," which was unfulfilled by marriage, the poet subsequently underwent "an acute crisis . . . and a change in character" that eventually produced the first and subsequent editions of *Leaves of Grass*.[16]

Generally, the reviewers thought Binns's book the best study of Whitman to date, and when they attacked, the target was more often Whitman than his British biographer. Whitman, many held, did not merit the name poet except for a select portion of his poetry. They also thought Binns lacked adequate evidence for his assertions about the high-born woman and the illegitimate children, and when they did accept the story they charged the poet with immorality and the social sin of abandoning his children. Furthermore, "the ascription of any such benign and fructifying influence to an illicit connection of this sort," offered Percy F. Bicknell in the *Dial*, "is what one might have expected rather from a writer on the other side of the Channel than from an Englishman." The Francophobic Bicknell also thought that the historical and political paralleling of America with Whitman was extraneous to the biography, but his anti-Whitman tone suggests that he also objected to the idea that Whitman's life, whose sordid aspects involved illegitimate children, was representative of his nation's.[17] To this last complaint, Traubel shot back from his editorial foxhole at the *Conservator* that Binns's early chapters on Whitman and the Republic got "Walt into the right historical perspective and instead of being superfluous [are] philosophically and psychically indispensable."[18]

One of the most interesting aspects of the Binns biography is Traubel's influence on the book (or the lack of it), considering that it has been hailed as the first "objective" biography. In their correspondence during the two years preceding its publication, there is evidence that at first Traubel was not completely cooperative in providing Binns the information he repeatedly requested, then that he tried to influence the book, especially the section alleging a heterosexual affair in New Orleans, perhaps thinking that Binns's argument would backfire. Traubel, who later claimed that Whitman had told him to "speak for me when I am dead" (HT, 1: vii), was determined to control the image of his poet, to protect it against what he considered distortion and trivialization. It is unlikely, therefore, that he was favorably impressed when Binns's first question concerned the poet's illegitimate children, which Binns considered "an important element in the life, and cannot be properly dismissed . . . in a mere aside."[19] After Binns finally met Traubel in Camden and was preparing to return to England, he told him: "I only hope the book will eventually seem worth while to you & others who have forwarded it."[20] Traubel may have also feared that the reception for his own work on Whitman, the first volume of *With Walt Whitman in Camden* (1906), coming down to publication about the same time as Binns's book, would be obscured by the biography—as well (so it turned out) as by the publication of Bliss Perry's life of the poet.

When Traubel reviewed Binns's book, he rejected the story of the New Orleans love affair as "not objectionable for any reason other than it is all in the air."[21] Apparently, Traubel never saw the completed manuscript before publication, but Binns did send him this section, which bears written corrections in a hand resembling Traubel's. The effect of his recommendations was to tone down the New Orleans love affair and to excise completely Binns's statement that a "Southern grandchild" had visited Whitman in Camden shortly before his death. There may have been other objections in other correspondences, but Traubel may have also been warned off by Binns's declaration to him in the months before the biography went to press that he would be true to his own idea of the poet. Feeling, as he told Traubel, "handicapped" by the lack of any personal knowledge of Whitman (which Traubel flaunted to the end of his days), Binns wrote him: "I am keeping as close to [Whitman] as I can in spirit, and I have Carpenter's help. . . . You understand, of course,—I am sure you do,—that I am going to say what I, personally, feel about Walt, and that I accept him as one of the fullest and highest utterances of Humanity: I am not going to be mum when I think some peculiarity in him made him less universal and more individual."[22]

It was in this spirit that Binns deplored in his biography the poet's anonymous reviews of *Leaves of Grass* and tempered his 1891 epistolary hagiography by declaring that "Whitman was, of course, no God among men, nor was he greater than other poets; in a sense he was even less than the least of them, so subjective was his genius; but since he consciously evokes a new emotion, he has his place among true artists. . . ."[23] This was essentially the view of Bliss Perry in 1906, who allowed only part of Whitman's verse into the current canon of American literature and criticized the poet's bohemian attitude toward middle-class society and the American family ("he writes glorious things about physical fatherhood and motherhood, but little about the home").[24] No doubt Traubel might have been more critical of Binns, but he was soon to expend his energy upon Perry, whose book—undeservedly, I think—eclipsed the Binns biography.

NOTES

1. Gay Wilson Allen, *The New Walt Whitman Handbook* (New York: New York University Press, 1975), 21. My essay on Binns is part of an ongoing study of Whitman's biographers. I would very much appreciate information pertaining to the private papers of the poet's biographers, especially those publishing between 1905 and 1926, the year in which Emory Holloway's biography was published.

2. Henry Bryan Binns, "Edward Carpenter's *Towards Democracy*," *Friend* (January 4, 1895): 11–13; Binns, *Abraham Lincoln* (London: J. M. Dent, 1907); Binns, *Walt Whitman and His Poetry* (London: G. G. Harrap, 1915).

3. Sculley Bradley, "Walt Whitman at Timber Creek," *American Literature* 5 (November 1933): 235–246.

4. Henry Bryan Binns to Horace Traubel, May 23, 1904, Charles E. Feinberg Collection, Library of Congress.

5. Henry Bryan Binns to Walt Whitman, April 2, 1891, Feinberg Collection. In CORR, 5:4–5, the letter is misdated as May 2 instead of April 2, 1891.

6. In his biography, Binns describes Marxism as a "brilliant, fatalistic theory" (*A Life of Walt Whitman* [London: Methuen, 1905], 309).

7. Henry Bryan Binns to Horace Traubel, July 6, 1906, Feinberg Collection.

8. Christopher Charlton, Introduction, in J. Wilhelm Rountree and Henry Bryan Binns, *A History of the Adult School Movement* (London: Headley Brothers, 1903; rpt., Nottingham: University of Nottingham Department of Adult Education, 1985), xiv.

9. Evelyn Noble Armitage, *The Quaker Poets of Great Britain and Ireland* (London: W. Andrews, 1896), 32–33.

10. Charlton, xv.

11. Ibid., xviii. At the time of his death, Binns's estate in Spark Haw, Crockham Hill, Edenbridge, Kent, was valued at £2,057. I am indebted to John Smurthwaite of Leeds for this information.

12. Ibid., xx.

13. Ibid., xiv.

14. Binns, *A Life*, vii.

15. Henry Bryan Binns to Johannes Schlaf, November 5 and 17, 1905, Johannes Schlaf Archives, Querfurt, Germany. I am indebted to Walter Grünzweig for this information.

16. Binns, *A Life*, 51, 71.

17. Percy F. Bicknell, "The Real and Ideal Whitman," *Dial* 40 (March 1, 1906): 144–146.

18. Horace Traubel, "Walt Whitman," *Conservator* 17 (June 1906): 59–60.

19. Henry Bryan Binns to Horace Traubel, May 23, 1904, Feinberg Collection.

20. Henry Bryan Binns to Horace Traubel, September 5, 1904, Feinberg Collection.

21. Traubel, 59–60.

22. Henry Bryan Binns to Horace Traubel, October 28, 1906, Feinberg Collection.

23. Binns, *A Life*, 109, 105.

24. Bliss Perry, *Walt Whitman* (Boston: Houghton Mifflin, 1906), 293, 268–308.

Whitman

Bibliography as Biography

"CAMERADO," writes Whitman at the end of *Leaves of Grass*, "this is no book, / Who touches this touches a man."[1] If Whitman's book is his life, then analytical or descriptive bibliography, the study of books, is also a way to practice biography. The bibliographical analysis of an author's career is a type of literary biography, one that can, in its description and analysis of physical evidence, tell us a great deal about an author's life. And when that author is Whitman, who equates his book with his self, then the challenge of applying bibliography to biography becomes not only irresistible but even necessary, for no other major American author more obviously serves this purpose than does the good gray poet.

Descriptive primary bibliographies are much more than listings of titles with selected full-scale physical descriptions of major works. They are literary biographies, showing the development of authors' careers—the number and variety of their works, the textual changes they made, their reception in other countries as indicated by non-native editions of their works, the popularity of individual works as shown by their being collected in anthologies and by their separate reprintings, the way in which they were viewed by contemporaries as reflected in the magazines in which they were published, the popularity of their works as measured by their sales, and the income they derived from these sales and how that affected their career choices.

There is, for example, no better example of how Emily Dickinson refused to auction her mind through publication than by noting that her first book was not published until five years after her death.[2] We can study how Thomas

Carlyle was initially received in America almost solely through the efforts (and according to the tastes) of Ralph Waldo Emerson. We can discover which of Emerson's essays were the most popular by checking which were most anthologized or separately reprinted. We can trace the beginnings of canon formation by checking the contents of nineteenth-century literary anthologies and, for American authors, the catalogs of Houghton Mifflin Company, whose lists of collected editions formed the basis for nearly every pre-1970 college American literature anthology. We can understand F. Scott Fitzgerald's immense popularity by documenting that most of his stories appeared in mass-circulation magazines, not in literary reviews with a narrow readership. We can understand why Emerson was a paid public lecturer for nearly all his life, why Henry David Thoreau never gave up surveying as a profession, why Nathaniel Hawthorne and Herman Melville took political appointments to support their families, and why Margaret Fuller joined the *New York Tribune* as a paid columnist when we discover that the monies they received from their writings did not provide them with a decent livelihood. And, conversely, we know why Louisa May Alcott was reluctant to bid farewell to Jo March when we learn how immensely popular and financially remunerative were the books written in the *Little Women* series in which she was featured.

G. Thomas Tanselle suggests that analytical bibliography has been overlooked as a scholarly tool with wide-ranging possibilities because it has "developed in the hands of literary scholars—particularly scholars of Elizabethan drama—and their primary interest in analyzing physical evidence has been the role it could play in determining the relative authority of variant readings in texts." This has, to Tanselle, "fostered the notion that analytical bibliography is primarily, or solely, a tool of editing and of literary study."[3] One person who has recognized the importance of the bibliographical study of Whitman is Ed Folsom, who has studied appearances of Whitman's works in nineteenth-century textbooks, handbooks, and anthologies to investigate "our working assumption about Whitman's reputation . . . that he was generally vilified or ignored by the literary establishment during his lifetime, was taken seriously by only a small coterie of American disciples and an idiosyncratic group of admirers from abroad, and thus was excluded from textbooks, which were after all the domain of established tastes and orthodox views." Folsom's comprehensive study conclusively disproves this long-held popular view and notes that the anthologists' repeated inclusion of works like "O Captain! My Captain!" and "Come Up from the Fields Father" showed their desire to "wrest Whitman's work into conventional forms and conventional sentiments."[4]

No American writer was as fully involved in the process of seeing a book into print as was Walt Whitman. Most authors ignored or evaded the publication process, feeling once their manuscript was complete, so was the book; they subsequently participated, if at all, by reading proofs. Some obtruded themselves into the process, as Fitzgerald did, by using the proof stage as an opportunity to indulge in a substantive, final rewriting of the work. But Whitman fully embraced the process by which his handwritten words were cast into metal and gift wrapped in paper or cloth for presentation to the world. He physically assisted in the setting of type and personally oversaw multiple proofings, chose the font styles and type sizes, decided what kind of paper and page size would be used, designed the bindings, wrote advertising copy for as well as published reviews of his works, and sold the books himself. In fact, if Whitman was not residing in the city in which his book was being printed, he moved there and requested office space inside the printing establishment. The production of a book was, to Whitman, a reproduction of self that required his extended personal involvement. As he later told Horace Traubel, his theory was that "we ought to get rid of the literary middleman. The author should be in more direct and vital touch with his reader. The formal publisher should be abolished. The printer was the mechanic in the affair. The author should sell his books direct to the consumer. In the ideal situation the author would have his own type and set the type of his book." Or Whitman "would laughingly say, to carry the ideal notion further, the author should not only set the type of his book and put on its cover, but, after doing this, should not sell it but should give it away." [5]

During his lifetime, Whitman published ten separate volumes, exclusive of the 1842 *Franklin Evans*, which falls outside the scope of this paper, and *Leaves of Grass*, which is its own special briar patch of bibliographical problems. For six of these, Whitman acted as his own publisher. For the other four, he was involved in significant ways in matters of design, printing, publication, and distribution. In some cases, he allowed David McKay of Philadelphia to publish a book while Whitman simultaneously sold copies from his house in Camden, New Jersey. For other books, he paid for the printing and binding and then sold bound copies to McKay, who made his profit by marking up the price. On only a few books did Whitman participate in the traditional author-publisher relationship, wherein he received royalties from his publisher, who took all the financial risks.

Even the distribution of Whitman's books in Britain followed an unusual pattern whereby bibliographical evidence leads us to literary biography. Although William Michael Rossetti had edited a selection of Whitman's poetry for publication in England in 1868, as a general rule, before the 1880s, Whitman's books were more or less "distributed" in Britain rather then being published there, and nearly every English issue is distinguished by the name of a British publisher either rubber-stamped in ink on the title page or pasted there on a printed paper label. The exception to this rule is the work of the London publisher John Camden Hotten. Copies of *Leaves of Grass* with an 1872 title page date, listed in the *English Catalogue* as an importation by Hotten, have usually been described as a later issue within the 1872 printing, but they are, in fact, an unauthorized type-facsimile edition.[6] Hotten's anonymous piracy was no doubt due to British censorship laws, under which one could be prosecuted for publishing an obscene book but not for merely distributing it, and which he probably thought he could avoid more easily by posing as the distributor of the book rather than as the publisher of it.

In the 1880s, more traditional methods of making Whitman's writings available in Britain were employed. Editions were published in Walter Scott's *Camelot* and *Scott Library* series, and English and Scottish issues of American sheets with cancel title leaves were common for *Leaves of Grass* and *Specimen Days & Collect*. But Whitman still continued his practice, started in the 1870s, of selling books directly to people in Britain, sending them out from his house in Camden.

One effect of this erratic British publication record is—to use a recent critical term—to demonstrate the concept of "the presence of absence." That is, because Whitman was not actually published in Britain before the 1880s, since he merely had his books distributed there, he had no serious concern about protecting his copyright in Britain. As a result, almost none of his works were deposited for copyright at the British Library, the universities at Oxford and Cambridge, or the National Library of Scotland. Nearly all the pre-1880 Whitman books in these libraries were obtained either through gift or purchase, and their holdings are quite spotty. But the absence of Whitman's books in British institutions does tell us a thing or two. First, the obvious point is that he was not seriously published in England, as seen by the lack of British copyright deposit copies. Second, the only fairly complete Whitman collections (those at the John Rylands Library at Manchester and the Bolton Public Library) were put together by enthusiasts rather than through organized institutional collecting practices. If we assume that libraries obtain the books their readers ask for—and this is not always a safe assumption—then we may suggest that Whitman was simply not all that popular in England before 1880. Hence, information may be inferred from the absence of information.[7]

But it is obviously in the American editions of Whitman's books, and particularly with *Leaves of Grass*, that Whitman's self-representation comes across best and bibliography becomes biography. In a way, the childless Whitman produced his prodigy in his publications, and a look at the genealogy of *Leaves of Grass* shows this, for the book has long been recognized as an almost unique work for biographical, literary, and bibliographical study. It is, in effect, the one book of poetry Whitman worked on and published during his long career, adding to it as much by accretion from his other books as by revision of the original texts, and each version was personalized in ways that bear examination.

The 1855 *Leaves of Grass*, while published without Whitman's name on the title page or binding, did bear his identity in three ways: the book's copyright notice was in his name,[8] he identified himself as "Walt Whitman, an American, one of the roughs, a kosmos," in the text,[9] and the Hollyer engraving of Whitman served as the book's frontispiece.[10] The 1856 second edition also lacked Whitman's name on the title page, although it did appear on the binding, and the Hollyer engraving again served as a frontispiece. As he did when he bound up later copies of the 1855 edition, Whitman appended press notices and other information about himself and his book, some of which he had published anonymously. And he added the famous quote from Emerson, greeting him at the beginning of a great career, in gold stamping on the spine.[11] Both these editions were printed by Fowler and Wells, whose name did not appear in the book as publisher, though they did advertise the volumes for sale from their establishment.

In 1860, the third edition of *Leaves of Grass* was published commercially by the Boston firm of Thayer and Eldridge. Whitman's name was not on the title page or binding, and the Schoff engraving of the Hine portrait of Whitman replaced the Hollyer engraving as the frontispiece.[12] Whitman even anonymously edited and partially wrote the separately published *Leaves of Grass Imprints* for the purpose of advertising this edition. But Thayer and Eldridge soon went out of business, and *Leaves of Grass* would not have another commercial publisher for two decades.

The fourth edition of *Leaves of Grass* appeared in 1867, privately printed in New York for Whitman, whose name did not appear on the title page or binding. It was the first edition to appear without a physical likeness of Whitman, as well as the first to show Whitman's process of adding to his text by accretion. Whereas earlier editions of *Leaves of Grass* had incorporated new poems into the text during the typesetting stage, now Whitman physically added sheets from other works to the book. The first issue of the 1867 *Leaves of Grass* contains the reset text of *Leaves* and three appendixes, each with separate pagination: the newly set "Songs Before Parting" and the remaining sheets from the separately published *Drum-Taps* with its *Sequel*. The following year, after having exhausted the supply of sheets from *Drum-Taps*, Whitman reissued *Leaves of Grass* with "Songs Before Parting" and then reissued *Leaves of Grass* by itself.

The 1871 fifth edition of *Leaves of Grass* was privately printed in New York for Whitman, lacks his name on the title page but has it on the binding, and was packaged in various ways. The first printing was issued in two formats: with *Leaves of Grass* only and with *Leaves of Grass* bound together with the sheets of the separately published *Passage to India*. Both *Leaves of Grass* and *Passage to India* were reprinted and bound together in 1872. Two years later, Whitman took these sheets and used them in his first attempt to collect his poetry and prose in one place.

The 1876 *Leaves of Grass* is technically the second issue of the second printing of the fifth edition of the book. In order to help celebrate the United States centennial, Whitman reissued *Leaves of Grass* along with a volume of his prose writing, *Two Rivulets*, both volumes bound alike as the *Centennial Edition*, limited to a hundred sets. Rather than reprinting *Leaves of Grass*, he inserted a cancel title leaf and printed four new poems on separate slips or intercalations, which he pasted on the blank parts of pages in the text. He signed the title page to each copy, making this the first time Whitman's name appeared on the title page of *Leaves of Grass*, albeit not in type. Two likenesses of Whitman appeared in this volume: the Hollyer engraving and the Linton engraving of the Potter photograph.[13] Later in 1876, Whitman reprinted these volumes, setting in type in the text the previously intercalated poems.

As mentioned, the sixth edition of *Leaves of Grass* was the type-facsimile piracy of the 1871 edition's second printing issued by Hotten in London in 1873.

Whitman was able to return to a commercial publisher, James R. Osgood of Boston, for the seventh edition (or sixth American edition) of *Leaves of Grass* in 1881. This is far and away the most bibliographically complex edition of the work, one which shows a total of fifteen printings, two states, and seventeen issues during Whitman's lifetime. This was the final American edition of *Leaves of Grass* published by Whitman, and, fittingly, from here on out his name appeared in a facsimile signature on the binding (but not on the title page) and the Hollyer engraving was inserted.[14] Osgood completed three printings, but when the district attorney of Massachusetts denounced the book as "obscene literature" (DN, 2:285–286n) and Whitman refused to bowdlerize it by revising it, they withdrew the book from publication and turned over the remaining sets of sheets to the author. Whitman took the sheets, added a cancel title leaf which he signed in each of the 225 copies, and bound them in casings without his name as the *Author's Edition* in 1882. Also in 1882, the book was reprinted by Rees Welsh of Philadelphia (which put Whitman's name back on the casings) and then by the firm's successor, David McKay, who also reprinted the book in 1883 and 1884. In 1888, McKay reprinted *Leaves of Grass* and added the annex "Sands at Seventy" from slightly altered duplicate plates of the separately published *November Boughs*. Also, since he had extra sheets left over from the 1884 printing, McKay added the "Sands at Seventy" sheets to these too, resulting in the oddity of an issue of *Leaves of Grass* bearing an 1884 date on the title page but with an annex of poems first published four years later.

In 1888, Whitman for a second time collected his prose and verse, this time in one volume as *Complete Poems & Prose*, limited to six hundred copies, composed of a new printing of *Leaves of Grass* along with *Specimen Days & Collect* and *November Boughs*, both reprinted from the plates of the separately published works. The volume contained the Hollyer and Linton engravings of Whitman, was signed by Whitman on the *Leaves of Grass* title page, and was framed by inserted autobiographical "Notes" at the beginning and end of the volume. Whitman designed the casings and spine labels for the book,[15] as well as the illustrated volume's title page, printed on glossy paper, the first on which Whitman's name was printed (rather than written in by hand), with the Spieler photograph[16] of him above the legend, "Authenticated & Personal Book (*handled by W.W.*)." Although McKay distributed most of the copies, many were sold by Whitman personally out of his house in Camden.

Whitman again reprinted *Leaves of Grass* in 1889, adding "Sands at Seventy" and a new annex, "A Blackward Glance O'er Travel'd Roads," in a limited printing of three hundred copies to be published on the occasion of his seventy-ninth birthday and distributed by Whitman personally. He signed each copy on the title page and inserted four photographs and two engravings of himself.

Whitman's final packaging of *Leaves of Grass* was the 1891–1892 "Deathbed Edition," published by McKay. In failing health, Whitman took the sheets from the 1888 printing of *Leaves of Grass*, inserted a cancel title leaf, and added "Sands at Seventy," "A Backward Glance O'er Travel'd Roads," and the reprinted sheets of the separately published *Good-Bye My Fancy*. Finished on December 6, 1891, this was the last version of *Leaves of Grass* that Whitman personally saw through the publication process.

Besides *Leaves of Grass*, Whitman published *Drum-Taps* (and its *Sequel*) (1865), *Democratic Vistas* (1870), *Passage to India* (1871), *After All, Not to Create Only* (1871), *As a Strong Bird, on Pinions Free* (1871), *Memoranda During the War* (1875–1876), *Two Rivulets* (1876), *Specimen Days & Collect* (1882–1883), *November Boughs* (1888), and *Good-Bye My Fancy* (1891). Four of these books were published by commercial firms, the others being privately printed and distributed by Whitman and by selected booksellers. Whitman's name appeared on the title pages of only five of them. The first five lacked physical likenesses of Whitman in the book, but the others were all personalized in various degrees. *Two Rivulets, November Boughs*, and *Good-Bye My Fancy* each had photographs of Whitman inserted. Most copies of *Specimen Days & Collect* had a photograph of Whitman inserted, while others were prepared in a large paper format with three pictures of Whitman plus ones of his mother and father. *Memoranda During the War* contained two engravings of Whitman plus a "Remembrance Copy" page, giving information about the book's author.

Toward the end of his life, as he became less interested in revising the existing texts of the poems in *Leaves of Grass* than in adding new poems to it, Whitman began in earnest a process he had used only sparingly before, of making proof slips of individual poems. As William H. Garrison recalled, "Each bit when it left his hands in manuscript was sent to a quaint old printing-establishment . . . where it was set up in type. It was then returned to the author, who made such corrections as seemed to him desirable, and after this a revised and re-corrected copy was struck off and sent out as the matter to be used *punctatim literatim*" by journal and newspaper editors.[17] Slips exist for nearly a hundred individual poems and brief prose pieces. Sometimes these are little more than extra copies of tear sheets ordered by Whitman, but more often they are conscious and original creations. Rather than sending off a handwritten copy of the poem, Whitman would send his manuscript to the local print shop, read and revise it in proof, order clean copies printed (both with and without his name), and submit them to editors and distribute them to friends.

These data represent an excellent basis for studying the development of books. They also suggest some interesting possibilities for biographical study. First, the very titles of Whitman's books show him paralleling his life with his work. His book and annex titles could serve as chapter titles to his own biography. We start in the springtime of *Leaves of Grass*, then move on to the important wartime activities of *Drum-Taps* and *Memoranda During the War*, with their resulting *Specimen Days* and *Democratic Vistas*. And as he ages, Whitman writes of "Sands at Seventy," of glancing backward over the roads he has traveled, of the November of his life, and, finally, he wishes his reader "Good-Bye."

Second, Whitman often put a part of himself in his books by including engravings or photographs of him or by signing each copy on the title page. Even the commercially published, mass-produced works of the 1880s were personalized through the presence of the gold-stamped facsimile signature on the front cover of the binding. Whitman's use of the pronoun "I" in the writing process, intended to facilitate a direct line of communication with the reader, is here neatly paralleled in the publishing process, as if Whitman is say-ing, "This book is given by me directly to you." To emphasize this, the title page to the 1888 *Complete Poems & Prose* states that the book was actually "handled" by Whitman.

Third—and perhaps the most tantalizing possibility—is the suggestion that Whitman is an author who from the first visualized his writings as being in print. After all, he began his career as a journalist, accustomed to meeting deadlines of time and space, intimately familiar with the processes by which manuscripts were converted into print. Imagine, if you can, the excitement Whitman must have felt in 1855, when, while writing his first book of poetry and helping to set it into type, he knew that his expression would not be re-stricted by the width of a newspaper column or by the three-inch-wide lines of the double-columned format of *Franklin Evans*, but could be let loose over a six-inch-long expanse of a page without the constraints of justified margins. Whitman's ability to visualize his work in print—to literally see the finished product and to plan it before and during the writing process—is perhaps best seen in the proof slips of the 1880s. If Whitman did indeed think in print, then we need to go beyond mere literary analysis into areas such as cognitive psychology and visual perception in order to understand more fully Whit-man's creative and poetic processes.

Anyone doubting the validity of applying bibliography to biography need go no further than the copyright page of the 1891–1892 "Deathbed Edition" for conclusive proof. There, filling virtually the entire page, is Whitman's list of the various editions of *Leaves of Grass* and their annexes; the Library of Congress's copyright acceptance of May 10, 1891, which Whitman notes holds good through 1919 and may be extended through 1933; and, finally, his state-ment that as "there are now several editions of L. of G., different texts and dates, I wish to say that I prefer and recommend this present one, complete, for future printing." Is this not a noble tombstone—far more Whitmanesque than the overbearing vault at Harleigh Cemetery—a tombstone that lists the important dates of his life, that states the acceptance of those dates and his works by America's national library, and that bequeaths an inheritance to his audience? Life and work, past and future, tombstone and will, are inextricably joined; the man and the book are finally one, joined forever on the printed page.

NOTES

1. "So Long," LG, 505. Information on Whitman's books is taken from my *Walt Whitman: A Descriptive Bibliography* (Pittsburgh: University of Pittsburgh Press, 1993).

2. "Publication—is the Auction / Of the Mind of Man—" (Poem 709), Thomas H. Johnson, ed., *The Poems of Emily Dickinson* (Cambridge: Harvard University Press, 1955), 2:544.

3. G. Thomas Tanselle, *The History of Books as a Field of Study* (Chapel Hill: University of North Carolina Press, 1981), 6–7.

4. Ed Folsom, "'Affording the Rising Generation an Adequate Notion': Whitman in Nineteenth-Century Textbooks, Handbooks, and Anthologies," in Joel Myerson, ed., *Studies in the American Renaissance 1991* (Charlottesville: University Press of Virginia, 1991), 345, 364.

5. Horace L. Traubel, "Walt Whitman at Fifty Dollars a Volume, and How He Came to It," *Era* 11 (June 1903): 525–526.

6. This volume contains, in addition to *Leaves of Grass*, the type-facsimile texts of *Passage to India* and *After All, Not to Create Only*, both published separately in 1871. It is a very close reproduction if glanced at quickly, but closer inspection shows different textual readings, line breaks, copyright date ("1871"), and ornaments between the poems that distinguish it from the American edition. For a full discussion, see Morton D. Paley, "John Camden Hotten and the First British Editions of Walt Whitman—'A Nice Milky Cocoa-Nut,'" *Publishing History* 6 (1979): 5–35.

7. An interesting example of how bibliographical sleuthing corroborates this assumption about the popularity of Whitman's works in Britain occurred in 1904, when the firm of Small, Maynard of Boston published two Whitman titles, *An American Primer* and *Walt Whitman's Diary in Canada*, each limited to five hundred copies. The copyright deposit copies of both at the British Library, with cancel title leaves bearing the imprint of G. P. Putnam's of London, are bound in unprinted gray wrappers, clearly not a format used for public sale. The deposit copies at Oxford and Cambridge universities, at Trinity College, and at the National Library of Scotland all have the same unprinted wrappers. No other copies besides these at the deposit libraries could be located. Finally, neither book was listed in the *English Catalogue* as an importation by Putnam's or anyone else. The answer to this puzzle seems to be that the copies with the cancel Putnam's title leaf were used solely for copyright deposit, to secure copyright in Britain, and were not actually sold there. This solution receives support from printed forms in the Feinberg Collection at the Library of Congress, which acknowledge receipt by the British stationer's office of copyright applications for both books.

8. In the first state, the printed copyright notice was omitted, and Whitman wrote the information in by hand.

9. This description was used in the first three editions of *Leaves of Grass* (it is on p. 29 of the 1855 edition); see LG, 52n, for information on its subsequent variations.

10. See Ed Folsom, "'This Heart's Geography Map': The Photographs of Walt Whitman," *Walt Whitman Quarterly Review* 4 (Fall/Winter 1986–1987): 7 (picture 1850.2).

11. C. Carroll Hollis, "Whitman's Sketches for the Spine of the 1856 Edition," *Walt Whitman Quarterly Review* 4 (Fall/Winter 1986–1987): 75–76 (reproduced in facsimile on the back cover verso).

12. Folsom, "Photographs of Whitman," 8 (picture 1850.4).

13. Ibid., 17 (picture 1870.9).

14. The 1886 edition of Whitman's *Poems* published by Walter Scott in England was supervised by Ernest Rhys, with Whitman's long-range assistance.

15. Reproduced in Joel Myerson, ed., *Whitman in His Own Time* (Detroit: Omnigraphics, 1991), 321.

16. Folsom, "Photographs of Whitman," 28 (picture 1880.19).

17. See "Walt Whitman," *Lippincott's Magazine* 49 (May 1892): 623–626.

Whitman Unperturbed

The Civil War and After

AFTER FOUR agonizing years the Civil War was over, and Whitman had returned to New York to see *Drum-Taps* through the press. Relieved to find his family in better health than anticipated, he was enjoying his visit home more than usual. Up early, he was looking forward to a lazy Saturday morning when he could dawdle over his mother's good strong coffee. But what Whitman later called "the foulest crime in history known in any land or age" had already stained the presidential box at Ford's Theater.[1] So on that stupefying Saturday morning of April 15, 1865, Whitman and his mother exchanged the papers silently. Neither of them could say much, and nothing more was eaten that day.[2] The night before, in Washington, Peter Doyle, who liked the theater and was attracted by celebrities, had gone to see the play, the President, and his wife. For his commemorative Lincoln lectures, which began in 1879, Whitman drew on Doyle's eyewitness account of the shooting.[3] Oddly enough, however, the poem that he completed by mid-September 1865 omits all direct reference to the violent human intervention that struck down Lincoln,[4] though the symbolism of "When Lilacs Last in the Dooryard Bloom'd"—the broken sprig, for example, that the persona offers to Lincoln's coffin at the end of Section 6—alludes obliquely to other possible ruptures. But a rupture is not necessarily a historical outrage or a political injustice. And the imagery seems to be working to exclude vulgar local associations, to exclude the trivial in favor of the exalted.

Criticism has tended to assume that in "Lilacs" Whitman sought to avert his gaze and that of his readers from the catastrophe wrought by John Wilkes

Booth. As the "wound-dresser" poet, so the story goes, Whitman was seeking to promote the psychology of peace. And there was no need for him to restate the obvious. His audience knew the unnarratable fact: Lincoln had been brutally assassinated. Without denying the partial validity of this reading, in what follows I would like to suggest that criticism has not yet fully accounted for the complexity of Whitman's griefwork. His cunningly creative omission of the assassin's hand serves to problematize, as do other anti-occasional elements of the poem, the origin(s) of the speaker's bereavement, if bereavement it be.[5]

With its nostalgia for the unbroken serenity of an earlier life and for inherited rituals that have the power to contain violence, "Lilacs" takes its time about its strange revelations. Writing after great pain, in the poem's opening lines the speaker is comforted by the idea that his grief is guaranteed to return each spring following the arrival of certain natural signs; he is also consoled by the belief that his grief shall be contained within discrete temporal moments. On the one hand, he laments the loss of pain; on the other, he fears its re-awakening. This beautifully paradoxical opening is ripe for plunder, and reading the poem now we cannot help but hear the Eliotic echo: April is indeed the cruelest month. Galway Kinnell, however, hears another part of the story when he observes that in "Lilacs" "the grief is too thoroughly consoled before the first line is uttered."[6] In my view, Whitman is compelled to celebrate death, "sane and sacred death," because he imagines that death alone has the power to interrupt a relentless socioerotic narrative in which he, "Whitman," is eternally marginalized. Eerily empowered now and at last by the loss of his beloved, who in this poem is all but called "Lincoln," Whitman discovers in the fact and in the idea of death a community of mourners when no other social relationships are imagined as capable of sustaining him. The poem takes the fantasy of an enduring socioerotic community as its subject.

After visiting the White House on October 31, 1863, Whitman recorded in his diary, "Saw Mr. Lincoln standing, talking with a gentleman, apparently a dear friend. His face & manner . . . are inexpressibly sweet—one hand on his friend's shoulder, the other holds his hand. I love the President personally."[7] These are the words of a man who wistfully watches other people's friendships and who romanticizes forbidden loves. Composing a sonorous hymn to endangered devotion that transformed the assassination from a political to a natural and even mythic event, Whitman was writing out of the context of earlier affectional losses, including the failure of his relationship with his father and the probable loss during the late 1850s of an idealized "Calamus" lover. He was also writing out of the more immediate failure of his love affair with the American public. His books had not sold, and despite his admiration for the common soldiers whom he encountered during his hospital visits, that fact still rankled. Though in Washington he had some ardent admirers, including John Burroughs to whom he was indebted for his knowledge of the reclusive hermit thrush ("likes shaded, dark, places in swamps— / is very shy / sings in May & June— / not much after June / is our best songster") ("Hermit Thrush," NUP, 2:766), his words were mainly unheard by the nation at large. Thus, Whitman's erotic anxieties were reinforced by his professional marginalization.

As a Lincoln lover, however, Whitman admits no erotic rivals, and he thrives on ahistorical fantasies of the power of psychic dissociation. Living beyond time, under no temporal circumstances can he be displaced by his beloved's beloved, and he celebrates an erotic life inviolable by third parties. This fantasy of imperial selfhood nevertheless proves, is proving, and has proven remarkably unstable. "Lincoln" in death becomes the speaker's permanent possession, but "Lincoln" in death also becomes the speaker's permanent loss. The tenuous balance that Whitman achieves between erotic expression and erotic self-suppression is continually threatened by a number of historical factors, including, in the more or less real world, the demonstrable rivalrous intervention of John Wilkes Booth, who notoriously figures in the poem through his absence. Evidently Whitman is determined to expunge Booth from his text: both his national, political text and his timeless, unconscious text. But here Whitman discovers that silencing Booth is easier said than done. Insofar as "Booth" represents unanchored, free-floating aggression— that which cannot be contained, normalized, or truly forgotten—he also represents a perpetual possibility in the human soul. Though he may not know it, grief is only one of the feelings that threaten the persona's psychic integrity at the poem's inception. Because of the uncanny coincidence between his personal and cultural work—in both spheres his mission is ruthlessly to silence Booth and Booth's impersonators, including himself—the bereaved lover may have trouble distinguishing the nation's mourning, in which he to some extent participates, from his own less social, more self-immortalizing project. Ironically, reviewing Whitman's attitudes toward the historical Lincoln may serve to reinforce this point.

Like other ardent Northern Unionists, Whitman had initially entertained substantial and, in the event, realistic reservations about Lincoln's ability to hold the country together. At one time, he hubristically imagined that Lincoln could profit from the benefit of his political advice. "Brochure," he projected: "Two characters as of a dialogue between A. L.——n and W. Whitman.—as in? a dream—or better? Lessons for a President elect—Dialogue between W. W. and 'President elect.'"[8] Commenting on the fabled

Lincoln-Douglas debates in August 1858, he observed that "of the two, Mr. Lincoln seems to have had the advantage thus far in the war of words."[9] But he supported Douglas, to whom he looked to reinvigorate the moribund Democratic party. And it was Douglas rather than Lincoln who, Whitman hoped, would organize "a great middle conservative party, neither proscribing slavery . . . nor fostering it."[10] Before the war, then, Lincoln struck him as too extreme in his opposition to the South's peculiar institution.

Moreover, the radically competitive Whitman was prejudiced against the institution of the presidency, disputing as he did the concept of "Supremes." "I praise no eminent man—I rebuke to his face the one that was thought most worthy," he announced in the 1860 consciousness-raising poem "Myself and Mine," a rather transparent example of his envious need to feel good about himself. "It is ended—I dally no more," he wrote,

> After to-day I inure myself to run, leap, swim, wrestle, fight,
> To stand the cold or heat—to take good aim with a gun—to sail a boat—to
>   manage horses—to beget superb children,
> To speak readily and clearly—to feel at home among common people,
> And to hold my own in terrible positions, on land and sea. (LG60, 224)

In the "Proto-Leaf" to the 1860 edition of *Leaves*, he declared that "I will make a song for the ears of the President, full of weapons with menacing points, / And behind the weapons countless dissatisfied faces" (10). With good reason, he hated Buchanan, but his antipresidential diatribes were part of a larger politics in which there had to be room at the top for the ordinary men and women whom he imagined as his readers. "Have you outstript the rest? Are you the President?" he inquired. "It is a trifle—they will more than arrive there every one, and still pass on" (50). Thus, he had asked:

> Is it you that thought the President greater than you?
> Or the rich better off than you? or the educated wiser than you?
> .   ..   .
> The President is there in the White House for you—it is not you who are
>   here for him. . . .
> .   .   .
> You workwomen and workmen of These States having your own divine and
>   strong life,
> Looking the President always sternly in the face, unbending, nonchalant,
> Understanding that he is to be kept by you to short and sharp account of
>   himself,
> And all else thus far giving place to men and women like you. (145, 149, 157)

Along with the 1855 Preface, the first three editions of *Leaves of Grass* are filled with this kind of populism: antipatriarchal, anti-establishment, and antipresidential. There is also a demagogic edge to Whitman's rhetoric. When the "Presidents shall not be their common referee so much as their poets shall" (115), power shall be transferred not just to any poet but to Whitman in particular.

Associating presidents with tyrannical fathers as he does in "Song of the Broad-Axe," where he urges that children are to be "taught from the jump . . . to be laws to themselves, and to depend on themselves" (LG60, 133), Whitman also announced in the "Apostroph" to the "Chants Democratic" of the 1860 *Leaves*, "O you grand Presidentiads! I wait for you!" (108), which is not surprising considering that he had always been fascinated by visionary fantasies of perfected paternity and, more generally, by the notion of "supremes," such as God. This vital contradiction between the conservative and radical, the hierarchical and antihierarchical Whitman is inscribed in "Lilacs," where the dead president is both a melancholy comrade (not a supreme) and "the sweetest, wisest soul of all my days and lands" (a supreme of a democratic sort).

Whitman first saw Lincoln in person in mid-February 1861. From the top of an omnibus, he observed a silent, sulky crowd observing the blackclad president-elect in front of the Astor House on Broadway. Though Lincoln's life was already being threatened—both Lincoln and his wife feared that he would never return to Springfield alive—at the suggestion of New York Senator William Henry Seward he was deliberately taking a circuitous route on his journey to the capital, so as to rally support in the North. "The crowd that hemm'd around consisted I should think," Whitman recalled in his anniversary lecture,

> of thirty to forty thousand men, not a single one his personal friend—while
> I have no doubt, (so frenzied were the ferments of the time,) many an as-
> sassin's knife and pistol lurk'd in hip or breast-pocket there, ready, soon as
> break and riot came. But no break or riot came. The tall figure gave another
> relieving stretch or two of arms and legs; then with moderate pace, and ac-
> companied by a few unknown looking persons, ascended the portico-steps
> of the Astor House, disappear'd through its broad entrance—and the dumb-
> show ended.[11]

So frenzied were the ferments of the time that in the homiletic 1860 poem beginning "Respondez! Respondez!" Whitman had commanded apocalyptically, "Let Death be inaugurated! / Let nothing remain upon the earth except the ashes of teachers, artists, moralists, lawyers, and learned and polite persons! / Let him who is without my poems be assassinated!" (LG60, 168). It was galling to the poet who called himself the Answerer to find his ideas slighted, ignored, or even violently rebuffed by America's thinking elite. Whitman could play a part no longer; he was incensed with a little success.[12]

Following his own move to Washington in December 1862, Whitman was able to observe Lincoln more closely. The two men were never introduced and never spoke, but Whitman often saw the president as he was driven through the streets of Washington in his carriage. And he began to identify with Lincoln's plight. Writing to his friends Nat Bloom and Fred Gray, whom he called his "gossips & darlings," on March 19, 1863, Whitman noted:

I think well of the President. He has a face like a hoosier Michael Angelo, so awful ugly it becomes beautiful, with its strange mouth, its deep cut, criss-cross lines, and its doughnut complexion. My notion is, too, that underneath his outside smutched mannerism, and stories from third-class county barrooms, (it is his humor,) Mr. Lincoln keeps a fountain of first-class practical telling wisdom. I do not dwell on the supposed failures of his government; he has shown, I sometimes think, an almost supernatural tact in keeping the ship afloat at all, with head steady, not only not going down, and now certain not to, but with proud and resolute spirit, and flag flying in sight of the world, menacing and high as ever. I say never yet captain, never ruler, had such a perplexing, dangerous task as his, the past two years. I more and more rely upon his idiomatic western genius, careless of court dress or court decorums. (CORR, 1:82–83)

"I had a good view of the President last evening," the poet, who remained concerned for Lincoln's safety, wrote to his mother on June 30, 1863:

He looks more careworn even than usual—his face with deep cut lines, seams, & his *complexion gray*, through very dark skin, a curious looking man, very sad—I said to a lady who was looking with me, "Who can see that man without losing all wish to be sharp upon him personally? Who can say he has not a good soul?" The lady assented, although she is almost vindictive on the course of the administration, (thinks it wants nerve &c., the usual complaint). (CORR, 1:113)

This complaint was shared by Whitman's brother Jeff, who found him indecisive, "not a man for the times, not big enough . . . an old woman."[13] For his part, Whitman tried not to blame Lincoln for Union losses. "I believe fully in Lincoln," he wrote to Abby Price as Meade was unable to slow the Confederate advance across Virginia's Rapidan River; again, Whitman employed the ship of state metaphor that figured prominently in his letters home: "Few know the rocks & quicksands he has to steer through" (163–164).

The ship of state metaphor also figured prominently in one of Lincoln's re-current anxiety dreams, which, despite its murky symbolism, the president himself considered an omen of Union victory. And so it happened that on Good Friday, April 14, 1865, when Lincoln held his last cabinet meeting,

> General Grant, who attended the meeting, was asked for late news from Sherman, but had none. Lincoln remarked that it would come soon, and be favorable, for last night he had dreamed a familiar dream. In a strange inde-scribable ship he seemed to be moving with great rapidity towards a dark and undefined shore. He had had this same dream before Sumter, Bull Run, Antietam, Murfreesborough, Vicksburg, and Wilmington. Matter-of-fact Grant remarked that Murfreesborough was no victory—"a few such fights would have ruined us." Lincoln looked at him curiously and said, however that might be, his dream preceded that battle.[14]

So Whitman's fears for Lincoln's safety, as expressed in his most popular poem, "O Captain! My Captain!," and as represented by the thoroughly con-ventional ship of state metaphor, had a dense history in the poet's thoughts and in the president's. With good reason, then, both Mutlu Konuk Blasing and Kenneth M. Price refer to Lincoln as Whitman's political alter ego.[15] He had not always been so, but so he became. To say this, however, is to recognize the possibility of a divided or even fractured self, a self terribly in need of rec-onciliation. Reconciliation would, though, depend on some external integrat-ing power. If Whitman is completely identified with Lincoln, the collapse of difference bodes ill for the persona's future force—unless, that is, the absenc-ing power of language itself should prove sufficient, should prove to be that external integrating power so necessary for the poet's psychic salvation.

"Must not worry about George, for I hope the worst is over—must keep up a stout heart," Whitman had cautioned himself in a notebook entry written early in 1863. But then he had exploded, "My opinion is *to stop the war now*" (NUP, 2:548–549). Whatever his reservations about Lincoln's leadership, by the end of October he explained to his mother, "I have finally made up my mind that Mr. Lincoln has done as good as a human man could do—I still think him a pretty big President" (CORR, 1:174). Thereafter, he continued to reiterate his support for a beleaguered president, though it could be argued that he was almost equally taken with General Grant, "the most in earnest of any man in command or in the government either" (211). "Others may say what they like, I believe in Grant & in Lincoln too" (213). By May 6, 1864, he was convinced that "Grant has taken the reins entirely in his own hands—he is really dictator at present—we shall hear something important within two or three days—Grant is very secretive indeed—he bothers himself very little about sending news even to the President or Stanton—time only can develope his plans—I still think *he is going to take Richmond & soon*, (but I may be mistaken as I have been in past)—" (219–220).

Many of these contradictory attitudes toward Lincoln and male heroism are exemplified by a letter Whitman wrote to his mother following the assassination. On May 25, he praised the new president, Andrew Johnson, extolled Grant, who had been instrumental in effecting the exchange of Captain George Whitman from a Confederate prison camp, as "the noblest Roman of them all," and proffered an oblique dismissal of both leaders, Johnson and Grant, with the statement, "but the *rank & file* was the greatest sight of all." So the point is not that Whitman was more or less indifferent to Lincoln before John Wilkes Booth changed history. The seeds of his Lincoln cult had been planted, as had the seeds of a Grant cult. But following Whitman's attitudes in his contemporaneous writings, we are far from a vision of Lincoln as "the grandest figure yet, on all the crowded canvas of the Nineteenth Century," as he became in the somewhat ironically titled "Personal Reminiscences of Abraham Lincoln."[16]

Nevertheless, Whitman's finest Lincoln elegy, "When Lilacs Last in the Dooryard Bloom'd," is strikingly free of such particularizing detail as he could have provided from personal observation, from the firsthand accounts of others, or from his reading—had he wished to memorialize the historical Lincoln. As Helen Vendler has noted, "Lilacs" does not really contain "Memories of President Lincoln," which is the title of the *Leaves* cluster to which the poem was eventually assigned.[17] Other elegists provided "memories" of President Lincoln, evoking his rise from obscure origins, early losses, "cunning with the pen" (the phrase is Richard Henry Stoddard's), proverbial honesty, penchant for telling humorous stories, hatred of slavery, clemency toward the South, and political martyrdom—to name just a few themes in the voluminous Lincoln literature of the postbellum era.[18] Instead, Whitman histrionically foregrounded himself as the leading character in Lincoln's drama and dissolved the actual Abe into a national panorama of lost men. Given this dramatic repression of Lincoln's personal history and particular qualities ("the sweetest, wisest soul of all my days and lands" does not really qualify in the way of particularizing historical detail) and Whitman's almost complete repression of the murder as murder, it is evident that the poet's literary aggression had targets other than Booth. In short, Whitman's envy and distrust of powerful men were so great as to covertly determine the structure of any serious poem that he might write in praise of a fallen leader.

How does one compete with the honored dead, the dead whom one also wishes to honor? To say that Whitman identifies positively or even narcissistically with Lincoln, as to some extent he surely does, is not to suggest that he identifies with a unitary phenomenon. The poet who earlier in his career prided himself on his contradictions knew whereof he spoke. Caught as he is between a regenerative ideal ("fresh as the morning") and the night-stricken actual, the persona is determined to transcend his very representative grief and is committed to his personal, isolating quarrel with what, in his shrewd psychic economy, the dead president also represents: the power of the presidency, the power of the father, the power of the modern, technological, military state. Let's not be foolish here and claim that Whitman is in love with an aristocratic ideal. But just as at one time John Fitzgerald Kennedy seemed to represent a witty and humane alternative to his lackluster predecessor, so, too, Lincoln, even as a "hoosier Michael Angelo," accumulated some of the trappings of an imperial presidency.[19] From a distance, Whitman had been starstruck by the handsome young Prince of Wales, the future King Edward VII.[20] Now Lincoln is associated with voluptuous Venus, the evening star, as Whitman with his strong interest in astronomy well knew. The "lustrous" orb possesses the brilliance of a masculine supreme tempered by the obscurity of the feminized dead. Just as in the opening poem of Wordsworth's "Lucy" sequence a dropping moon portends her death ("'O mercy!' to myself I cried, / 'If Lucy should be dead!'"), in "Lilacs" the star's disappearance portends the president's death, stagily. Considered as a democratic performance, "Lilacs" brilliantly encapsulates the American fascination with royalty, with "Yous up there" and with "Supremes."

The poem has two emotional projects: transcending grief and transcending aggression. In "Lilacs," when the speaker praises the dead president as "the sweetest, wisest soul of all my days and lands" or as his "dear," then "dearest" comrade, he is specifically denying Lincoln's political power and robbing him of his phallic force. Vaguely reminiscent of Wordsworth's Lucy, "Fair as a star, when only one / Is shining in the sky," Lincoln is associated with the evening star Whitman later called "voluptuous Venus . . . languid and shorn of her beams, as if from some divine excess."[21] In "Strange Fits of Passion Have I Known," a disappearing moon portends Lucy's death; in "Out of the Cradle Endlessly Rocking," the low-hanging moon becomes a dynamic symbol of the beloved's fate; in "Lilacs," a heavenly sign portends the president's death. In keeping with the poem's ambiguous emotional project, Whitman's "lustrous star" is both masculinized and feminized, empowered and disempowered.

The persona's need to evade his aggression, to cover it all over with "bouquets of roses . . . with roses and early lilies . . . [and with] the lilac that blooms the first" (DT, 5), has two main literary consequences. First, in offering Lincoln's coffin his sprig of lilac, he renounces his vision of himself as a romantic rebel in the Shelleyean tradition, a vision allied with his sense of himself as a primitive phallic force. Second, having renounced this sociopolitical conception of his poetic mission, he is compelled to sing "Death's outlet song of life," "Song of the bleeding throat" (DT, 4). Glancing obliquely at Lincoln's martyrdom, the self-dramatizing Whitman stages his own demise. Empathetically merging with Lincoln, he defuses "Lincoln's" structural power.

At the same time, however, Whitman's still-powerful need to compete with his beloved, with "Lincoln," erupts in Section 18 when he compares the welfare of the living and the dead. Such comparisons were conventional in sentimental literature where, as in Susanna Rowson's *Charlotte Temple*, they usually functioned as devices to resolve otherwise irreconcilable political and literary conflicts.[22] The belief that the dead are better off than the living also influenced how people thought about hardship. Consider the memoirs of Private Henry Robinson Berkeley, a Confederate soldier who, like Peter Doyle, was a member of a Virginia militia unit when the war began. Unlike Doyle, Berkeley lasted out the entire conflict, though he was captured in March 1865 and imprisoned at Fort Delaware, Delaware. Along with other Southern prisoners, he was released in mid-June on the condition that he take an oath of allegiance to the United States government. Berkeley was a Virginia native, the son of a farmer. A future schoolteacher, he was not a particularly reflective man and was thoroughly demoralized by the war's conclusion. He was convinced that Lincoln should have been in church rather than at the theater on that fatal Good Friday and was personally embittered by the rough treatment he and other Confederate prisoners received in the weeks following Lincoln's death, when there was talk of a national conspiracy afoot that caused Confederate prisoners to be subjected to further reprisals.

Searching for a way to conclude a diary that had become a record of his humiliations, Berkeley, who was by then waiting in Richmond for a ride back to his home in Hanover County, recorded:

> As I had an hour, I thought I would walk a little way down Main Street and take a look at the burnt district. One could hardly tell where Main Street had been. It was one big pile of ruins from the Custom House to the wharf at Rocketts. At this point, the Yanks had collected all kinds of debris of war: cannon, muskets, bayonets, cartridge boxes, swords, broken guncarriages, broken wagons, etc. I had never imagined that the Confederacy had one-half as many siege guns in and around Richmond. As I gazed sadly over all this war wreckage for a few moments, my thoughts were with our noble dead, "the unreturning brave." Is it better with them or with us? We hope, aye, we almost know it is well with them. But who knows what the future

holds for us; only God. I turned away and with a sad and gloomy heart
bent my steps towards the Depot.[23]

"Is it better with them or with us?" Berkeley asked. "We hope, aye, we almost know it is well with them. But who knows what the future holds for us;
only God." With greater assurance and considerably less deference to any God-
centered religious hopes for an afterlife, Whitman cannily and categorically
asserts that whereas the living remain and suffer, the dead are fully at rest:

> I saw battle-corpses, myriads of them,
> And the white skeletons of young men—I saw them,
> I saw the debris and debris of all the dead soldiers;
> But I saw they were not as was thought;
> They themselves were fully at rest—they suffer'd not;
> The living remain'd and suffer'd—the mother suffer'd,
> And the wife and the child, and the musing comrade suffer'd,
> And the armies that remain'd suffer'd. (DT, 11)[24]

But why enter into a competition with the dead for primacy of suffering?
"Companionless," cries Shelley at a comparable moment in "Adonais":

> Oh, weep for Adonais—he is dead!
> Wake, melancholy Mother, wake and weep!
> Yet wherefore? Quench within their burning bed
> Thy fiery tears, and let thy loud heart keep
> Like his, a mute and uncomplaining sleep;
> For he is gone, where all things wise and fair
> Descend;—oh, dream not that the amorous Deep
> Will yet restore him to the vital air;
> Death feeds on his mute voice, and laughs at our despair.[25]

Companionless yet unable to accept his existential solitude, companioned
only by the thought of death and the knowledge of death, to escape from
erotic desolation Whitman is tempted by suicide—just as following his
mother's death in 1873 he expressed the wish to Ellen O'Connor that he, too,
could die. On the one hand, despair; on the other, a powerful determination
to enact the role of a suffering secular saint, to become the president of despair. But in rescuing the dead from further suffering, the speaker celebrates
the heroism of the living. The living remain and suffer, and in "Lilacs" suffering commands center stage.

"The death of the late President," Lincoln had declared in July 1850, following the sudden death of Zachary Taylor, "may not be without its use in
reminding us that we, too, must die. Death, abstractly considered, is the same

with the high as with the low; but practically, we are not so much aroused to the contemplation of our own mortal natures, by the fall of *many* undistinguished, as that of one great, and well known name."[26] Lincoln's death caused Whitman to contemplate the problem of death, "abstractly considered," just as the deaths of many undistinguished people, including his brother Andrew, during the "parturition years" of the Civil War contributed to his ambivalent sense of himself as a guilty survivor. In "Lilacs," the poet of the body becomes the poet of the body's tragedies. He seems to blame himself in Section 8 for not having prevented Lincoln's death and to blame himself in Section 18 for not having fought in the war. Psychically battle-fatigued, "all splinter'd and broken" (DT, 11), he finds it necessary to insist somewhat tactlessly, as I have been suggesting, that the dead, who are at rest, are better off than the living— whose lives, at that point in the poem, are superficially projected as unremittingly miserable. Yet perhaps the vision is not so much tragic as fatalistic, and this fatalism eventuates in Whitman's intimacy with death, the "Dark Mother, always gliding near, with soft feet" (9). Balanced against this fatalism is Whitman's muscular sense of life as a struggle, a competition from which he is not yet willing to withdraw, however much he is tempted by his emblematic bird's somewhat inhuman praise of death. Haunted as he is by earlier songs of fresher selves, he looks back to a central work in his own career, to "Out of the Cradle Endlessly Rocking," a poem that critics have also been quick to label as morbid. Here, in "Lilacs," Whitman reincarnates his mockingbird as a hermit thrush who, in avoiding the settlements, attempts to jettison the hubristic agonies of the romantic artist. In "Lilacs," the bird exemplifies the speaker's death wish, which Whitman is not yet ready to claim as his own.

Despite Whitman's fatalism, throughout the poem there are ebbs and flows in his access to somatic and psychic power. Cruel hands hold him powerless; he uses his hands to break off a sprig of lilac with its flower; he contributes his sprig of lilac to the coffin that slowly passes and then to all conceivable coffins, discovering joyously and paradoxically the copiousness of nature in his feverish efforts to celebrate death; he imagines himself as a tomb decorator, hanging pictures on the walls of "the burial-house of him I love" (DT, 7); he holds hands with the thought and the knowledge, with the anticipation and the retrospective awareness of death; he hymns "the sure-enwinding arms of cool-enfolding Death" (9) in Section 16; and, following his visionary experience in Section 18, he frees himself from death's grasp, "unloosing the hold of my comrades' hands" (11). Finally, in Section 20, his hands are at rest and he leaves the lilac with heart-shaped leaves, "there in the door-yard, blooming, returning with spring" (12). He doesn't need to break it or to use it to smother his grief. He can afford to leave it alone.

Can it be, then, as Harold Bloom has wickedly suggested, that hands are more than merely totemistic in "Lilacs" and that the poem is centrally concerned with masturbation? He explains that the sprig of lilac represents what the poet, in Section 25 of "Song of Myself," calls his "live parts" and that "the voice of the bird will represent those ardors so intense, so wrenched from Whitman, that he did not know he possessed them." Moreover, "a failed masturbation is the concealed reference in Section 2 of the *Lilacs* elegy":

> O powerful, western, fallen star!
> O shades of night! O moody, tearful night!
> O great star disappear'd! O the black murk that hides the star!
> O cruel hands that hold me powerless! O helpless soul of me!
> O harsh surrounding cloud that will not free my soul! (DT, 3)

Bloom further explains that "the cruel hands are Whitman's own, as he vainly seeks relief from his repressed guilt, since the death of Father Abraham has rekindled the death, a decade before, of the drunken Quaker carpenter-father, Walter Whitman, Senior." [27]

However implausibly lurid, Bloom's father-centered analysis accounts for the fact that Whitman writes like a man whose only resource was Lincoln and whose world has collapsed because of his hero's death. This melodramatic perspective, as Bloom hints when he refers to "the supposed elegy for Lincoln" and then, several pages later, to the "elegy for President Lincoln," is more appropriate to the child than to the man. Or we may say that the still-living child in all of us is father to Whitman's man. Hence the attractiveness of death as a "Dark Mother." Losing his father, whose potency he covets, the speaker turns to his mother; she alleviates his loss, but she cannot fully initiate him into or restore his manhood. The helpless child will not be stilled, the child who cannot believe that his dearest, most protective comrade would desert him, leaving him prey to a red marauder. Reaching out to the symbolic romantic father, Whitman's hands grasp the democratic mother instead. But she, too, is a language silencer. Bloom's narrow insistence on failed masturbation provides an explanation for the speaker's psychic vulnerability—castration figuring as perhaps the most fundamental violation of male sexuality—but in so doing it mistakes a possible troping effect for a specific historical cause. As I suggested earlier, "Lilacs" takes as its subject the fantasy of an enduring socioerotic community and tests this fantasy against history. Ironically, Bloom's reductive conclusion underscores the poem's concern with the unforced transmission of power from father (here "Lincoln") to son (here "Whitman"); it also obscures those impalpable psychic fault lines on which the greatness of Whitman's never-to-be-completed utterance depends.

"Drum Taps has none of the perturbations of Leaves of Grass," Whitman proudly told William Douglas O'Connor in January 1865 (CORR, 1:247). As many critics have noted, Whitman unperturbed was not much of a poet, since his struggle with masculine literary, political, and familial tradition had energized his art. Once he became the good gray poet, the benevolent patriarch, and, as I have attempted to show, the Lincoln lover, his story was over. Mostly, after the war, there was no more need for symbolic language and for the estranging power of poetry. In the ghostly pines and the cedars dusk and dim there was nothing left to obscure, not even anything sexual. Whatever Whitman's personal temptations in the future—with Peter Doyle, with Anne Gilchrist, with Harry Stafford—with bereavement and ill health and old age and envy, his poetic temptations were a thing of the past. Lincoln's death had occasioned one last major poetic perturbation, but following the war, as he lived beyond "Lincoln" and beyond rage, Whitman's violent quarrel with patriarchal tradition was so muted as to be almost inaudible. There were still brilliant exceptions—lines, images, short poems—but mainly the postwar Whitman recommitted himself to prose. "Lilacs" prophetically demonstrates, as I have tried to show, what may happen to a "wound-dresser" with too many wounds.

NOTES

1. LG, 339. "This Dust Was Once the Man" was first published in 1871.

2. "Mother prepared breakfast," he later recalled, "and other meals afterwards—as usual; but not a mouthful was eaten all day by either of us. We each drank half a cup of coffee; that was all. Little was said. We got every newspaper morning and evening, and the frequent extras of that period, and pass'd them silently to each other" ("The Stupor Passes—Something Else Begins," PW, 2:31). He further recalled that "I remember where I was stopping at the time, the season being advanced, there were many lilacs in full bloom. By one of those caprices that enter and give tinge to events without being at all a part of them, I find myself always reminded of the great tragedy of that day by the sight and odor of these blossoms. It never fails" (see "Death of Abraham Lincoln," PW, 2:503). Lilacs were also in full bloom in Washington outside the Peterson House where Lincoln was taken after the shooting. For a fascinating account of this and other historical matters, see Dorothy Meserve Kunhardt and Philip B. Kunhardt, *Twenty Days: A Narrative in Text and Pictures of Abraham Lincoln and the Twenty Days and Nights that Followed—The Nation in Mourning, The Long Trip Home to Springfield* (New York: Harper and Row, 1965).

3. Richard Maurice Bucke, ed., *Calamus: A Series of Letters Written during the Years 1868–1880 by Walt Whitman to a Young Friend (Peter Doyle)* (Boston: Small,

Maynard, 1897), 25–26. Whitman first mentioned Doyle in his diary in December 1865 but had not yet made his acquaintance while writing "Lilacs." In correspondence with Whitman, Doyle's love of the theater, including burlesque, is evident. See Charley Shively, ed., *Calamus Lovers: Walt Whitman's Working Class Camerados* (San Francisco: Gay Sunshine Press, 1987), 106.

4. Exactly when Whitman first drafted "Lilacs" is unknown. Presumably the poem was written and rewritten. In mid-September, John Burroughs wrote to his friend Myron Benton that "Walt's book will be out in a week or two. . . . He is deeply interested in what I tell him of the Hermit Thrush, and says he has used largely the information I have given him in one of his principal poems" (quoted in Clara Barrus, *Whitman and Burroughs, Comrades* [Boston: Houghton Mifflin, 1931], 24). Mid-September is a terminus ad quem for the poem's composition. Since the book appears to have been in press at this time, it seems likely that the poem had been completed by the end of August. Possibly Whitman began drafting the poem in May and June and finished it by the end of August.

5. A strong reading that challenges the usual unified poem tradition is offered by Kerry C. Larson in *Whitman's Drama of Consensus* (Chicago: University of Chicago Press, 1988), 231–243. Drawing attention to the provisional, multiple beginnings, the splintered, centerless point of view, and the static, nonincremental mode of development, Larson nevertheless argues that "Lilacs" is "unquestionably the greatest of his 'great poems of death': this elegy for Lincoln marks a special advance in understanding by formulating a distinction between 'the thought of death' and 'the knowledge of death' in the climactic recognition scene of section fourteen" (231). But the poem is more concerned with preserving emotional hegemony than with abstruse advances in understanding that turn on death's temporality.

6. Galway Kinnell, "Whitman's Indicative Words," in Stephen Railton, ed., *Walt Whitman: Walt Whitman's Autograph Revision of the Analysis of Leaves of Grass (For Dr. R. M. Bucke's Walt Whitman)* (New York: New York University Press, 1974), 58.

7. DT, xviii–xix.

8. Charles I. Glicksburg, ed., *Walt Whitman and the Civil War* (New York: A. S. Barnes, 1963), 174.

9. Emory Holloway and Vernolian Schwarz, eds., *I Sit and Look Out: Editorials from the "Brooklyn Daily Times"* (New York: Columbia University Press, 1932), 96.

10. Holloway and Schwarz, 98.

11. "Death of Abraham Lincoln" (PW, 2:501).

12. According to Henry B. Rankin, had Whitman only known it, one of his readers was none other than the prepresidential lawyer himself. In *Personal Recollections of Abraham Lincoln* (New York: G. P. Putnam's Sons, 1916), Rankin

writes that "Lincoln . . . who had been . . . in the unapproachable depths of one of his glum moods . . . took up *Leaves of Grass* for his first reading of it. After half an hour or more of devotion to it, he turned back to the first pages and, to our general surprise, began to read aloud. . . . His rendering revealed a charm of new life in Whitman's versification. Save for a few comments on some broad allusions that Lincoln suggested could have been veiled, or left out, he commended the new poet's verses for their virility, freshness, unconventional sentiments, and unique forms of expression, and claimed that Whitman gave promise of a new school of poetry" (91). Alas, the tale is a hoax, according to William E. Barton. In *Abraham Lincoln and Walt Whitman* (Indianapolis: Bobbs-Merrill, 1928), Barton claims that Rankin was never one of Lincoln's law clerks (90–94).

13. Dennis Berthold and Kenneth M. Price, eds., *Dear Brother Walt: The Letters of Thomas Jefferson Whitman* (Kent, Ohio: Kent State University Press, 1984), 59, 61.

14. Samuel Eliot Morison and Henry Steele Commager, *The Growth of the American Republic* (New York: Oxford University Press, 1934), 613.

15. See Mutlu Konuk Blasing, "Whitman's 'Lilacs' and the Grammars of Time," *PMLA* 97 (January 1982): 31; Kenneth M. Price, *Whitman and Tradition: The Poet in His Century* (New Haven: Yale University Press, 1990), 77.

16. *North American Review* (1886), as reprinted in Barton, 83–89. The essay is also reprinted with the title "Abraham Lincoln" in PW, 2:601–604.

17. Helen Vendler, "Whitman's 'When Lilacs Last in the Dooryard Bloom'd,'" in Mary Ann Caws, ed., *Textual Analysis: Some Readers Reading* (New York: Modern Language Association of America, 1986), 132–143.

18. Richard Henry Stoddard, "An Horatian Ode," in A. Dallas Williams, ed., *The Praise of Lincoln* (Indianapolis: Bobbs-Merrill, 1911), 102–108. In addition to Whitman, among the authors represented in this volume are Thomas Bailey Aldrich, William Cullen Bryant, Alice Cary, Phoebe Cary, Rose Terry Cooke, Richard Watson Gilder, Oliver Wendell Holmes, Lucy Larcom, James Russell Lowell, Edmund Clarence Stedman, Bayard Taylor, John Townsend Trowbridge, Jones Very, John Greenleaf Whittier, and Whitman's Washington friend, John James Piatt. For a study of Lincoln mythology that is a bit dated but still very helpful, see Roy P. Basler, *The Lincoln Legend: A Study in Changing Conceptions* (Boston: Houghton Mifflin, 1935). Basler lists other anthologies of Lincolniana. Further, for the kind of material that Whitman censored, see "A Lincoln Reminiscence," beginning, "As is well known, story-telling was often with President Lincoln a weapon which he employ'd with great skill" (PW, 2:537).

19. According to Don E. Fehrenbacher, "Serious scholars have applied the word 'dictator' more often to Lincoln than to any other president. The list of his presidential actions inspiring such judgments is a rather long one. With Congress, by

his arrangement, not in session, he responded to the attack on Fort Sumter by enlarging the army, proclaiming a blockade of Southern ports, suspending the writ of habeas corpus in certain areas, authorizing arbitrary arrests and imprisonments on a large scale, and spending public funds without legal warrant. He never yielded the initiative seized at this time, and, in later bold assertions of executive authority, he introduced conscription, proclaimed emancipation and inaugurated a program of reconstruction" ("Lincoln and the Constitution," in Cullom Davis, Charles B. Strozier, Rebecca Monroe Veach, and Geoffrey C. Ward, eds., *The Public and the Private Lincoln: Contemporary Perspectives* [Carbondale: Southern Illinois University Press, 1979], 127).

20. The love letter to the future King Edward VII that Whitman embedded within "Year of Meteors (1859–60)" is possibly the most embarrassing vignette in *Leaves of Grass*.

> Remember you surging Manhattan's crowds, as you passed with your cortege of nobles?
> There in the crowds stood I, and singled you out with attachment;
> I know not why, but I loved you . . . (and so go forth little song,
> Far over sea speed like an arrow, carrying my love all folded,
> And find in his palace the youth I love, and drop these lines at his feet).
> (DT, 51–52)

See also "A Broadway Pageant" in the same volume.

21. Whitman, *Specimen Days*, in PW, 150.

22. According to Cathy N. Davidson, "*Charlotte Temple* became America's first best-selling novel in the earliest years of the Republic, when the fledgling nation was yet defining its own cultural and political identity, and it remained a best-seller well into the beginning of the twentieth century and America's ascendancy as a world power"; see Susanna Rowson, *Charlotte Temple*, ed. Cathy N. Davidson (New York: Oxford University Press, 1986), xi.

23. William H. Runge, ed., *Four Years in the Confederate Artillery: The Diary of Private Henry Robinson Berkeley* (Chapel Hill: University of North Carolina Press, 1961), 144.

24. Vendler sees this passage as an example of Whitman's great delicacy of feeling. She writes, "It is, as the poem says, the living who remain and suffer. Only the dead are excused from suffering, insanity, and the gross inflictions of war. With characteristic delicacy, Whitman puts himself in a minor place in the list of survivors: For each dead soldier 'the mother suffer'd, / And the wife and child and musing comrade suffer'd / And the armies that remain'd suffer'd. . . .' The thrice-repeated 'suffer'd' is paired inextricably with the twice-repeated 'remain'd' until the two verbs become synonymous: to remain is to suffer" (140).

25. "Adonais," in *Shelley's Poetry and Prose*, ed. Donald H. Reiman and Sharon B. Powers (New York: W. W. Norton, 1977), 393.

26. Roy P. Basler, ed., *The Collected Works of Abraham Lincoln* (New Brunswick: Rutgers University Press, 1953), 2:90. The address was delivered at City Hall in Chicago.

27. Harold Bloom, "Whitman's Image of Voice: To the Tally of My Soul," in *Agon: Towards a Theory of Revisionism* (New York: Oxford University Press, 1982), 179–199. The quoted passages are from 188–190.

ORIGINS AND STYLE

He most honors my style who learns under it to destroy the teacher.

("Song of Myself," LG, 84)

The European Roots of *Leaves of Grass*

M Y TITLE must not be taken literally. The grass which decorated the cover of the first edition of *Leaves of Grass* had roots as well as leaves, but these roots were firmly sunk in American soil, and this grass could not at the same time have roots in Europe—where Whitman never set foot. But this grass, figuratively, had European roots, too—which, incidentally, helped its acclimatization in Europe later. However original, Whitman's poetry was not an alien body and an absolute novelty in the literature of the Western world. It was as much influenced by European writers as were the works of his more conventional compatriots. Unlike the transcendentalists, he was a New Yorker, not a New Englander, and, even in those days, New York was both the most American city on account of its gigantism and dynamism and the most cosmopolitan, the most European city in the United States. It was a beachhead of Europe in America, and Whitman breathed there a European atmosphere uncontaminated on the whole by the puritanism which subsisted in New England and was even reinforced by the Catholic puritanism of the Irish immigrants.

Whitman, however, found himself in a difficult position. On the one hand, he wanted to practice what Emerson preached in his "American Scholar Address" two decades before, namely to lay the foundations of a purely American literature, independent of Europe; on the other hand, he realized that it was impossible completely to break with the past. He was no new Adam starting from scratch, obliged to invent a new language. He had a ready-made one at his disposal, which came from Europe. He knew that, generally speaking, "no result exists now without being from its long antecedent result, and that from its antecedent. . . ."[1] The very first words of the 1855 Preface were unambiguous in this respect: "America does not repel the past or what it has produced . . ." (LG, 709). And he specified: "The New World receives with joy the poems of the antique, with European feudalism's rich fund of epics, plays, ballads. . . . If I had not stood before those poems with uncover'd head, fully aware of their colossal grandeur of form and spirit, I could not have written 'Leaves of Grass.'"[2] In short, since the language was the same, he regarded English literature as the past of the nascent American literature.

A contemporary of Whitman's reading *Leaves of Grass* and knowing nothing about its author, could not have suspected the "long foreground" that preceded it (except Emerson, from whom I borrow the phrase). Yet, the "turbulent, fleshy, sensual, eating, drinking and breeding" "rough" Whitman claims to be in "Song of Myself," the "rough" who led no one to a hateful "indoor library," actually was, as we all know, not the manual worker we see on the frontispiece of the 1855 *Leaves of Grass* but a journalist, a man who lived by his pen, an intellectual, an "American scholar" in a way, though he had never been to college. True, he was self-taught, but he was widely read, as is amply shown by the notes he took, which were collected by Richard Maurice Bucke in *Notes and Fragments* and by Clifton J. Furness in his *Walt Whitman's Workshop*. He was led by an insatiable intellectual curiosity, which impelled him systematically to explore human history and the literatures of the past. In so doing, his purpose was not to garner up materials which he would use later in his own writings; it was a disinterested pursuit. His ideal (as he defined it for critics—that is to say, for himself, for he was a critic as well as a poet) was to comprehend "the universal, the all, yet with keen eye to detail, and with quick ear, well aware of passions and emotions, intuitive, intellectual, yet more than merely intellectual." He wished to have "at command the whole arsenal of books," to be possessed of "the special instinct of the love of books," and to acquire "a distinct perception and recognition of the wonders of Humanity and Nature" which would eventually lead to some suggestive explanation on those "tremendous wonders" and to the knowledge "that man and the universe have a fitting purpose and that Soul *is*." Thus, reading was not for him an accumulative process but an active search. It kept him simmering and simmering until he reached the boiling point (NF, 53).

With such an aim and such a method, he went straight to essentials when reading. Very often he did not bother to read a book from cover to cover, he merely skimmed through it, but despite this cursory examination, he managed to have a searching and valid estimate of it thanks to "that skimming tact which an editor gets after some experience, [that] enables him to take out at a dash the meaning of a book."[3] If one reads the pages he has devoted to writers in *Specimen Days* or in his journalist writings—or what he confided to Traubel in his old age when they discussed literature—one realizes that he was a shrewd literary critic. Sometimes he did not even bother to read the books he was discussing. In his notes on Dante, for instance, he writes: "The *Paradiso*, I've not read," but he had read the *Inferno* and that sufficed (NF, 96). He had not read *Don Quixote* either, for he states: "The second part . . . *is said* to be better than the first" (84, emphasis added). He seems to have read Virgil, for he wrote in his notes: "Oct. and Nov. 1857. Reading Virgil's Bucolics, Eclogues and Aeneid" (100). Very often, too, his notes are merely condensations of articles or notices he found in magazines or encyclopedias, but through them he skillfully knew how to reach the heart of the matter. However, he seems to have been quite interested in Lucretius, whose *De rerum natura* contained a noble though too negative philosophy to which he was still referring in *Specimen Days*.[4]

Thus, there were three sorts of books for Whitman: books he did not read because they were mere fiction in particular, books he read cursorily, and books he loved and read with reverence or admiration. But for him there would never be imitation: "Books, as now produced, have reached their twentieth remove from verities. Our writers have apparently forgotten that there is anything to be aimed at except Literary Literature" (NF, 146). He wanted above all to be intrepidly himself. There was no fear or anxiety of influence in his case. He was absolutely self-reliant and wrote in his notes: "The great poet [i.e., himself] absorbs the identity of others and the experience of others and they are definite in him and from him; but he presses them all throughout the powerful press of himself . . . loads his own masterly identity" (109). His purpose, when reading, was to become "well saturated with the originality of others" ("Death of Longfellow").[5] He had that courage praised by Emerson, which consists in the conviction that "they with whom you contend, are no more than you."[6] "Who wants to be any man's follower?" he proudly asked. As Harold Bloom had to acknowledge, Emerson, like Whitman after him, denied the anxiety of influence: "We need not fear excessive influence," Emerson said in "Uses of Great Men," ". . . the wheels of tendency [i.e., of evolution] will not stop. On and forever onward." Those whom we recognize as our masters or precursors only reveal to us and bring to the surface our own inner latencies: "Instead of feeling a poverty when we encounter a great man, let us treat the newcomer like a traveling geologist who passes through our estate and shows us good slate, or limestone, or anthracite, in our brush pasture."[7]

Whitman was certainly never intimidated when he discovered a great writer. He immediately regarded such an author as, at best, his equal and in no case his superior—whether it was Shakespeare or the Hebrew prophets of the Bible or Milton. Of all the English poets, he most admired Shakespeare, but he objected to his ornate style and his feudalistic themes. He respected Milton but did not consider him a great poet; his subjects seemed to Whitman uninteresting and anachronistic. Whitman treated his British contemporaries or quasi-contemporaries, like Scott and Tennyson, in a similar fashion: he enjoyed their poetry, but he disapproved of their vestigial feudalism. He seems to have known most of the British romantics primarily by hearsay. While he was attracted to Robert Burns as a democratic poet after his own heart, he found Keats and Shelley and Byron oddly incomplete, "perhaps because they all died too young."[8] Blake seemed to him a half-mad visionary. Wordsworth and Coleridge, whose poetry (surprisingly, especially in the case of Wordsworth) Whitman seems not to have known well, were "lost leaders" whose promising early work was betrayed by their later admiration for "kingcraft, obedience and so forth" (NF, 107). Swinburne was all "pretty thoughts, pretty chime, pretty arrangements" (HT, 2:188), and Browning was too difficult, "free of the desire to be at once understood" (93). Carlyle had a "rapt, weird, (grotesque?) style," but Whitman could not help admiring him.

As was natural and inevitable, *Leaves of Grass* drew its sap more from these British writers than from continental European authors. It has been calculated that "numerically, more critical comments were made in the *Eagle* on the British than all the continental nations combined."[9] But this does not mean that Whitman ignored or underrated European writers to whose works he had access through translations. He concluded his essay on "British Literature" in *Specimen Days* with this exhortation: "I strongly recommend all the young men and women of the United States . . . to overhaul the well-freighted fleets, the literatures of Italy, Spain, France, Germany, so full of those elements of freedom, self-possession, gay-heartedness, subtlety, dilation, needed in preparation for the future of the States. I only wish we could have really good translations."[10]

In the notes published by Richard Maurice Bucke, Whitman lists a number of Greek and Latin classics: the *Iliad* and the *Odyssey*, and works by Aeschylus, Euripides, Sophocles, Aristophanes, Aristotle, Pindar, and Virgil, whom he despised because the *Aeneid* is merely "a second-hand article," but he considered the *Bucolics* and *Georgics* first-rate (NF, 99). He seems to have read these poems as well as the *De rerum natura*, as we have seen, but it is unlikely that he read the other authors. His notes read as if they had been compiled from some encyclopedia. Their works are every bit as "second-hand" as he believed the *Aeneid* was.

Among the Italians, Whitman seems to have been familiar with Dante, at least with the *Inferno*. He knowingly praises its "lean and muscular ruggedness; no superfluous flesh . . ." and adds that "some of its idioms must, in Italian, cut like a knife. . . . A great study for diffuse moderns." He may have been thinking of himself. He quite candidly admits he did not read the *Paradiso* (NF, 95–96). Tasso is the other Italian writer he mentions, but his notes on him are purely biographical; he certainly did not read any of Tasso's works (130–131).

Whitman preferred German and French writers. When Heine died in 1856, Whitman read some of his poems and noted: "fanciful and vivacious, rather ironical and melancholy with a dash of poetical craziness" (NF, 94). A very sound judgment but only a fleeting impression.

He was more interested in Goethe. He reviewed Goethe's autobiography in the *Brooklyn Eagle* in 1846 and described it as "the simple easy *truthful* narrative of the existence and experience of a man of genius." He proposed it as a model for the way it showed "how his mind unfolded . . . how and where the religious sentiment dawned in him, what he thought of God. . . ."[11] He knew Goethe mostly through Carlyle and two works of popularization: Joseph Gostwick's *German Literature* and Frederic Henry Hedge's *Prose Writers of Germany*, both of which he owned and read assiduously.[12] In his notes on Goethe, he very frankly confessed: "Had I not better read more of Goethe before giving an opinion?" He gave one nonetheless: "Goethe's was the faith of a physical well-being, a good digestion and appetite; it was not the faith of the masters, poets, prophets, divine persons" (NF, 105–106). (In this respect, he probably considered himself superior to Goethe.) He did not accept Goethe's doctrine "that the artist or poet is to live in art or poetry alone apart from affairs, politics, facts, vulgar life, persons and things—seeking his 'high ideal.'" So, to his mind, though great as the embodiment of culture, Goethe was no model for American authors. Yet he had "almost boundless pleasure in Goethe's works" and, to some extent, tried to emulate him.

As was often the case, Whitman was more interested in Goethe's personality than in his works, and he was thus curiously attracted by the autobiography of an obscure contemporary of Goethe, Heinrich Zschokke, whose "great natural goodness" and "sense of living at home in Heaven with [God] in this wonderful place" (the world) had struck him (NUP, 5:1,831). In his eyes, it was almost "Song of Myself" in prose.

But the strongest impact of Germany on Whitman's mind came from the philosophers of the idealist school: Kant, Fichte, Schelling, and Hegel. He celebrated their philosophy in *Specimen Days* in "Carlyle from American Points of View," for it was Carlyle who had discovered them and brought them into fashion. Whitman knew them through Gostwick and Hedge, for their aridity repelled him and mere abstracts of their often abstruse treatises sufficed for him. Their conclusions became "The Base of All Metaphysics," as he explained in *Leaves of Grass*. His favorite was Hegel. "Only Hegel is fit for America—is large enough and free enough" for "the heavens and earth and all things within their compass—all the events of history—the facts of the present and the development of the future . . . all forms . . . a succession of steps in the one eternal process of creative thought" (NF, 134). He rated Hegel "as Humanity's chiefest teacher and the choicest physician of [his] mind and soul" because, "penetrating beneath the shows and materials of the objective world," he showed "that in respect to human cognition of them, all and several are pervaded by *the only absolute substance* which is SPIRIT" (135). There resulted from his vision "a curious triplicate process," Hegel's dialectic: thesis, antithesis, and from the clash of the two, synthesis, a process which "goes on without end." This philosophy seemed to Whitman to answer all questions, and he adopted it unreservedly. ("History, with all its long trains of baffling, contradictory elements . . . the dark problem of evil, forming half of the infinite scheme, etc. . . . .")

As to France, the land of revolutions and militant (but not triumphant) Democracy, "ma femme," as he apostrophized her, it supplied Whitman with more precise answers on the political plane. He was a child of the Age of Enlightenment and had absorbed the motto of the first French Republic: Liberty, Equality, Fraternity. His father was a freethinker, and from childhood Whitman had been familiar with Volney's *The Ruins*, a very popular translation of a French book first published in 1791 during the revolution. It was the work of a French "philosophe," later a member of the French Convention, who, after meditating on the ruins of ancient cities in the Middle East, reached the conclusion that religions have only a relative and temporary value and, all being ephemeral, are all equal. It helped Whitman to detach himself from Christianity. He knew of Voltaire, too, and published an article about him in *Life Illustrated* in 1856. He saw in him "a fit precursor, in one or two points, of the American era" and summed up Voltaire's contribution to history: "He had no belief in the soul—none in immortality. He had a clear head, never to be cheated by the traditions of those who made a good thing out of churches and courts. . . . He helped on a great work—he did his part," but "he had no democracy."[13]

Volney and Voltaire (whose works he knew only at secondhand) finally had a negative influence on him. They were above all denigrators. Rousseau's case was different. Whitman read his *Social Contract* very carefully. There is even among his papers a manuscript translation of part of it in his own hand; of course, he did not do it himself, since he did not know French. He sympathized in particular with Rousseau's affirmation of human rights and sentences like, "Man is born free, yet he is everywhere in fetters," but he objected to the way the individual was sacrificed to the state in Rousseau's utopia: "Where Rousseau is yet undeveloped is in not realizing that the individual man or woman is the head, and the State, City, Government, or what not, is a servant, subordinate—with nothing sacred about it. . . ."[14] This already sounds like *Leaves of Grass*.

When reading Michelet, however, Whitman had no reservations. Michelet, like him, believed in the people. The people were the heroes of his *History of France*, which Whitman briefly reviewed in the *Brooklyn Eagle* in 1847 (UPP, 1:134). He probably also read *The People* (published in the U.S. in 1846), for there are strange resemblances between Michelet's book and *Leaves of Grass*, as Gay Wilson Allen pointed out in his *Walt Whitman Handbook*.[15] He may even have read Michelet's book, *The Bird*, which, though in prose, is pure poetry. He transcribed the passage on "l'oiseau frégate," which became "To the Man-of-War Bird"—an early instance of "found poetry."

Victor Hugo was another contemporary author with whom Whitman sympathized. Like Michelet, Hugo had exalted the people in *Les Misérables*, which Whitman had read, and in his poetry, especially *La Légende des siècles*. Besides, Victor Hugo violently attacked Napoléon III, whom he called Napoléon the Lesser in *Les Châtiments*, and he spent the twenty years of Napoléon III's reign in exile in the Channel Islands. But poetry like wine does not travel well, and Victor Hugo was not well served by his translators. Whitman read some of Hugo's poems in the Canterbury Poets series, and the translation by a clergyman named Carrington was so bad that he considered the poems "mere skim milk." Fortunately, a friend of his in Washington translated some of the poems orally in a very lively manner. Anne Gilchrist later translated part of the *Légende des siècles* for him, and "it was nobly done," he said. As a result, he deeply admired Hugo's works: "He was a masculine genius. There are some signs of flare, peculiar Frenchiness in *Légende des siècles*, but after that a real sublimity of power" (HT, 2:335). "He always appeals to what is deepest in me" (329). But he objected to what he called the "flatulent literary blotches and excesses" of Hugo's poetry, without realizing that his own might incur the same reproach. Their careers ran along parallel lines. In one of his pictures Whitman even looked exactly like Hugo (1:338). But there was never any real contact between them. They may even have been somewhat jealous of each other, each regarding the other as a rival. "I do not like his insularity," Whitman confided to Traubel, "he never said a good word for us—was rather inclined towards the Carlylean point of view with regard to America. Hugo was full of contempt for all things not Parisian—at least not French" (223). (This in 1888; Hugo died in 1885.)

The French writer Whitman was most enthusiastic about was certainly George Sand. Even in his old age he grew dithyrambic when her name was mentioned. "I regard her as the brightest woman ever born," he said in 1888. "Better than Hugo as a novel writer?" asked Traubel. "Oh! greatly! Why, read *Consuelo* . . . it displays the most marvelous verity and temperance: no false color—not a bit: no superfluous flesh—not an ounce: suggests an athlete, a soldier . . . prepared for the fight . . . She was Dantesque in her rigid fidelity to Nature . . ." (HT, 3:35). He was especially fond of *Consuelo* and its sequel, *The Countess of Rudolstadt*. "I find," he said in 1888, "I have the volumes complete: five of them: three of the story proper: two of the sequel—*The Countess of Rudolstadt*. . . . I have had the books—or my mother—I think since '41— nearly fifty years. . . . The book is a masterpiece: truly a masterpiece: the noblest work left by George Sand—the noblest in many respects, on its own field, in all literature" (423). (This incidentally shows that, contrary to Esther Shephard's claim, he never concealed the fact that he knew this book.) He also read another of George Sand's novels, *The Journeyman Joiner*, which he reviewed in 1847 (UPP, 1:135). In *The Countess of Rudolstadt*, there is a "rhapsode vagabond" dressed as a worker or a peasant, who, during a mystic trance, composes "the most magnificent poem that can be conceived." He is a poet-prophet who wants to be anonymous, because, he says, "my name is a man and I am nothing more than any other man." To him everything is beautiful. The only evil is tyranny, which goes against nature, since all men are born brothers in freedom and equality. Is he not just like Whitman as he described and sang himself in *Leaves of Grass*? So Esther Shephard jumped to the conclusion that Whitman was not inspired by a transcendentalist mysticism but deliberately and slyly borrowed the main themes of his poems from George Sand. And, to make things worse, according to her, he also plundered *The Journeyman Joiner*, which told the story of a handsome young carpenter as noble as Christ, who worked with his father, just like Whitman, and talked eloquently about art. And, like Whitman again, he one day experienced an ecstasy and spoke afterward with the eloquence of a great orator or writer.

The analogies are striking, but are they sufficient to explain the sudden birth of *Leaves of Grass*? What Whitman found in these verbose novels (they are verbose, despite Whitman's praise of their style) were mere vague suggestions which confirmed tendencies already present in him. Some of the analogies were more apparent than real. The ecstasy of George Sand's hero has nothing in common with the rapture described by Whitman in "Song of Myself," and as to the trance into which the Count of Rudolstadt falls, it is of a totally different nature: it enables him immediately to express his ideas with passion and eloquence, while Whitman's ecstasy was the source of his inspiration but had no content. It only put him in a state of poetic grace and was not immediately translatable into poetry. As to his philosophical and social ideas, they were not Sand's exclusive monopoly. They were in the air, in Carlyle's and Emerson's works in particular, and they were not even hers to begin with; she derived them from a socialist friend of hers, Pierre Leroux, as Henri Roddier has shown.[16] At the most, Whitman may have found in these two novels an encouragement to become himself, to become what he had for a long time confusedly dreamed of being but had not dared to realize for fear of appearing abnormal or ridiculous. After reading George Sand's novels, it seemed natural to him to become a poet-prophet like the Count of Rudolstadt and to make a living as a carpenter like the Journeyman Joiner—and like his own father. The fact that his father was a carpenter must have seemed to him a happy and auspicious coincidence. There is absolutely no reason, therefore, for accusing Whitman of cheating or insincerity, but there is no doubt, nevertheless, that some of the roots of *Leaves of Grass* drew their sap from Sand's novels, whereas, as we have seen, other potential roots, on the contrary, dried up and died. One reason for this dearth of influence was that Whitman did not want to absorb the morbid elements in European literatures and "the rankest and foulest poison" of their antidemocratic doctrines.

What Whitman wanted to extract from the literatures of the Old World was in particular "the element of courageous and lofty manhood" which "from the Iliad to Shakespeare" remained "unchanged" (PW, 2:727). He wanted above all to be "a master after [his] own kind, making the poems of emotions, as they pass or stay, the poems of freedom and the exposé of personality [his own], singing in high tones Democracy and the New World of it through These States" (a statement written before 1850, according to Bucke, NF, 92)—and his success is due in part to the European roots of *Leaves of Grass*.

NOTES

1. 1855 Preface, LG, 725; see also 562–564.

2. "A Backward Glance O'er Travel'd Roads," LG, 567, 568.

3. Cleveland Rogers and John Black, eds., *The Gathering of the Forces* (New York: G. P. Putnam's Sons, 1920), 2:279.

4. See Roger Asselineau, *The Evolution of Walt Whitman* (Cambridge: Harvard University Press, 1962), 2:290, 117n.

5. *Specimen Days*, PW, 1:286.

6. Merton M. Sealts, ed., *The Journals and Miscellaneous Notebooks of Ralph Waldo Emerson* (Cambridge: Harvard University Press, 1965), 5:344.

7. Quoted in Harold Bloom, *A Map of Misreading* (New York: Oxford University Press, 1975).

8. "Old Poets," PW, 2:658.

9. Thomas Brasher, *Whitman as Editor of the "Brooklyn Daily Eagle"* (Detroit: Wayne State University Press, 1970), 97.

10. "British Literature," PW, 2:523.

11. Rogers and Black, 2:294–295.

12. See Floyd Stovall, *The Foreground of Leaves of Grass* (Charlottesville: University Press of Virginia, 1974), 195–196.

13. Emory Holloway and Ralph Adimari, eds., *New York Dissected* (New York: Rufus Rockwell Wilson, 1936), 70, 73.

14. Clarence Gohdes and Rollo Silver, eds., *Faint Clews and Indirections* (Durham: Duke University Press, 1959), 33 *et seq.*

15. Gay Wilson Allen, *Walt Whitman Handbook* (Chicago: Packard, 1946), 469–470.

16. Henri Roddier, "Pierre Leroux, George Sand et Walt Whitman," *Revue de Littérature Comparée* 31 (January–March 1957): 5–33. See Esther Shephard, *Walt Whitman's Pose* (New York: Harcourt, Brace, 1938), especially 178–271.

"Tallying, Vocalizing All"

Discourse Markers in *Leaves of Grass*

M Y TITLE comes from line 8 in "Proto-Leaf," the opening poem in the 1860 edition of *Leaves of Grass*. It begins the line and announces the mode and manner of Whitman's utterance, or, I should say, his intended utterance, for there is no record that he ever spoke these words. But I've been thinking about them, off and on, for many months now, for they indicate an oral (spoken) mode that I have always sensed in *Leaves* (especially the early poems) but have never been able to get a handle on. The two classic studies of Whitman's early manuscripts (Fredson Bowers's *Whitman's Manuscripts* and Arthur Golden's *Walt Whitman's Blue Book*) provide much parallel information on other aspects of this poem as it evolved into "Starting from Paumanok." Bowers spots various manuscript lines that might support the oral as well as the written intention behind some of these poetic attempts, such as "Hear the loud echo of my songs there! Read the hints come at last" or "Listen to me, / Out from Paumanok, where I was born" (MLG, 35, 49).

I have never found evidence that Whitman made public platform presentations of his poems in the early years of his poetic career (1854–1860), though I've often wondered whether he ever thought of going up to Central Park some Saturday afternoon, climbing on a park bench, and belting out a "chant democratic" or so. He respected and admired Elias Hicks and Edward Thompson Taylor, knew and seemed to approve both Beechers, and was familiar with books on oratory. In creating his poems, he certainly would have tested the lines out loud to himself and thought about their impact on the audience he hoped was there. I am not, however, concerned here with the possibility that Whitman actually recited the early *Leaves* but rather with the probability that he wrote with the intention that they be read aloud. In brief, is there any evidence of an oral style in *Leaves*?

A few years ago Ed Folsom alerted me to a passage in Horace Traubel's *With Walt Whitman in Camden* that I had overlooked. On March 20, 1889, Walt and Horace were talking about their English friend, the socialist Edward Carpenter, who had written about one of his open-air lectures: "About seventy people came, old and young, respectable and non-respectable, and it was all very friendly and pleasant." Whitman picked up on Carpenter's terminology and said, "Respectables and non-respectables provide for us too: non-respectable—that's where we come in. Edward lectures: that should have been my business, too: if I'd gone direct to the people, read my poems, faced the crowds, got into immediate touch with Tom, Dick, and Harry, instead of writing to be interpreted, I'd had my audience at once" (HT, 4:392).

Since I had always believed that there was an oral basis in the early *Leaves*, Walt's confident statement that his poems should be said, not read, started me again looking for evidence. So for these last few years I've been examining assorted linguistic studies, seeking an explanation of the stylistic features I keep finding in the early editions of *Leaves*. I finally found one in Deborah Schiffrin's *Discourse markers*, volume 5 in *Studies in International Sociolinguistics*, under the general editorship of the anthropologist John Gumperz.[1]

Schiffrin is a member of that group of linguists at Georgetown University whose scholarship, under the direction of Deborah Tannen, has added significantly to recent language studies. Schiffrin's purpose is to demonstrate "how particular expressions are used to organize conversational interaction."[2] These "particular expressions" are known as "markers." All discourse markers are directed ideally and primarily to listeners (but also realistically and inevitably to readers), both to get their attention and to focus their attention on what follows. The markers Schiffrin investigates are *"oh, well, and, but, or, so, because, now, then, I mean,* and *y'know."*[3] The last two are truly conversational and do not apply to our project. Of the other nine, some are used by Whitman rarely and others extensively; I will only be able to examine a couple here. But if we make ourselves conscious of these markers and look for them in Whitman's early poetry, we will find them everywhere. My example will be "Proto-Leaf."[4]

Markers such as the ones we will discuss are so common in our daily conversation that it hardly seems necessary to explain them further,[5] especially since Schiffrin has a chapter on each one, with plenty of examples, all drawn from interviews she conducted in Philadelphia, which need not concern us here except to point out that they confirm the oral (spoken) origin and function of these words. Even as I was reading her examples, I was aware of parallels in *Leaves*, to which I *now* turn. Notice that discourse marker I just used—now—*and* which I am violating by not doing *so* (two more markers). *But* (still another marker) one other explanation—I will be using the 1860 edition, for discourse markers are integral to it.

Let me go back to explain why I called attention to my use of those four discourse markers (*now, and, so, but*). They appeared in my writing almost subconsciously, without my being specifically aware that I was practicing what I was going to preach; I became aware of them after the fact. These and other markers like them show up all the time in conversation, and our use of them is so habitual that we rarely are explicitly conscious of employing them in our talk or writing. The project I would like to initiate here is to see how discourse markers work, find what their place is in Whitman's poetry, discover how long his frequent use of markers lasted, and decide what we should do with this information.

Schiffrin's first three chapters are full of key explanations for amateurs in linguistic lore, but in chapter 4, "Oh: Marker of Information Management," she begins her most helpful explanation. I will summarize her findings but, rather than cite her examples, I will look at comparable uses from "Proto-Leaf." She points out that *oh* when spoken "is traditionally viewed as an exclamation or interjection" to suggest that its speaker "has undergone some kind of change" in his or her response to the situation under discussion.[6] Such an explanation certainly applies to Whitman's use of "O":

O such themes! Equalities!
O amazement of things! O divine average!
O warblings under the sun—ushered, or *now, or* at noon, *or* setting!
O strain musical, flowing through ages—*now* reaching hither,
I take to your reckless *and* composite chords—I add to them, *and* cheerfully
    pass them forward. (LG60, 14, emphasis added)

As far as we know, Walt never said or delivered these lines orally, but the record shows that he sometimes put O's in manuscript versions of his poems, perhaps in preparation for the performances that never occurred.

But is there any informational or poetic value in the five O's and their placement here in the opening of this major book of Whitman's early career? Deborah Tannen, in her *Talking Voices*, comments on the extensive repetition of some discourse markers: "Although these function words [discourse markers] are likely or even required to occur frequently in any English discourse, nonetheless their frequent occurrence plays a part in giving the discourse its characteristic shape and sound. In this sense, their repetition plays a significant role in establishing the shared universe of discourse created by conversational inter-action in that language."[7]

In "Proto-Leaf," the poet goes on to delineate just what in America he approves of and how he will treat it as he takes an imaginative tour of the country. Surveying and praising the country and its citizens, even those of the future, he cries out:

> *O* all and each well-loved by me! my intrepid nations! *O* I cannot be discharged from you!
> *O* Death! *O* for all that, I am yet of you, unseen this hour, with irrepressible love,
> Walking New England . . .
> [and through the nation] . . . welcoming every new brother,
> Hereby applying these leaves to the new ones, from the hour they unite with the old ones,
> Coming among the new ones myself, to be their companion—coming personally to you *now*,
> Enjoining you to acts, characters, spectacles, with me. (LG60, 18–19, emphasis added)

Note that the "you now" that ends the next-to-last line is expressly addressed to you, the listener and/or reader, whether in 1860 or 1992 or 2060.

In this excerpt, there is a central problem of interpretation that we should consider. In the third line, to what does "all that" refer? I presume it means "Death," and so he is saying "In spite of Death, I am yet of you." The "you" then is us, his future listener(s) and/or reader(s). Let's look at the passage closely: clearly "these leaves" are the pages of this new edition (which includes earlier poems mixed with these new ones). Note that he is "Coming among the new ones," not that he is the/a "new one." I'm suggesting that the printed words of the poem are comparable to the printed or written score of music: the poem must be played or sung or said to be affective. My claim is for the vital importance of oral rendition of *Leaves* to get the full affect of this song. When Whitman says, "Hereby applying these leaves to the new ones, from the hour they unite with the old ones, / Coming among the new ones myself, to be their companion—coming personally to you *now*, / Enjoining you to acts, characters, spectacles with me," the "you" of the "you *now*" is you the present reader, us, his future readers (listeners). Whitman thus accomplishes a transmigration, which seems confirmed at/with/in his lines. But as the old saying goes, "Saying doesn't make it so"—or does it? The ubiquitous discourse markers—signs of spoken discourse—certainly help to create the illusion.

It would be useful sometime to perform a full analysis of the variety of dis-course markers in Whitman's poetry—especially *and*, *but*, and *or*—but for now I will only suggest a couple of characteristics of his use of two other markers that have special interest in *Leaves*—*now* and *then*. In one of her chapters, Schiffrin discusses these markers, which she calls "temporal ad-verbs," and she explains their function in terms of conversational interchange. She makes it clear how different these two markers are in their discourse func-tion, explaining how "the deictic properties of *now* and *then* have an impact on their use as discourse markers" by relating them to "differentiation on a proximal/distal axis."[8] This axis contrasts time-deictics (*now* vs. *then*) but also person-deictics (*I* vs. *you*) and place deictics (*here* vs. *there*, *come* vs. *go*). As far as "Proto-Leaf" goes, Whitman uses *now* eleven times and *then* three times, clearly putting him at the "proximal" end of the axis. Schiffrin remarks: "Ele-ments on the proximal end are ego-centered: they are located closer to the speaker and to the speaker's space and time." She also refers to E. Clark, who in 1974 suggested "that ego-centered, proximal elements are used by a speaker to convey a positive personal orientation toward a particular state of affairs."[9]

This use of the "proximal/distal axis" was new to me, and it was surprising to see how this language analysis suggested things about Whitman and his po-etry that I would not have expected. "Time deictics" depend on the intention of the person uttering them, and they open up the whole complicated busi-ness of *time* in poetry. Let's look at a couple of lines in "Proto-Leaf": "I, *now* thirty-six years old, in perfect health, begin"; "*Then* take my place for good with my own day and race here" (MLG, 8, 7, emphasis added). Schiffrin ex-plains that there are two time relationships which are important for under-standing the discourse functions of *now* and *then*. These are "*event time* and *discourse time*,"[10] and here is where we get into complications. The "event time" is obviously 1860, when Whitman was thirty-six years old, but it is ob-viously false now, so we adjust at the cost of a little mental arithmetic. Similar adjustments are required when we take Whitman's place with his own day and race.

Even Roy Harvey Pearce's facsimile cannot make this text contemporary. We accept this, for even in 1860 the audience had to read, not hear, Walt's ut-terance. But since we are not ever going to get the true original, why not listen to (not read) *Leaves*? I cannot help but think how fascinating it would be to record a good actor reading the 1860 version of *Leaves*. Every page of the 1860 edition has discourse markers, so why not put them to use as Walt intended? Remember that such markers are not necessary in written discourse (a good critical exercise is to take a page of "Proto-Leaf" and remove all the markers and then decide which version is most effective and why). Markers simply direct language more intimately to the listener (and, when used in writing, to the reader cast as listener-on-the-page). They get and focus attention. It is difficult to demonstrate this vital feature of Walt's early style, but it comes close to being the aspect that most enthralled many poets in England and Europe for the rest of the nineteenth century.

In "Proto-Leaf" there are 293 instances of discourse markers. And how many in the whole 1860 edition: 5,403! I like to say that amazing number aloud, for it is surely something of a record. Someone should trace the decline in numbers in the succeeding editions of *Leaves*. The significance of markers in the history of poetry after Whitman is also yet to be studied, as is their role in the oral literature of this century. There is no time here to explore and to speculate upon the spoken (as contrasted with the written) poetry of the new century, but in the creation of the new literature, as well as in the appreciation of its new oral forms, discourse markers will be of increasing significance.

I'm sorry I didn't know more about these markers years ago. It would have been a stunner to conclude my study of language and style in *Leaves of Grass* with an analysis of the discourse markers in the first edition, then the 1860 edition, and then those appearing after the Civil War. Such a study should be done for the whole span of *Leaves*. Someone else will have to do it now; it could be an important book.

NOTES

1. Deborah Schiffrin, *Discourse markers* (Cambridge: Cambridge University Press, 1987). Various of Schiffrin's earlier articles are listed on 352–353.

2. Ibid., ix.

3. Ibid., 31.

4. LG60, 1–22. It should be noted that this introductory poem has a very complicated textual history that cannot be traced here. The evidence is provided in MLG; included in Bowers's study is the analysis of "Premonition" and other manuscript evidence from the Charles E. Feinberg Collection, Library of Congress. As "Proto-Leaf" is the basis of "Starting from Paumanok," "Premonition" is the basis of "Proto-Leaf." All the evidence confirms the oral (spoken) intention and aim of the poet at this stage of his career. That oral and/or spoken goal changed, and the poetic consequences are revealed in BB. As far as can be demonstrated from the surviving manuscript notes, Whitman started the poem in October 1856 and sometime in 1857 had enough pieces together to give it a title and organize different groups into sections, many of which still exist in the standard version today. Golden traces the growth. I have nothing but indebtedness and admiration for Bowers and Golden, and my work is a footnote to theirs, accentuating the oral intention that I find in Walt's poems.

5. Here is a list that provides a brief identification of the function of each of the nine markers important in Whitman's poetry.

O or Oh: usually an exclamation; when used alone, O is a sign of strong emotional states (surprise, fear, shock, grief, etc.)

O: in repairs: either in repair initiation: "O no!" or in completion: "O of course . . ."

O: marking focus of speaker's attention: "O say can you see . . ." or in the last section of "Proto-Leaf," "O power, liberty, eternity at last!"

Well: an interjection, filler, particle, hesitator, initiator; almost always a response marker

CONNECTIVES

And: coordinates idea units (series), and continues a speaker's action

But: contrasting ideas

Or: an option marker (hearer directed)

CAUSE and RESULT

So: in communication: shifts responsibility to hearer

Because: in communication: indicates cause

TEMPORAL ADVERBS (Deictic)

Now: at the time the word is uttered (points forward)

Then: at the time the word is uttered (points backward)

6. Schiffrin, 73, 74.

7. Deborah Tannen, *Talking Voices: Repetition, Dialogue, and Imagery in Conversational Discourse* (Cambridge: Cambridge University Press, 1989), 76.

8. Schiffrin, 228.

9. Ibid., 228, 229.

10. Ibid., 229.

Whitman's Physical Eloquence

A NUMBER OF the papers presented at the Centennial Conference suggest how Whitman's special manipulation of the physical medium of his poems affected the rhetoric and potential reception of *Leaves of Grass*. Joel Myerson demonstrates how Whitman's knowledge of printing shaped visually effective innovations in his poetic art. As if to balance this implicit appeal to an increasingly literate (and thus visually oriented) readership, Whitman also strived—as Carroll Hollis suggests—to create an illusion of orality that would echo the still-powerful strains of oratory from the early nineteenth-century pulpit and political forum. From James Miller, we learn how Whitman's commitment to the human body—and the body of his lovers—thoroughly infused his conception of language and spirit. Finally, Wynn Thomas, in commenting on the politics of *Leaves of Grass*, questions the rhetoric of identification often attributed to Whitman, and Alan Trachtenberg likewise notes the "coming closer of you and I" as a political and poetic problem in the poems. I want to explore these themes further by means of a concept I will refer to as "physical eloquence," Whitman's attempt to replace a rhetoric of identification with a rhetoric of interpenetration based on sexual experience. As much as it was an effort to express the author's own physical experience and desire, Whitman's poetry of the body evokes the physical experience of the ideal or implied reader and attempts radically to extend that experience, thus connecting literate and political life in a way that transforms both aspects of the reader's experience.

Whitman's experiment with physical eloquence began in the 1855 *Leaves of Grass*; indeed, it distinguishes the poems written in the 1850s and early 1860s from his earlier writing and from the poems and prose written after the Civil War. In the poetry of the body he cultivated an extreme application of prosopopoeia, which Paul de Man, true to the literate bias of deconstruction, has identified as "the master trope of poetic discourse," the means by which the author restores the illusion of his own presence to the written text, but also "as the trope of address, the very figure of the reader and reading."[1] Whitman wanted to come before his reader as a human being, not as a book, interposing not only the illusion of the author's bodily presence but also the figures that will bring the reader's own body to attention. Instead of a mere spectator, the ideal reader becomes a fellow performer, a bodily presence, and, ultimately, a lover. "Come closer to me," the poet had encouraged an audience of lovingly imagined but unknown readers in 1855, "Push close my lovers and take the best I possess"; then shifting attention from his own person to that of his readers, he urged further: "Yield closer and closer and give me the best you possess" (LG55, 87). In the face of such boldness, Calvin Bedient asks, "Who before him so relentlessly buttonholed the 'strangers' of his own and future days, spoke up so breath-near, asked so much of them, characterized them so lovingly, imposed on them so insinuating, so whispered an intimacy?" In the provocative trope of Alan Helms, Whitman "cruised the reader," offering signs of companionship and desire in a continual search for an accepting, indeed a loving, readership.[2]

The distance implicit in the literate medium is undermined by the figures and conventions of orality and physical presence. And yet, though complaining that he "pass[ed] . . . poorly with paper and types" (LG55, 87), Whitman would have passed not at all without paper and types. His notebooks are full of lectures and speeches never given; his early attempts to address political gatherings fell flat. It was not orality or literacy in the pure and simple dichotomy so often gleaned from the work of Marshall McLuhan and Walter J. Ong that made Whitman's poems effective in their special way but rather the curious interplay of speech and poetic writing. The very failure of Whitman's voice in public speech was transformed into an effort to give voice to the silent text and to "pass with the contact of bodies and souls" of absent and future readers (87). To these readers—most especially to those of us reading one hundred years after his death—he could say with truth, "every atom belonging to me as good belongs to you" (25), for only the corpus of the poems, now the "property" of us latter-day readers, is left as the trace of the once-living poet's material existence and possessions. The poems that can no longer sustain him sustain us. "The words of the dead man," as W. H. Auden writes in his elegy on Yeats, "are modified in the guts of the living."[3]

The evocations of—and the impositions upon—the reader's body pass nearly unnoticed at times. Mere tugs at the unconscious, they restrain the reader from an easy passage into a fully mental experience that would exclude the life of the body. In "Song of Myself," for example, we encounter the line, "Only the lull I like, the hum of your valved voice" (LG55, 28). The liquid *l*'s move the tongue despite the repressive efforts of a silent yet subvocalizing reader. The motion of the tongue in pronouncing "the lull I like" prepares the reader to take the part of the lover who ravishes the poet in the lines that follow: "You settled your head athwart my hips"—the *h*'s breathing forth the short breaths of sexual excitement—"and gently turned over upon me, / And parted the shirt from my bosom-bone, and plunged your tongue to my bare-stript heart"—the plosive *p*'s and *b*'s bursting the envelope of body and text, allowing the reader to come inside, to "get into" the poem (28–29). The heart, which itself has already spoken—"the hum of your valved voice" mimicking the vibrations and quiet roar of the internal organs, the "voice of God" (om) acknowledged by the meditating yogi—now becomes the seat of the reader positioned within the body of the poet.

The internal and the external, container and contained, public and private, the poet's body and the reader's mind, words and gestures, the acted upon and the actor, the oral and the literate, while retaining their binary identities, interpenetrate in this passage. Multiple possibilities for substitution arise from the fervid tropes. Urged by Whitman's words, the invading reader comes away with a mouthful of the poet's loving heart. The metaphor of the heart—moribund in the sentimental literature of Whitman's day, if not dead—is resurrected with a shocking intensity in these lines, the key trope of which is reiterated in a later passage. Here it is the poet who receives the favors: "My lovers suffocate me!" he writes, "Bussing my body with soft and balsamic busses, / Noiselessly passing handfuls out of their hearts and giving them to be mine" (LG55, 78).

As physical lovers share one another's actual flesh and fluids, entering one another's bodies, so the physically eloquent poet enters the body of the reader and opens his own in a seductive invitation. Alliteration and tropic replacements generate a sexual and mystical passage that goes beyond identification—the modified aim of rhetorical appeals in Kenneth Burke's theory—and enacts a kind of interpenetration. In another line from "Song of Myself," the poet plays the part of the audience to model the response he seeks: "I hear the trained soprano," he says, "she convulses me like the climax of my love-grip"

(LG55, 52). Reception can thus be bodily as well as mentally effective; the words can enter the body, can stir the listener to new possibilities. Whitman could therefore speak of his "language experiment" as "an attempt to give the spirit, the body, the man, new words, new potentialities of speech" (AP, viii–ix).

The rhetoric of interpenetration, modeled on the sexual experience, was a first step in this direction, a positive gain over the less sophisticated and more traditional rhetoric of identification over distance, which he had used in early stories like "The Child's Champion." There the author creates characters, both pursued and pursuer in scenes pitting manly love against rough desire. Often unconventional in their homoeroticism, these stories were formally conventional.[4] Having invested in the textual experience, the reader is welcome to join the author in identifying with the hero or victim. But this identification can be at best a distant experience, a spectacle viewed from a grandstand seat, a second-order semiotic relation without the pretense of reader-author involvement in the plot. Narrator and reader—"I" and "you"—stand aside like a chorus or a jury.

To cite the opposition of responses that the 1855 Preface assigns to the great poet encountering the materials of his work, the writer and reader of the early stories are more prudent than sympathetic. Prudence and sympathy—withholding identification and granting it—became in 1855 the contrary impulses between which physical eloquence would unfold.[5] As the poet of the body gives himself to writing, he simultaneously withdraws from the world of physical contact in an act of prudence (that is, an act of writing) and creates, in an act of sympathy, a world of physical contact that, though empty itself of physical presence, strives to inspire (literally, to breathe) within the reader—prudently withdrawn into reading—the sympathetic desire for physical contact which reading cannot finally satisfy.[6] The poetry of the body is an open semiotic system; it opens out into potential physical action. By contrast, the earlier stories work within relatively closed systems of signification that posit a reader who leaves the story satisfied, having functioned not as an actor but as an observer of action, who may now give an account as a witness to action but is in no particular way moved toward further action. By the time of "Calamus," however, the poet of the body in full career can rest content neither with storytelling nor with a reflective or appreciative readership. Of his primary phallic symbol, the calamus root, he writes, "Interchange it, youths, with each other!" (LG60, 348). And, lending weight to Lewis Hyde's interpretation of art as gift-giving, a system of circularity rather than capitalist exchange, the "Calamus" poet adds, "Let none render it back!" (348). Once the cycle of interchange has begun, the phallic token must continue to circulate, promiscuously and ritually opening new paths for the "dear love of comrades."

The poetry of the body thus directs the reader toward an openness to experience, creating a desire without satisfying it, indeed drawing attention to the inability of language to satisfy bodily desires. Such intrusions upon the reading experience are characteristic of eloquence, which always seems to burst the illusion of transparency created by the fluent text. It draws attention to the language of a text or to the performance of an orator and therefore distracts that attention away from the message of the text, the so-called content.

"Eloquence," says Kenneth Burke, "is a frequency of Symbolic and formal effects. One work is more eloquent than another if it contains Symbolic and formal charges in greater profusion."[7] Reading a work that is "non-eloquent," that conforms to the stylistic objective of "clarity," readers are able to forget they are reading.[8] But an eloquent profusion of effects, which can produce either irritation or admiration, recalls the reader's attention to language. In addition, *physical* eloquence brings special attention to the material conditions of existence, the body *of* the text and *in* the text, as well as the body engaged in reading the text. Outside of the text, the reader's experience looms; into this world, the poet of the body outlandishly insinuates himself by means of his characteristic rhetoric.

Rhetoric, Richard Weaver has said, "is an art of emphasis embodying an order of desire."[9] In the same vein, Burke notes, "Form in literature is an arousing and fulfillment of desires."[10] Enabled by the classical tradition, the view of rhetoric in Weaver and Burke gives us a rhetor in full command not only of technique and subject matter but also of audience. An alternative view encourages us to consider the circumstances under which the text is produced and received, with the understanding that the author's powers of control over the reader's response may be related in some deep way to these circumstances, that the "order of desire" the author is embodying may be historically and socially conditioned, momentary and contingent rather than universal and ideal. Burke suggests something similar in his definition of one aspect of eloquence, which he calls "Symbolic intensity." This, he says, "arises when the artist uses subject-matter 'charged' by the reader's experience outside the work of art."[11]

In Whitman's day, the body of the reader was rendered prominent for cultural and political reasons. The cultural climate was strongly affected by the shift from a primarily oral to a primarily literate medium of public exchange. This shift was accompanied by a failure of public discourse to mediate effectively the differences of North and South. In the middle 1850s, North and

South struck once and for all an adversarial posture toward one another, foregoing union and choosing to see each other as a problem to be solved. This mutual objectifying of opposing regions assured the failure of dialogue and foretold the conflict of bodies.

The clearest instance of this breakdown occurred in May 1856 while Whitman was working on the second edition of *Leaves of Grass*. On May 23, Charles Sumner of Massachusetts delivered an impassioned abolitionist discourse on the floor of the Senate, using the tropes of sexual violence to oppose the extension of slave power into Kansas. "It is the rape of a virgin Territory, compelling it to the hateful embrace of Slavery," he said, "and it may be clearly traced to a depraved desire for a new Slave State, hideous offspring of such a crime." Of Senator Andrew P. Butler of South Carolina, Sumner said, "He has chosen a mistress . . . who, though ugly to others, is always lovely to him,—though polluted in the sight of the world, is chaste in his sight: I mean the harlot Slavery."[12] The trope, like Whitman's own, admits multiple substitutions and replacements, with rape and slavery interpenetrating one another's semantic space and circling through various other states of meaning. Read allegorically, it comes down to this: the "harlot Slavery" is forced upon the virgin Kansas by the depraved pimp, Senator Butler, representative of the slaveholding South. In this ad hominem vein, Sumner went further yet, drawing upon alliteration and onomatopoeia in his complaint that Butler "overflows with rage, . . . and, with incoherent phrase, discharges the loose expectoration of his speech" upon the representatives and people of Kansas.[13] In David Potter's view, this figure of speech not only insulted Butler's manners and morals but also depicted the "imperfect labial control of an old man."[14] For this exposure of the slaveholder's body, this graphic hint at the loss of bodily control, and this evocation of the body of slavery, exploited by the southern economy in an act at once represented by and including sexual exploitation, Sumner's physical eloquence was answered with a beating on the Senate floor, delivered by Butler's kinsman, Preston Brooks, with a metal-tipped cane. On the very next day, over a thousand miles away, decades of verbal exchange over the question of free soil collapsed completely into the violence of Bleeding Kansas as John Brown and a band of free-soil raiders carried out the brutal Pottawatomie Massacre, using broad swords to hack to death five proslavery settlers.[15] In the events of these few days, violence entered speech, and speech gave way to bodily violence.

If, as Paul Zweig has said, "Whitman experienced public crises in his flesh,"[16] he was typical of Americans facing the onset of the Civil War. Like him, they responded physically to the political demands of the day, not only with warlike violence but also with aroused sexual appetites. In the 1850s,

Americans produced and purchased health and sex manuals with a body-conscious enthusiasm unmatched in earlier decades. What made Whitman different from the majority of his fellow Americans was that, like the abolitionists, though without their puritanical self-righteousness and their "mad fanaticism" and "ranting," which he disdained,[17] he realized the psychological and social connections of the sexual body and the body politic. In the 1855 poem that would later become "I Sing the Body Electric," for example, he exposes slavery as a spiritual and moral evil with roots in the refusal to recognize the human body of the slave and to acknowledge openly its sexual power. The slaver, he says, "does not half know his business" and does not know that, within the body of the slave, runs "the same old blood"; "There swells and jets his heart," the seat of "all passions and desires," "reachings and aspirations" (LG55, 121). The pun on the dead metaphors "to reach" and "to aspire" unveils the physical basis for emotions that, in polite society, come to seem disembodied. Claiming the presence of strong emotions for all who possess a human body, including the black slaves, Whitman asks his pointed question, "Do you think they are not there because they are not expressed in parlors and lecture-rooms?" (122). Applying the doctrine of evolution, the sophisticated product of the lecture room, to his presentation of the slave's body, he says, "For him the globe lay preparing quintillions of years without one animal or plant, / For him the revolving cycles truly and steadily rolled" (121). He also applies the generative principle of representation, hinting at both political and poetic significance: "This is not only one man. . . . he is the father of those who shall be fathers in their turns" (122).

At the time these lines appeared in print, John Brown—whose body "a-mouldering in the grave" would fill the songs of Yankee soldiers—was already dreaming of a conspiracy of violence against the keepers of slaves. As for the keepers themselves, their anxiety broke forth in a discourse that, over and against Whitman's pleas for a union (Union) based on sexual sympathy, hatefully inverted the abolitionists' tropes of sexual violence. The abolitionists, their opponents said, would not be satisfied until slaves killed their masters and violated the white women of the South. The bodies once possessed and controlled—both black and female, Whitman's matching pair "A slave at auction" and "A woman at auction" (LG55, 121–122)—now were imagined as out of control, the objects of the slaveholders' worst fears. In exposing these bodies to the public eye, Whitman defied a repressive social system that made a routine of covert violence and sexual exploitation. His message is clear in the penultimate line of the poem, "Who degrades or defiles the living human body is cursed" (123).

The rhetoric of bodily exposure—featured in the speeches of Sumner and transformed into written discourse in the poems of the 1855 *Leaves of Grass*—stands in bold contrast to a conventional eloquence based upon what Burke calls a "categorical appeal," a purified "literary" convention. Whereas the author of "derivative" poetry and the speaker who cultivates a "purified diction" of polite address will draw their "Symbolic charges from the Symbolic charges of [their] forbears," physically eloquent authors will base "their inclusions and exclusions not on traditional definitions of the ceremonious, but upon those aspects of an ideology which can be associated with the ceremonious in [their] environment"; their eloquence will be "based upon the contemporaneously charged, rather than upon the traditionally charged." [18]

But why, according to this logic, has the rhetoric of Whitman's poetry of the body, now missing the contemporaneous charge of the body electrified by the Civil War, not passed into the realm of the categorically charged, the traditional? Why does it retain its appeal?

One reason may arise from Whitman's special handling of his genre and medium. Sumner's oratory depended upon the moment of history in which it appeared; the inflamed public speaker makes only the slightest appeal to readers removed by the distance of future ages, little effort to inspire in that audience a vibrating, living discourse that calls the body to attention and brings the absent reader into the heart of the writing. "The Crime against Kansas" thus becomes the corpse of archives and historical memory—enlivened perhaps for readers in times of racial tension and civil disorder—while *Leaves of Grass* silently breathes a seemingly continuous appeal to present-day readers.

Another possible explanation is provided by Kenneth Cmiel, the historian of "democratic eloquence": "Far from being a uniquely American dilemma or one experienced only in the mid-nineteenth century," he writes, "[a 'middling rhetoric'] alternating between the refined and the coarse, between public reserve and private informality"—between the prudent and the sympathetic—"touches the heart of modernity." [19] The modern reader can still respond to Whitman's invocation of the body, not necessarily because the repetitive structures of the poetry have a universal or inevitably continuous appeal but because the cultural and social forces unleashed by the Civil War, the first modern war, have continued to rage in the twentieth century.

These forces, no doubt, have been felt unevenly. Whitman himself gave up writing the poetry of the body. After the war, in his elegy to Lincoln, he wearily buried the corpse of radical conflict. [20] Indeed, the poet of the 1850s at times appears to have had more in common with the high modern writers of the period between the world wars than he had in common with the good gray poet he became in his own later years. In this light, it is no wonder that the poems of the 1850s can be so nicely framed by Burke's theory of categorical and environmental appeals, a theory developed in the 1930s as Europe simmered between the wars. Nor is it any wonder that, under the postwar influence of Malcolm Cowley and the academic critics of the 1950s, when the Cold War presented a daily threat to the body of the whole earth, Whitman's reputation improved—and improved yet again with the succeeding social movements that have culminated modernity: the civil rights movement, the sexual revolution that accompanied the war in Vietnam, the peace movement, feminism, gay liberation, environmentalism, and now multiculturalism. Each of these ventures would set a high value on Whitman's physical eloquence. If the plain style, the American version of Barthes's writing degree zero, "submerge[s] civic contention" by allowing the reader to sink comfortably into the observer's posture,[21] physical eloquence revives dead metaphors, irritating the ear and the eye of the passive reader and renewing the tensions that both reflect and create the politically sensitized body.

NOTES

1. Paul de Man, *The Resistance to Theory* (Minneapolis: University of Minnesota Press, 1986), 45–48.

2. Calvin Bedient, "Orality and Power (Whitman's 'Song of Myself')," *Delta* 16 (1983): 91; Alan Helms, "Whitman's Homosexual Disguises," in Joann P. Krieg, ed., *Walt Whitman: Here and Now* (Westport, Conn.: Greenwood Press, 1985), 67.

3. W. H. Auden, "In Memory of W. B. Yeats," *The Oxford Book of Twentieth-Century Verse* (Oxford: Clarendon, 1973), 418.

4. See Michael Moon, *Disseminating Whitman: Revision and Corporeality in Leaves of Grass* (Cambridge: Harvard University Press, 1991), 26–36.

5. These two poles of reading experience—prudence and sympathy—correspond roughly to the conflicting aims of what Elaine Scarry has defined as a materialist theory of textuality, a concern with how language both "absorbs the material world and empties itself of material content" (Elaine Scarry, ed., *Literature and the Body: Essays on Populations and Persons* [Baltimore: Johns Hopkins University Press, 1988], xx). The vexed question of reference comes into play here. Insisting that poetry can not only refer to extratextual life but can even exemplify if not contain it, materialist practice also recognizes, with some anxiety, that, though "language is sometimes highly referential," it is not always so (Scarry, xx). The "I" in *Leaves of Grass* may well represent a man named Walt Whitman alive in 1855, whose photograph accompanies the text, but this reference hardly fixes the meaning of the pronoun once and for all, not even within the immediate context.

In fact, the first-person pronoun is particularly fluid; its alternation between an "empty" and a "full" semantic state is notorious among linguists, as is the similar behavior of the second-person *you* (Emile Benveniste, *Problems in General Linguistics*, trans. Mary Elizabeth Meeks [Coral Gables, Fla.: University of Miami Press, 1971], 218–219). As Scarry concludes, "If language had no [such] referential freedom or fluidity, many of its advantages, its ways of supplementing 'the sensuously obvious,' would be immediately gone" (xx). The materialist writer or reader does not have to be merely a positivist or even a realist but can aspire to a utopian purpose because of the very linguistic fluidity that seems to challenge cruder versions of materialism. In emptying the poem of its content, utopian materialists can carry away not only a sense of historical personage but also a heightened desire, not the poet's but their own, imposed upon them by the desiring (and designing) poet. Language that evokes a reader's awareness of physical possibility leaves a valence that it cannot complete, an open link in the signifying chain connecting the writer's physical experience to the writer's act of writing and then to the reader's reading. It directs the reader back to the realm of physical experience outside the poem, though it does not, cannot, embody that experience. The chain of sympathy is broken at this crucial point of prudence.

6. Literacy theory is useful on this point. Deborah Brandt, for example, in *Literacy as Involvement: The Acts of Writers, Readers, and Texts* (Carbondale: Southern Illinois University Press, 1990), suggests that the act of writing is at once among the most social and the most private acts human beings accomplish: "Functionally speaking, literacy is the most social of all imaginable practices—hypersocial, actually, because it epitomizes the role of culture in human exchange and condenses into the channels of reading and writing some of the most crucial of our joint enterprises. Yet there is another current that says to be literate one must be able to pull away from the demanding solidarity with the social world, to put deliberate space and time *between* oneself and others" (1). Whitman uses this "paradox of literacy" in his interpenetrating exploration of public and private, political and poetic spaces.

7. Kenneth Burke, *Counter-Statement* (Los Altos, Calif.: Hermes, 1953), 165.

8. Ibid., 166.

9. Richard Weaver, "Language Is Sermonic," in Patricia Bizzell and Bruce Herzberg, eds., *The Rhetorical Tradition: Readings from Classical Times to the Present,* (New York: St. Martin's, 1990), 1,048.

10. Burke, 124.

11. Ibid., 163.

12. Charles Sumner, "The Crime against Kansas," *Complete Works* (New York: Negro Universities Press, 1969), 140, 144.

13. Ibid., 239–240.

14. David M. Potter, *The Impending Crisis: 1848–1861* (New York: Harper and Row, 1976), 210.

15. Ibid., 211–212.

16. Paul Zweig, *Walt Whitman: The Making of a Poet* (New York: Basic Books, 1984), 324.

17. Betsy Erkkila, *Whitman the Political Poet* (New York: Oxford University Press, 1989), 47.

18. Burke, 170.

19. Kenneth Cmiel, *Democratic Eloquence: The Fight over Popular Speech in Nineteenth-Century America* (Berkeley: University of California Press, 1990), 92.

20. M. Jimmie Killingsworth, *Whitman's Poetry of The Body: Sexuality, Politics, and the Text* (Chapel Hill: University of North Carolina Press, 1989).

21. Cmiel, 261.

Reconstructing Language
in *Democratic Vistas*

ONE OF the consistent tendencies in Walt Whitman's career is his penchant for self-advertisement. The most famous examples are the anonymous reviews of the 1855 *Leaves of Grass* and the 1856 "Letter" to Emerson. I want to begin by adding an example. A manuscript in the Charles E. Feinberg Collection shows Whitman drafting an anonymous review/advertisement of *Democratic Vistas*, probably soon after its publication in 1871:

> Any criticism worthy this tremendous & electric pamphlet would need far
> more space than I here command. I can will briefly say here, Among much
> else
> An inquiry into the political, social, & literary United States of to-day—
> not merely into the surface & show United States—but the inmost tissues,
> blood, vitality, morality, heart & brain—and what the reality, good &
> bad.—what the *philosophy*, (as the modern term is) Beneath the fine show
> on the surface of all these are there can lie cancers chasms? Suggestions are
> given of new orders of authors and artists.—a new *priesthood* and knight-
> hood. Religion & conscience are boldly advanced as the only lasting basis
> of Democracy. The purport of America is not as was supposed, merely to
> revolutionize & reconstruct politics, but Religion, Sociology, Manners, Lit-
> erature & Art.[1]

In summarizing the "purport" of *Democratic Vistas*, Whitman clearly defines
his role as a cultural diagnostician, one who can see "beneath the fine show on

the surface" in order to examine "the inmost tissues, blood, vitality, morality, heart & brain" of America's cultural "body." The diagnosis suggests that "cancers chasms" lie beneath the surface, though the faltering style of the trial sentence indicates a certain unwillingness, on Whitman's part, to dwell on disease. Instead, he moves to the cure—"new orders of authors and artists.— a new *priesthood* and knighthood." The cure Whitman proposes is spiritual, moral, and aesthetic, and in the final sentence of the draft he associates that cure with reconstruction: "The purport of America is not as was supposed, merely to revolutionize & reconstruct politics, but Religion, Sociology, Manners, Literature & Art." Whitman's reduction of the complex program of political reconstruction parallels it to the "fine show on the surface," for in both sentences he uses the adverb "merely" to qualify a superficial inquiry into the "surface & show United States." Whitman instead calls for a deeper, more far-reaching revolutionizing and reconstructing of America.

Whitman's clear aim is to deepen the sense of the word *reconstruction*, and I take as my own aim to explore the various ways in which reconstruction can be applied to *Democratic Vistas*. Most fundamentally, the text itself is a reconstruction. As Whitman admits in the third paragraph of the essay, "it is, in fact, a collection of memoranda, perhaps for future designers, comprehenders" (PW, 2:362). I have pointed out elsewhere that Whitman's description is quite accurate, since *Democratic Vistas* is composed of memoranda written from as early as the middle 1850s.[2] Moreover, the essay exists, like other Whitman texts, in several versions: besides the manuscript "Rough Draft" and the two *Galaxy* essays on "Democracy" and "Personalism," there are the 1871 pamphlet, the version in *Two Rivulets* (1876), the version in *Specimen Days & Collect* (1882), and, finally, the version in Floyd Stovall's edition of *Prose Works 1892*, which includes all of the variants from previous versions. Not all of these versions differ significantly from one another, but they do suggest that for over ten years Whitman continued to construct and reconstruct *Democratic Vistas*.

The textual reconstruction is further complicated by Whitman's use of other texts in constructing *Democratic Vistas*. One striking example of this reconstructive strategy is Whitman's incorporating parts of "The Eighteenth Presidency!" into the 1871 text. Whitman records the "doubt and gloom" he experienced "before the war" and then quotes a "foreigner" who puts "in form, indeed, my own observations." The observations focus on the "infidelism" of party politics and "how the millions of sturdy farmers and mechanics are thus the helpless supple-jacks of comparatively few politicians" (PW, 2:386). The final sentence echoes Whitman's 1856 pamphlet, but by putting his words in a foreigner's mouth Whitman distances himself from his own "doubt and gloom." Thus, he can pronounce the foreigner's speech as "sad, serious, deep truths" but then add:

Yet are there other, still deeper, amply confronting, dominating truths.
Over those politicians and great and little rings, and over all their insolence
and wiles, and over the powerfulest parties, looms a power, too sluggish
maybe, but ever holding decisions and decrees in hand, ready, with stern
process, to execute them as soon as plainly needed—and at times, indeed,
summarily crushing to atoms the mightiest parties, even in the hour of
their pride. (387)

Whitman's reconstructive strategy is also apparent in the short essay "Origins of Attempted Secession," which follows *Democratic Vistas* in the 1882 *Specimen Days & Collect*. "Origins" is constructed of several previously published texts, most notably "The Eighteenth Presidency!" but also part of a note on "The Late War" that appeared in the 1871 and 1876 versions of *Democratic Vistas* (PW, 2:426–433). All of these details point to the appropriateness of Whitman's title *Collect* for the miscellany of essays, "Notes Left Over," and "Pieces in Early Youth" that fill out the 1882 collection of prose. They also suggest that reconstruction is a basic textual strategy, both for Whitman and for his "future designers, comprehenders."

A reconstructive critical strategy could take any of several directions: for example, Stovall's edition allows a reader to reconstruct the two-paragraph note on "The Late War" (PW, 2:431–432, 756). The note begins with the image of the war as "the last great material and military outcropping of the Feudal spirit" and marks the result as "the abolition of Slavery, and the extirpation of the Slaveholding Class, (cut out and thrown away like a tumor by surgical operation)" (756). In the second paragraph, Whitman characteristically turns from the immediate diagnosis to the future cure: "But immensest results, not only in politics, but in literature, poems, and sociology, are doubtless waiting yet unform'd in the future. How long they will wait I cannot tell" (432). By reconstructing the note on "The Late War," we can see clearly the elements of Whitman's reconstructive strategy, which situates him between a reconstructing of the past and a reconstructing of the future. A more detailed reading of "The Late War" note would show, among other things, how Whitman constructs his vision of feudalism around the figure of the crusades, how he refigures the crusades as the "embryo, the start" of European civilization, and how he thus implies that the "late war" will become a parallel "embryo" for future "immensest results" in America.

A critical strategy of textual reconstruction plays upon the primary, literal sense of the verb *reconstruct* as "to construct anew," but it also implies two figural senses of *reconstruct*: as "to construct anew in the mind" and as "to re-store (something past) mentally" (*OED*). And just as the history of the word leads from literal to figural reconstructings, so the reconstructive strategy leads from textual to rhetorical criticism. In perhaps the most basic figural strategy of *Democratic Vistas*, Whitman seeks to reconstruct not only the newly reunit-ing United States but also his own eloquent voice. In other words, *Democratic Vistas* focuses on the power of language to construct anew and to restore American culture, but its strategies also construct anew and restore the power of Whitman's own language.

Several related problems arise from this turn to the figure of voice. First, there is the problem of the prewar and postwar Whitman: the narrative most generally accepted and retold among Whitman scholars is that the postwar Whitman loses the power of language in stylistic mannerisms and archaisms, that Whitman's voice becomes conventionally "poetic" in the late work. Sec-ond, there is the problem of reconstruction versus deconstruction: "voice" is itself a mystifying metaphor, so that in reconstructing Whitman's figure of eloquence we should be on our guard against a naively phonocentric reading of the oratorical style. Third, given these two problems of textuality, the prob-lem of context becomes quite insistent: after all, the most specific sense of the word *reconstruction* regards "the process by which after the Civil War the States which had seceded were restored to the rights and privileges of the Union" (*OED*). In *Democratic Vistas*, Whitman positions himself within that process, although the anonymous review suggests a larger—and more accurate—defi-nition both of the term and of the process. Indeed, the word *reconstruction* was used as early as 1861 to signify "the reorganization of the government of the U.S."[3] The definitions and problems of *reconstruction* suggest that Whit-man constructs the "voice" of *Democratic Vistas* out of several opposed figures, creating a style that combines a backward-looking vision and a forward-looking vision, history and idealism, the literary and the more broadly cul-tural, the cultural and the political.

These general considerations become more specific when we consider three concrete elements of the oratorical style in *Democratic Vistas*. Two are charac-teristic of the oracular voice that dominates *Leaves of Grass* from 1855 to 1867: syntactic parallelism and cataloging. A two-paragraph passage from the intro-ductory section of the 1871 essay illustrates the style as well as Whitman's thesis, that "it is as if we were somehow being endow'd with a vast and more and more thoroughly-appointed body, and then left with little or no soul" (PW, 2:370):

> Let me illustrate further, as I write, with current observations, localities,
> &c. The subject is important, and will bear repetition. After an absence, I

am now again (September, 1870) in New York city and Brooklyn, on a few
weeks' vacation. The splendor, picturesqueness, and oceanic amplitude and
rush of these great cities, the unsurpass'd situation, rivers and bay, sparkling
sea-tides, costly and lofty new buildings, facades of marble and iron, of
original grandeur and elegance of design, with the masses of gay color, the
preponderance of white and blue, the flags flying, the endless ships, the tu-
multuous streets, Broadway, the heavy, low, musical roar, hardly ever inter-
mitted, even at night; the jobbers' houses, the rich shops, the wharves, the
great Central Park, and the Brooklyn Park of hills, (as I wander among
them this beautiful fall weather, musing, watching, absorbing)—the assem-
blages of the citizens in their groups, conversations, trades, evening amuse-
ments, or along the by-quarters—these, I say, and the like of these, completely
satisfy my senses of power, fulness, motion, &c., and give me, through such
senses and appetites, and through my esthetic conscience, a continued exal-
tation and absolute fulfilment. Always and more and more, as I cross the
East and North rivers, the ferries, or with the pilots in their pilot-houses, or
pass an hour in Wall street, or the gold exchange, I realize, (if we must admit
such partialisms,) that not Nature alone is great in her fields of freedom and
the open air, in her storms, the shows of night and day, the mountains, forests,
seas—but in the artificial, the work of man too is equally great—in this
profusion of teeming humanity—in these ingenuities, streets, goods, houses,
ships—these hurrying, feverish, electric crowds of men, their complicated
business genius, (not least among the geniuses,) and all this mighty, many-
threaded wealth and industry concentrated here. (371)

In this first paragraph, Whitman illustrates the "vast and more and more
thoroughly-appointed body" of New York City, and his style enacts the
"oceanic amplitude and rush" of the city through extended catalogs of sights,
sounds, characters, and activities. None of the particular details is allowed to
become the central focus of the description, for the purpose of the cataloging
is to evoke the sense of a vast and limitless panorama. Whitman's catalog
rhetoric mixes the orderliness of repeated syntactic formulas with the continual shifting of syntactic repetends from one parallel to another. That is one
way of describing the dynamic catalog, which is certainly more than a mere
list. Equally important, however, is the role of the "I" in the paragraph. Whitman begins by noting "as I write," and he locates the scene of writing precisely—"I am now again (September, 1870) in New York city and Brooklyn."
But about two-thirds of the way through the panoramic cataloging, he parenthetically represents himself as active observer: "as I wander among them this
beautiful fall weather, musing, watching, absorbing." And this shift becomes
more pronounced as the paragraph proceeds: "these, I say, and the like of
these," "as I cross the East and North rivers," "I realize." From the act of

writing, Whitman crosses over to the combined acts of saying and seeing, but it is through the act of writing that Whitman constructs a figural bridge between past, present, and future.

These figural crossings recall, most immediately, the style of "Crossing Brooklyn Ferry," just as the description itself echoes the 1856 poem. But the figural transition from writing to speaking also recalls the 1856 pamphlet, "The Eighteenth Presidency!," subtitled "Voice of Walt Whitman to each Young Man in the Nation, North, South, East, and West" (NUP, 6:2,120). And the quality of the second paragraph, a kind of mini-jeremiad upon America's "little or no soul," recalls the 1856 "Letter" to Emerson: "Not a man faces round at the rest with terrible negative voice, refusing all terms to be bought off from his own eye-sight, or from the soul that he is, or from friendship, or from the body that he is, or from the soil and sea" (LG, 737).

The second paragraph of the 1871 passage creates the figure of a "terrible negative voice," but that voice does not speak like an individual, just as the vision it announces does not finally issue from one person's "eye-sight."

> But sternly discarding, shutting our eyes to the glow and grandeur of the general superficial effect, coming down to what is of the only real importance, Personalities, and examining minutely, we question, we ask, Are there, indeed, *men* here worthy the name? Are there athletes? Are there perfect women, to match the generous material luxuriance? Is there a pervading atmosphere of beautiful manners? Are there crops of fine youths, and majestic old persons? Are there arts worthy freedom and a rich people? Is there a great moral and religious civilization—the only justification of a great material one? Confess that to severe eyes, using the moral microscope upon humanity, a sort of dry and flat Sahara appears, these cities, crowded with petty grotesques, malformations, phantoms, playing meaningless antics. Confess that everywhere, in shop, street, church, theatre, barroom, official chair, are pervading flippancy and vulgarity, low cunning, infidelity—everywhere the youth puny, impudent, foppish, prematurely ripe—everywhere an abnormal libidinousness, unhealthy forms, male, female, painted, padded, dyed, chignon'd, muddy complexions, bad blood, the capacity for good motherhood deceasing or deceas'd, shallow notions of beauty, with a range of manners, or rather lack of manners, (considering the advantages enjoy'd,) probably the meanest to be seen in the world. (PW, 2:371–372)

The parallel rhetorical questions all ask for a negative response, but more important is the framing of the questions by "we question, we ask." This is a corporate or aggregate "we," a figure of communal interests and agreements, of common ground. Moreover, though the diagnosing writer acts as the mediator of this corporate figure, the repeated command to "confess" figures the

writer and reader as joining in a ritualized speech act. The confession takes the
shape of another set of catalogs, but the catalogs effectively subvert the
"oceanic amplitude and rush" of the first paragraph. Thus, in the first paragraph the oratorical style creates a figure of lyric power and individual
eloquence, while in the second it creates a figure of corporate, reciprocal
eloquence.

If these familiar poetic techniques create a complex sense of Whitman's
voice—or, as I have also called it, the figure of eloquence he constructs—the
third stylistic trait makes Whitman's construction yet more complex. This is
the compound word, a construction subject to a great deal of variety and
capable of producing a number of effects. The compounds lingering-bequeathed,
health-action, birth-stock, monkish-feudal, culmination-expression, stock-
personality, return-expressions, origin-idea, artist-mind, secession-slave-power,
moral-spiritual, crisis-crash, gravitation-hold, dominion-heart, and spine-
character appear in the first third of the essay, and a complete list and analysis
would run several pages. The common characteristic of the fifteen examples,
however, is fairly clear: Whitman joins two terms in order to construct a third,
synthesizing term. The compound words thus enact, on a miniature scale, the
Hegelian dialectic that structures the essay as well as Whitman's vision of history. And in constructing the compounds, Whitman clearly foregrounds the
synthesizing power of language.

But how, we may well ask, is the compound related to the oratorical style?
The answer lies in Whitman's tendency to construct a series of clauses and
phrases. Syntactic parallelism and cataloging are two forms that tendency
takes, and *Democratic Vistas* features countless examples of a short series of
two or three terms used in parallel. So, for example, in the sentence, "To-day,
ahead, though dimly yet, we see, in vistas, a copious, sane, gigantic offspring"
(PW, 2:362), the three adjectives form a cumulative series modifying "offspring." In another sentence nearby, Whitman employs three different series
which, while each is quite brief, together create a cumulative effect of a mini-
catalog: "To him or her within whose thought rages the battle, advancing,
retreating, between democracy's convictions, aspirations, and the people's
crudeness, vice, caprices, I mainly write this essay" (363). The compound
words that Whitman constructs become, in this context, a synthetic series of
two or occasionally three terms. And though the compound seems to be a
stylistic trait of the later Whitman, it has clear antecedents in the prose of
"The Eighteenth Presidency!" and the "Letter" to Emerson, both of which
repeatedly employ the parallel series to create oratorical effects.

The style of *Democratic Vistas* recalls, then, Whitman's attempts at becoming an orator/pamphleteer in the 1850s, and there are fundamental

continuities between the early style and the late style, even though the late style marks itself as different from the early. If nothing more, I hope this reconstructing of Whitman's language also points toward our need, as scholars, to reconstruct our visions of the poet and his career-achievement. Similarly, my reconstruction is intended to invite the subversive strategies of deconstruction. But I have also hinted at a third step in this critical reconstruction. The figure of eloquence that Whitman reconstructs out of the "collection of memoranda" depends, finally, on the reconstruction of an audience that will respond to that eloquence. Perhaps the most important connection between the prewar and postwar Whitman, then, is this figure of an audience.

Wynn Thomas has argued persuasively that Whitman's antebellum poetry addresses an idealized and disappearing class of artisans and that after the war the change to industrial, entrepreneurial capitalism makes such an address virtually impossible.[4] My reading of *Democratic Vistas* suggests that one of Whitman's fundamental strategies is to reconstruct an audience, an "aggregate," for whom and to whom he can speak/write. This is to read the essay as itself an example of "the great literature" that "penetrates all, gives hue to all, shapes aggregates and individuals, and, after subtle ways, with irresistible power, constructs, sustains, demolishes at will" (PW, 2:366).

But my reading requires a second, parallel recognition—that the reconstructing power of language functions within a larger cultural space, always competing with other cultural discourses or "voices." In postbellum America, Whitman looks backward to the vanished artisan class and projects an idealized version of it into the future: "I should demand a programme of culture, drawn out, not for a single class alone, or for the parlors or lecture-rooms, but with an eye to practical life, the west, the working-men, the facts of farms and jack-planes and engineers, and of the broad range of the women also of the middle and working strata, and with reference to the perfect equality of women, and of a grand and powerful motherhood" (PW, 2:396). By defining democratic culture in terms of audience, Whitman effectively dissolves the boundaries between high and low or elite and popular culture. And by reconstructing the very category of culture, Whitman's reconstructing language attempts to construct a cultural space for his own work, including *Democratic Vistas*. The reconstructing language in *Democratic Vistas* thus attempts to construct a new reciprocal relationship between speech and writing, between the orator-poet and the audience, between the text and cultural context. If Whitman's reconstructive strategies do not appear wholly successful, if they seem colored as much by nostalgia as by hope, perhaps that is because the process of reconstruction has not been, and cannot be, completed.

NOTES

1. The manuscript is included in Container 36 of the Charles E. Feinberg Collection, Library of Congress.

2. James Perrin Warren, *Walt Whitman's Language Experiment* (University Park: Penn State University Press, 1990), 114–115.

3. Mitford M. Mathews, *A Dictionary of Americanisms: On Historical Principles* (Chicago: University of Chicago Press, 1951), 1,367.

4. M. Wynn Thomas, *The Lunar Light of Whitman's Poetry* (Cambridge: Harvard University Press, 1987), 2–3, 178–280.

The Obfuscations of Rhetoric

Whitman and the Visionary Experience

WHITMAN SPENT a lifetime writing poetry, establishing various public personalities, and covering his tracks. With the help of his early disciples, he more or less successfully managed all three.

Over the years he had written too much on a variety of subjects—poetry, newspaper editorials, essays, letters—to keep intact for long the portrait of himself he wished to project of the fiercely democratic bard, the apostle of simple comradely friendship, the good gray poet. And he saved everything: manuscripts, worksheets, scraps, clippings. He was right about his being a major poet, but given the vast amount of material available to critics over the years, his carefully nurtured images gave way to the reality of a very private, manipulative, defensive person fighting demons within himself, idealizing in his poetry what in his prose he often had grave and bitter doubts about.

For the most part, *Leaves of Grass* perfects the ideal visionary experience of becoming. Whitman's objective correlative in *Leaves of Grass* might be defined as the guiltless yearnings of common people toward the freest possible fulfillment of the self in a constrictive world of sharply defined social and sexual taboos. In the 1855 Preface to *Leaves of Grass*, itself one long lovely poem, Whitman exalts the ideal, common people:

> The genius of the United States is . . . always most in the common people. Their manners speech dress friendships—the freshness and candor of their physiognomy—the picturesque looseness of their carriage . . . their deathless attachment to freedom—their aversion to anything indecorous or soft or mean—the practical acknowledgment of the citizens of one state by the

citizens of all other states—the fierceness of their roused resentment—their curiosity and welcome of novelty—their self-esteem and wonderful sympathy—their susceptibility to a slight—the air they have of persons who never knew how it felt to stand in the presence of superiors—the fluency of their speech—their delight in music, the sure symptom of manly tenderness and native elegance of soul . . . their good temper and openhandedness—the terrible significance of their elections—the President's taking off his hat to them not they to him—these too are unrhymed poetry. It awaits the gigantic and generous treatment worthy of it. (LG, 710)[1]

And in the 1860 poem "Starting from Paumanok," he deifies the common people in the lines "O such themes! Equalities! / O Amazement of things! O divine average" (TV, 2:281).[2] The "divine average" becomes a central image in *Leaves of Grass* and, to paraphrase Yeats, brings him metaphors to create his ideal prophetic, visionary democracy.

However, an assessment of the exalted "divine average" outside of *Leaves of Grass* by the *prose* Whitman, the writer of editorials, essays, unpublished essays, and letters, is quite different. Beginning as a journalist in his early twenties and, over the years, writing for such newspapers as the *New York Aurora*, *Brooklyn Eagle*, and *Brooklyn Daily Times*, and witnessing the ongoing corruption in Washington, D.C., Whitman had seen too much of the seamier side of political "quackery," to use one of his milder terms, to have any illusions about officeholders and politicians or about the gullibility of the people who were swayed into voting for such frauds by vague promises and soothing oratory.[3]

We are not here dealing either with Whitman's daily one-to-one cordial or close relationships with friends, workers, or hospitalized soldiers but, rather, with people "En-Masse" (TV, 2:558)—to use another of his unifying *Leaves of Grass* images—who in Whitman's prose were derisively termed on occasion "ignorant and unfit." Whitman's disenchantment with the democratic process—the failure of the average American to realize the full potentialities of the Jeffersonian ideal by rejecting the third-raters who ran for office and thus elevate the democratic process—is at the heart of his frustrations over the direction the republic was taking. *He* knew what should be done, but he could vote only once. When it came down to it, it appeared that the people could not be counted on to advance even their own interests. What might have become a great republic founders in a morass of political corruption. At the heart of it all is the knavish, corrupt politician, enchanting the average voter.

Two major texts written some fifteen years apart, "The Eighteenth Presidency!" in 1856 and *Democratic Vistas* in 1871, give us an insight into Whitman's thinking on the prose "divine average." With a "ruthless lucidity," to use Roger Asselineau's apt phrase, Whitman focuses in both works on the negative social and political conditions confronting the American people, the reasons for them, and his assessment of the entire situation.

"The Eighteenth Presidency! Voice of Walt Whitman to each Young Man in the Nation, North, South, East, and West" was, so far as is known, never published in Whitman's lifetime.[4] Written one year after the first edition of *Leaves of Grass*, it carries over in parts the visionary resonances of the 1855 Preface. But in "The Eighteenth Presidency!" his intended affirmation dissolves into vaporous generalizations, given his immediate incisive overall assessment of the political situation at hand, the campaign for the presidency of the United States between the inept proslavery candidate, James Buchanan, and the equally inept Millard Fillmore, who ran on the nativist Know-Nothing movement's American party ticket. The new Republican party nominated John C. Frémont, who had explored the West and was antislavery, but Whitman shied away from him, mentioning him only once, and that in passing, possibly fearing "that his election would split the Union, as the election of Republican Abraham Lincoln four years later actually did."[5] Whitman describes Buchanan and Fillmore as "two debauched old disunionist politicians, the lees and dregs of more than sixty years! A pretty time for two dead corpses to go walking up and down the earth, to guide by feebleness and ashes a proud, young, friendly, fresh, heroic nation of thirty million of live and electric men!" (NUP, 6:2,135).

As in his newspaper editorials, Whitman's analysis of the political situation confronting the nation on the matter of the extension of slavery into new territories is clear and precise:

> At present, we are environed with nonsense under the name of respectability. . . . The people, credulous, generous, deferential, allow the American government to be managed in many respects as is only proper under the personnel of a king and hereditary lords; or, more truly, not proper under any decent men anywhere. If this were to go on, we ought to change the title of the President, and issue patents of nobility. Of course it is not to go on; the Americans are no fools! (NUP, 6:2,121–2,122)

Elsewhere in the essay he is not so sure. A year after his humane identification in "Song of Myself" with a brutally "hounded [runaway] slave,"—"Agonies are one of my changes of garments, / I do not ask the wounded person how he feels. . . . I myself became the wounded person" (TV, 1:51–52)[6]—in "The Eighteenth Presidency!" he echoes an earlier editorial stand dating back to 1847, which over the years in his prose remained more or less constant, on the place of blacks in American society.[7] In "The Eighteenth Presidency!" he speaks of "the true people, the millions of white citizens, mechanics, farmers, boatmen" (NUP, 6:2,124). He is in favor of keeping slavery in the slave states: "Where slavery is, there it is," but slavery should not be extended into new territories (2,134). And under the heading "Must Runaway Slaves be Delivered Back?" his precise response is, "They must" (2,132).[8] In other words, when the prose Whitman speaks outside of *Leaves of Grass* of an "American" he is typically talking about a white native American.

It was also in "The Eighteenth Presidency!" that Whitman polished his rhetorical approach to the political and social realities he had clearly delineated. That is, when confronted with the reality and immediacy of his disenchantment both with the ongoing democratic process in the hands of political quacks and the "credulous, generous, deferential" voters (NUP, 6:2,121), Whitman envelops his discussion with prophetic visionary rhetoric on the potentialities for political acumen in mechanics and farmers that are at once belied by his previous analysis of their basic ineptitude in implementing the democratic process. Thus, Whitman intermixes reality with soothing visionary cadences that would certainly be more at home in the 1855 Preface. Typically:

> Races are marching and countermarching by swift millions and tens of millions. Never was justice so mighty amid injustice; never did the idea of equality erect itself so haughty and uncompromising amid inequality, as today. . . . Never was the representative man more energetic, more like a god, than to-day. He urges on the myriads before him, he crowds them aside, his daring step approaches the arctic and the antarctic poles, he colonizes the shores of the Pacific, the Asiatic Indias, the birthplace of languages and of races, the archipelagoes, Australia; he explores Africa, he unearths Assyria and Egypt, he re-states history, he enlarges morality. . . . (2,135)

Nevertheless, it remained that voters in 1856 were not yet capable of coping with the vacuity of American politics.[9] Of course, that would be for some mystical future time: "A new race copiously appears, with resolute tread, soon to confront Presidents, Congresses and parties, to look them sternly in the face, to stand no nonsense; American young men, the offspring and proof of These States, the West the same as the East, and the South alike with the North" (NUP, 6:2,125). And so on.

Whitman's newspaper editorials for the most part are devoid of such visionary experiences couched in obfuscating rhetoric. When he is talking about the immediate reality of some political or social dilemma, whatever the merits of his argument, he leaves little doubt as to what he perceives to be the essence of the situation. By way of example, in 1858, two years after "The Eighteenth Presidency!," he again defined his views on a critical issue of the time in the editorial "Prohibition of Colored Persons."[10] The views Whitman supported here were, at the time, shared by many. On the other hand, they did not write *Leaves of Grass*. In fact, between the years 1856 and 1859, when he wrote this editorial, Whitman was deeply involved in revising the poems that had previously appeared in the 1855 and 1856 editions of *Leaves of Grass* and creating the bulk of the new poems that would appear in the next, 1860 edition, which he termed his "New Bible," namely the "Calamus," "Children of Adam," and the patriotic-programmatic "Chants Democratic and Native American" clusters, and others.[11] There was here, and elsewhere, one might add, except for the omnipresent "Calamus" motif, very little cross-fertilization of attitudes, especially racial, from poetry to prose.[12]

The issue in "Prohibition of Colored Persons" was the viability of Oregon's prohibition of blacks, free or slave, from entering the state, thus giving Oregon "an exclusively white population." Whitman put it simply: "It will be a conflict between the totality of White Labor [and] the interference and competition of Black Labor, or of bringing in colored persons on any terms. . . ." Although at "first sight it seems a cruel prohibition," Whitman, upon examination, finds "much to commend it, and much that will be likely to carry the judgment of the masses of the nation in its favor." He summarizes the exclusionist position: "White Labor will not demean itself to stand, walk, sit, work, or what not, side by side with blacks, and on an equality with them." Whitman shows no indignation. On the contrary, he says that "zealous persons may speak of this as a prejudice, but we think every man has a right to his taste in such things—and the white workingman has in this."

Yet apparently something was bothering him: "Can any person of moral and benevolent feelings, then countenance for a moment, such a plan as the total exclusion of an unfortunate race, merely on account of their color, and because there is a prejudice against them? No, not if there is a shadow of a hope that battling against this prejudice will succeed in rooting it out of America." This was mainly the argument of the abolitionists, but Whitman opposed them. Nor is there a characteristic grandiose appeal as in "The Eighteenth Presidency!" to some future amelioration of this situation. Whitman takes "a deep and wide view of the whole question . . . [and] the answer might *perhaps* be Yes—strange as it sounds at first" (emphasis added). Whitman then gets to the point: "Who believes that the Whites and Blacks can ever amalgamate in America? Or who wishes it to happen? Nature has set an impassable seal against it. Besides, is not America for Whites? And is it not better so?" He then fudges the implications of this argument with some familiar cadences: "As long as the Blacks remain here, how can they become anything like an independent and heroic race? There is no chance for it." Finally he invokes the old Jeffersonian argument about shipping blacks elsewhere, so that "they would have a chance to develop themselves, to gradually form a race, a nation. . . ." He does not say where.

Actually, Whitman had some difficulty in deciding exactly what to do with blacks. In an editorial written but a year earlier, he thought that blacks actually were better off *in* the United States; sending them back to Africa would not do, and for a curious reason. "The blacks, mulattos, etc., either in the Northern or Southern States, might bear in mind that had their forefathers remained in Africa, and their birth occurred there, they would now be roaming Krumen and Ashanteemen, wild, filthy, paganistic—not *residents* of a land of light, and bearing their share, *to some extent* in all its civilizations" (emphasis added).[13]

For the most part, this straightforward clarity of expression in Whitman's prose dissolves when he is caught up in strongly conflicting inner emotions in detailing what might be termed An Important Statement. Such a statement is his best-known prose work, *Democratic Vistas*. Here Whitman touches all bases. *Democratic Vistas*, written after the Civil War, is a compendium of his mature thinking on such questions as the vitality of American democracy, the nature of contemporary society, and the direction the United States would take in the future. In this loose, discursive essay, he paints a sorry picture of the state of the Republic a few years after the end of the war.

Whitman, the complex delineator of visionary hopes and dreams, takes a long, hard look at what has happened after almost a century to the early theoretical promise of a new democratic Eden. His concern is with day-to-day living at every level of American society.

The 1871 eighty-four page pamphlet *Democratic Vistas* originated from two previously published essays, "Democracy" (1867) and "Personalism" (1868), and part of a third essay that was rejected for publication.[14] In "Democracy," Whitman had heatedly responded to Carlyle's vituperative attack in "Shooting Niagara: And After?" on American democracy and the enfranchisement of blacks, although Whitman's own assessment of the direction of American democracy, as he was soon to acknowledge at the onset of the Gilded Age, was not too far from Carlyle's. In *Democratic Vistas*, he replaced his lengthy attack on Carlyle with a conciliatory note that puts *Vistas* in a proper perspective. "I was at first roused to much anger and abuse by this essay from Mr. Carlyle, so insulting to the theory of America—but happening to think afterwards how I had more than once been in the like mood, . . . and seen persons and things in the same light. . . ." With rare understatement he added parenthetically, "Indeed some might say there are signs of the same feeling in these Vistas" (PW, 2:375, 76n).[15]

Quite early in *Democratic Vistas*, he states the essential theme of the essay: "The battle . . . between democracy's convictions, aspirations, and the people's crudeness, vice, caprices . . . [and the] appaling [*sic*] dangers of universal suffrage in the United States . . . The United States are destined either to surmount the gorgeous history of feudalism, or else prove the most tremendous failure of time. Not the least doubtful am I on any prospects of their material success . . . [and] the priceless value of our political institutions [and] general suffrage . . ." (PW, 2:363–364). I would suggest that, for the most part, the overwhelming evidence *Democratic Vistas* provides would support the opening lines of this quotation; in the face of this evidence, the latter sentences in *Democratic Vistas* become simply idealistic wishful thinking.

Underlying the whole process of the failure he describes is his ongoing disenchantment with "society, in these States, [which] is canker'd, crude, superstitious, and rotten. Political or law-made society is, and private, or voluntary society, is also. . . . [T]he element of the moral conscience . . . seems to me either entirely lacking, or seriously enfeebled or ungrown" (PW, 2:369).

When Whitman fixes his "moral microscope upon humanity," he sees "a sort of dry and flat Sahara, . . . [the] cities, crowded with petty grotesques, malformations playing meaningless antics everywhere, in shop, street, church, theatre, barroom, official chair, . . . are . . . vulgarity, low cunning, infidelity— everywhere the youth puny, impudent, foppish . . . everywhere an abnormal libidinousness, unhealthy forms, male, female, painted, padded, dyed, . . . bad blood, the capacity for good motherhood deceasing or deceas'd, . . . probably the meanest to be seen in the world" (PW, 2:372).

His by now automatic verbal responses and standard tricks provide the underpinnings for the rhetorical obfuscations that inform *Vistas*. That is, when the dreadful reality of his indictment in *Democratic Vistas* becomes too compelling, he routinely shifts, often within the same paragraph, to a more soothing palliative recollection of the visionary *poetic* potentialities of his "divine average":

> Meantime, general humanity . . . has always . . . been full of perverse maleficence, and is so yet. . . . I myself see clearly enough the crude, defective streaks in all the strata of the common people; the specimens and vast collections of the ignorant, the credulous, the unfit and uncouth, the incapable, and the very low and poor. . . . [Can] we expect to elevate and improve a nation's politics by absorbing such morbid collections and qualities therein[?] The point is a formidable one. . . . We believe the ulterior object of political and all other government . . . [is] to develop, to open up to cultivation, to encourage the possibilities of all beneficent and manly outcroppage,

and of that aspiration for independence, and the pride and self-respect latent
in all characters. (PW, 2:379)

There is typically more of the same elsewhere: "The average man of a land at
last only is important. He, in these States, remains immortal owner and boss,
deriving good uses, somehow, out of any sort of servant in office, even the
basest" (387).

The essay "Personalism," Whitman's general term for his program of the development of the individual, apparently was written to soften his appraisal of
conditions in the United States that had appeared a year earlier in the essay
"Democracy." In *Democratic Vistas*, "Personalism" immediately follows "Democracy." We are at once more or less back to the rolling visionary cadences of
the 1855 Preface or perhaps the 1855 poem "A Song for Occupations" or the 1856
"Salut au Monde!" or the 1860 "Starting from Paumanok." It is all very familiar, especially the emphasis on a eugenics program for a new breed of healthier
men and women, on the "adhesive" comradeship of men, on the importance to
the United States of future great American writers, or "literatuses," as he
termed them, and on his distaste for "feudalism," which, he acknowledged,
had produced great literature, although it viewed humanity "in the lump" (PW,
2:376)—which he did as well in *Democratic Vistas*. Whitman here appears to
be standing still. It is as though nothing had changed since 1855.

That is, in the "Personalism" section of *Vistas*, through uplifting metaphor,
we get a reflexive denial of reality, of failed social and political formulations.
Whitman seems to be saying, "It should be, ergo, it will be," despite the mas-
sive evidence to the contrary that he had previously delineated on his loss of
faith in the ongoing democratic process and in his "divine average."

Certainly the tone here is softer, despite such familiar imperatives as "I
should demand a programme." The "Personalism" section, for the most part,
is a lovely rhapsody of all-too-familiar cadences and adjective-noun pairings,
an oasis in his earlier Sahara, as in this typical example:

> Assuming Democracy to be at present in its embryo condition, and that the
> only large and satisfactory justification of it resides in the future, mainly
> through the copious production of perfect characters among people, and
> through the advent of the sane and pervading religiousness, it is with regard
> to the atmosphere and spaciousness fit for such characters, and of certain
> nutriment . . . proper for them, and indicating them for New World pur-
> poses, that I continue the present statement—an exploration, as *of new
> ground*, wherein, like other primitive surveyors, I must do the best I can
> leaving it to those who come after me to do much better. (PW, 2:392–393,
> emphasis added)

Or again, in returning to familiar territory, he catalogs the attributes required of ideal parents for the creation of a greater republic: "To our model, a clear-blooded, strong-fibred physique is indispensable" (PW, 2:397), in a sentence burdened with repetitive clauses that runs an additional eight lines.

Occasionally his either-or approach to life in the United States leads him into some silly business, as when, in rehearsing his familiar insistence of the primacy of a native American literature culturally to elevate the United States over one predicated on European "feudal" models, he says that "America has yet morally and artistically originated nothing. She seems singularly unaware that the models of persons, books, manners, &c., appropriate for former conditions and for European lands, are but exiles and exotics here" (PW, 2:395). Apparently to make his point, he modestly excludes himself, but as Richard Chase points out, what of such writers, or "literatuses," as Cooper, Poe, Emerson, Thoreau, Melville, and Hawthorne?[16]

In the final pages of *Vistas*, Whitman returns once more to the realities of post–Civil War American society. "Democracy grows rankly up the thickest, noxious, deadliest plants and fruits of all—brings worse and worse invaders. . . ." The reason is clear: "Even to-day, amid these whirls, incredible flippancy, and blind fury of parties, infidelity, entire lack of first-class captains and leaders, added to the plentiful meanness and vulgarity of the ostensible masses . . ." (PW, 2:422).

Given this overwhelming indictment in his prose of his "divine average," it would appear that the masses, despite his idealistic programs for them, would not get any wiser or be consistently more politically or socially receptive to their own needs. In fact, some ten years later, he admits as much in *Collect*. Following a discussion in the essay "Democracy in the New World" on the need to expose the "weakness . . . and infinite corruptions of democracy," he concludes with the sad confession that "man is about the same, in the main, whether with despotism, or whether with freedom" (PW, 2:529).[17] Put simply, the redemption of the masses in *Democratic Vistas* lies in a rhetorically safe shelter, the vague but comforting future.[18] And, it might be added, it was also in this volume that, when he reprinted the 1855 Preface, Whitman excised his inspiriting hymn to the common people cited at the beginning of this essay and substituted instead, after "common people," the by now reflexive "south, north, west, east, in all its States, through all its mighty amplitude" (LG, 710, 30n).

The same year he wrote "The Eighteenth Presidency!," the savagely ironical poem "Respondez!"—along with such other poems as "Salut au Monde!," "Song of the Broad-Axe," "Crossing Brooklyn Ferry," and "Song of the Open Road"—appeared among the twenty new poems of the 1856 edition of *Leaves*, with such typical lines as "Let churches accommodate serpents, vermin, and the corpses of those who have died of the most filthy diseases!" (TV, 1:262). In the 1871 edition, around the time he was putting *Democratic Vistas* together, he added to "Respondez!" some new lines that proved to be a capsule summary of *Vistas*:

(The war is completed—the price is paid—the title is settled beyond recall;) . . .
.   .   .
(Stifled, O Days! O lands! in every public and private corruption!
Smother'd in thievery, impotence, shamelessness, mountain-high;
Brazen effrontery, scheming, rolling like ocean's waves around and upon you,
   O my days! my lands!
For not even those thunderstorms, nor fiercest lightnings of the war, have pu-
   rified the atmosphere.) (260–261)[19]

Within the context of the 1856 edition of *Leaves*, the irony of "Respondez!" was clearly understood. But too much had happened between 1856 and 1871, and the double-edged sword of irony was now cutting the other way. Given the Civil War (the "Great Barbeque," one critic termed it[20]), and its aftermath, what Whitman had earlier intended as irony had in the intervening years become for him a progression of ineluctable truisms. It may well have been for this reason that he dropped "Respondez!" from the final 1881 edition of *Leaves of Grass* after its appearance in four consecutive editions.

However, some ten years later, he appears to have had second thoughts about excluding from *Leaves* a poem of this sort. The sentiments conveyed in "Respondez!" appear in the rarely anthologized poem "The Rounded Catalogue Divine Complete," included in *Good-Bye My Fancy*, the 1891–1892 annex to *Leaves of Grass*. This grim, unflinching appraisal of the human condition seems lost among such benign decorative pieces as "My 71st Year," "On, On the Same, Ye Jocund Twain," "An Ended Day," "Unseen Buds," and the title poem. We get resonances of the 1856 line from "Respondez!" cited above, but here totally without ironical intent.

In the epigraph to the poem, Whitman universalizes the theme by not specifying a particular time or place. The minister could give his sermon on any Sunday, in any church, but to Whitman the uplifting message boiled down to the same old sad story. The learned minister had missed the point of what life was all about below the cosmetic surface of things:

"The Rounded Catalogue Divine Complete."

[Sunday,— — —.—Went this forenoon to church. A college professor, Rev. Dr. ———, gave us a fine sermon, during which I caught the above words; but the minister included in his "rounded catalogue" letter and spirit, only the esthetic things, and entirely ignored what I name in the following:]

The devilish and the dark, the dying and diseas'd,
The countless (nineteen-twentieths) low and evil, crude and savage,
The crazed, prisoners in jail, the horrible, rank, malignant,
Venom and filth, serpents, the ravenous sharks, liars, the dissolute;
(What is the part the wicked and the loathesome bear within earth's orbic scheme?)
Newts, crawling things in slime and mud, poisons,
The barren soil, the evil men, the slag and hideous rot. (TV, 3:747)

Howard Mumford Jones saw *Democratic Vistas* as "a sort of Götterdämmerung" with a happy ending.[21] On the other hand, Whitman's necessarily vague futuristic optimism was denied at every turn by his sound, rigorous appraisal of a "canker'd" social and political situation that he wished would simply go away. *Vistas* may well be likened to Götterdämmerung, but given Whitman's inability substantively to justify his fabled "divine average" as a vital factor in day-to-day living in a viable democratic society, I would suggest that the ending, for Whitman, was far from happy.[22]

NOTES

1. Whitman had incorporated some seventy lines from the 1855 Preface into the 1856 poem "By Blue Ontario's Shore" (throughout this essay only final titles are given) and all but two lines of the 1856 poem "Song of Prudence," along with a few other poems (see LG, 340–341n, 372n, and 708n). William Everson followed Whitman's lead by reworking the entire Preface into stanzaic form in *American Bard* (New York: Viking Press, 1982).

2. In the final 1881 edition, "O Amazement of things!" was dropped.

3. See Joseph Jay Rubin and Charles H. Brown, eds., *Walt Whitman of the "New York Aurora": Editor at Twenty-Two* (State College, Penn.: Bald Eagle Press, 1950); Cleveland Rodgers and John Black, eds., *The Gathering of the Forces, Editorials, Essays . . . by Walt Whitman . . . as Editor of the "Brooklyn Daily Eagle" in 1846 and 1847* (New York: G. P. Putnam's Sons, 1920), 2 vols.; Thomas L. Brasher, *Whitman as Editor of the "Brooklyn Daily Eagle"* (Detroit: Wayne State University Press, 1970); Emory Holloway and Vernolian Schwarz, eds., *I Sit and Look Out: Editorials from the "Brooklyn Daily Times"* (New York: Columbia University Press, 1932); Emory Holloway and Ralph Adimari, eds., *New York Dissected . . . Newspaper Articles* (New York: Rufus Rockwell Wilson, 1936); Vincent Freimarck and Bernard Rosenthal, eds., *Race and the American Romantics . . . Writings on Slavery* (New York: Schocken Books, 1971).

4. Whitman had set this essay in type and apparently distributed it in proof to editors of the "independent press." So far as is known, no editor actually printed it. See Gay Wilson Allen, *The New Walt Whitman Handbook*, rev. ed. (New York: New York University Press, 1986), 170–171.

5. See Allen, 170. See also T. Harry Williams, Richard N. Current, and Frank Freidel, *A History of the United States to 1876* (New York: Knopf, 1961), 542–566. The election actually became a contest between Buchanan and Frémont. Buchanan, who won the popular vote by some 500,000 votes, carried all the slave states except Maryland and five Northern states; he polled 174 electoral votes, Frémont 114, and Fillmore 8 (from Maryland) (544).

6. For early trial lines on this 1855 passage, see NUP, 1:109–110. See also TV, 1:12, for the persona's sympathetic ministering to a runaway slave until he "pass'd north"; TV, 1:13–14, for Whitman's idealization of a black drayman; and TV, 1:172, for the line in the 1856 poem "Salut au Monde!": "You dim-descended, black, divine-souled African, large fine-headed, nobly-formed, superbly-destined, on equal terms with me!" Also see UPP, 2:69, for other early trial lines on the persona's identification with slaves in "Song of Myself" and NUP, 1:115, for Whitman's apotheosis of the slave in trial lines for the 1855 "Song of Myself": "Where others see a slave a pariah an emptier of privies the Poet beholds what when the days of the soul are accomplished shall be peer of God."

7. See, for example, the 1847 editorial "American Workingmen, Versus Slavery" in the *Brooklyn Eagle*, in which Whitman opposes slavery on the grounds that white labor is totally degraded by slavery, and thus he is against the extension of slavery into "new territories" (Freimarck and Rosenthal, 38–41).

8. Whitman's concern here was with the integrity of the "organic compact" between the states. He put it succinctly: "These States compact each with the other, that any person held to service or labor in one State under its laws, and escaping into another State, shall not be absolved from service by any law of that other State, but shall be delivered up to the persons to whom such service or labor is due" (NUP, 6:2,132). His opposition to the Fugitive Slave Law (1850) was that it "contravenes the whole of the organic compacts" (2,132–2,133) or interferes with states' rights, that is, with protecting equally the integrity of the slave states.

In 1854, a fugitive slave, Anthony Burns, was seized in Boston and returned to his owner in Virginia. Whitman's poem "A Boston Ballad," a satirical pillorying of the federal authorities who had seized Burns, was probably written around this time and appeared in the 1855 edition of *Leaves of Grass*. A year later in "The Eighteenth Presidency!" the *prose* Whitman saw the capture of runaway slaves quite differently. See also, Williams, Current, and Freidel, 507, 530–531.

9. See Whitman's 1860 poem "To the States; To Identify the 16th, 17th, or 18th Presidentiad" (TV, 2:414–415)—i.e., the administrations of Millard Fillmore,

Franklin Pierce, and James Buchanan—and the summary line: "What a filthy Presidentiad!"

10. See the May 6, 1858, editorial in the *Brooklyn Daily Times* (Freimarck and Rosenthal, 46–47).

11. See MLG.

12. It was the *prose* Whitman whose attitudes inform his 1867 poem "Ethiopia Saluting the Colors," published in the 1871 edition of *Leaves of Grass*. Through the speaker in the poem, a Union soldier, Whitman's earlier empathy with blacks in *Leaves* gave way to a stereotypical image of an old black woman as she curtsies to a regiment of Union soldiers and "rolls her darkling eye." She is "so ancient, hardly human," with "bare bony feet," wearing a colorful turban. Though in one stanza she is quite capable of reflecting on the cruelty of her former servitude— "What is it, fateful woman—so blear, hardly human?"—nevertheless she looks at the soldiers through the eyes of a simple child: "Are the things so strange and marvelous, you see or have seen?" (TV, 3:631–632). An undated manuscript fragment apparently reflects this later approach to the "black person": "Poem of the black person.—Infuse the sentiment of a sweeping, surrounding, shielding protection of the blacks—their passiveness—their character of sudden fits—the abstracted fit—(the three *picturesque blacks*—in the men's cabin in the Fulton ferry boat)— their costumes—dinner kettles—describe them in the poem" (emphasis added). Such a passage does not appear in *Leaves of Grass*. See Richard M. Bucke, Thomas B. Harned, and Horace L. Traubel, eds., *Complete Writings* (New York: G. P. Putnam's Son's, 1902), 10:19.

13. See "On the Old Subject—The Origin of It All," July 17, 1857 editorial in the *Brooklyn Daily Times* (Freimarck and Rosenthal, 43–45). Whitman also noted here, "It is also to be remembered that no race ever can remain slaves if they have it in them to become free. Why do slave-ships go to Africa only?"

Alan Trachtenberg has pointed out to me that twenty-three years later, in 1890, Whitman spoke directly about what he termed "the nigger question": "'I never went full on the nigger question—the nigger would not turn—would not do anything for himself—he would only act when prompted to act. No! no! I should not like to see the nigger in the saddle—it seems unnatural; for he is only there when propped there, and propping don't civilize. I have always had a latent sympathy for the Southerner—and even for those in Europe—the Cavalier-folk— hateful as they are to me abstractly—un-democratic—from putting myself in a way in their shoes. Till the nigger can do something for himself, little can be done *for* him!' He spoke of 'the line of social demarkation [*sic*] in the lower orders' as 'very much more obvious than that higher up'" (HT, 6:323).

Six months later, Whitman returned to the subject: "Discussed Watterson's Boston speech, in which, in the Negro question, he took the ground that the

Negro franchise would never be truly granted till the Negro vote was divided, not a class one. W. said, 'I know enough of Southern affairs, have associated enough with Southern people to feel convinced that if I lived South I should side with the Southern whites.' But how did that consist with his democracy? 'I should be forced not to explain that: I would have to evade the issue. And yet I feel with Watterson strongly'" (HT, 7:158).

14. See PW, 2:361–362n. See Edward F. Grier, "Walt Whitman, the *Galaxy*, and *Democratic Vistas*," *American Literature* 23 (November 1951): 332–350, for an account of Whitman's dealings with the *Galaxy*. See also CORR, 1:82n, 338ff., 2:15n, 18–19ff.

Over the years, the scholarship on *Democratic Vistas* has been extensive, reflecting the wide variety of approaches to this work. Of special interest for those critics who more or less accept Whitman's affirmations of the democratic ideal after a close analysis of his negative responses, see Frederik Schyberg, *Walt Whitman* (New York: Columbia University Press, 1951), 220–225; James E. Miller, Jr., *A Critical Guide to Leaves of Grass* (Chicago: University of Chicago Press, 1957), 54–56; Roger Asselineau, *Walt Whitman: The Creation of a Book* (Cambridge: Harvard University Press, 1962), 163–169; Howard Mumford Jones, *The Age of Energy: Varieties of American Experience, 1865–1915* (New York: Viking Compass, 1971), 107; Betsy Erkkila, *Whitman the Political Poet* (New York: Oxford University Press, 1989), 247–257; Alan Trachtenberg, "Whitman's Visionary Politics," *Mickle Street Review* 10 (1988): 15–31.

Of special interest for negative critical assessments of *Vistas*, see Gay Wilson Allen, *A Reader's Guide to Walt Whitman* (New York: Farrar, Straus and Giroux, 1970), 93–97; Richard Chase, *Walt Whitman Reconsidered* (New York: William Sloane Associates, 1955), 153–165; M. Wynn Thomas, *The Lunar Light of Whitman's Poetry* (Cambridge: Harvard University Press, 1987), 266, 292, 35n, 308, 8n; Edwin Haviland Miller, *Walt Whitman: A Psychological Journey* (Boston: Houghton Mifflin, 1968), 129, 147. See also note 18.

15. For Whitman's deleted attack on Carlyle, see PW, 2:749–750; for his later, somewhat favorable consideration of Carlyle, see his essays "Death of Thomas Carlyle" and "Later Thoughts and Jottings. Carlyle from American Points of View," in *Specimen Days* (1882), PW, 1:248–253, 254–262.

For a full discussion of Whitman and Carlyle, see Gregory Paine, "The Literary Relations of Whitman and Carlyle with Especial Reference to Their Contrasting Views of Democracy," *Studies in Philology* 36 (July 1939): 550–563. Alice L. Cooke, "Whitman as a Critic: *Democratic Vistas* with Special Reference to Carlyle," *Walt Whitman Newsletter* 4 (June 1958): 91–95, stresses their points of agreement.

16. Chase, 161.

17. Asselineau, 334, 67n, has acutely noticed that Whitman had drawn the same conclusions, and in almost the same phrasing, some forty years earlier, when he was the twenty-three-year-old editor of the *New York Aurora*: "Human nature is the same, whether in a republic or [under] despotism" (Rubin and Brown, 98).

In this connection, some of Whitman's earlier comments regarding his prose "divine average" have recently surfaced in a group of nine letters that he wrote to a friend in 1840 and 1841. At the time, Whitman taught school in Woodbury, Long Island, and boarded with the families of his pupils. In these letters, Whitman, at twenty-two, and apparently to impress his correspondent, offers labored allusions to Chesterfield, Homeric and Italian poetry, *Hamlet* (misquoted), "salad and champagne," and the like. Nevertheless, his early contempt for the farmers, their gross personal and eating habits, and their "ignorance, vulgarity, rudeness," comes through clearly in such references to them as "the fag ends, the scraps and refuse," "bog-trotters," "contemptible ninnies," "brutes," "Woodbury animals," "clowns and country bumpkins," "flat-heads," "coarse gump-heads" (foolish or dull-witted persons), "unqualified infernal jackasses," "the grossest, the most low-minded of the human race," and the like. See Arthur Golden, "Nine Early Whitman Letters, 1840–1841," *American Literature* 58 (October 1986): 342–360.

18. In this connection, Rudolf Schmidt, who had translated *Democratic Vistas* into Danish as early as 1874, wrote perceptively in his Introduction that Whitman's "democracy transcends the personal limitations, the personal programs. It is a cosmic, pantheistic democracy" (Schyberg, 220). See also V. K. Chari, *Whitman in the Light of Vedantic Mysticism* (Lincoln: University of Nebraska Press, 1964), 136–137, 148–149, for the development of similar ideas.

19. See also, for example, Whitman's additions to "By Blue Ontario's Shore" in the 1867 edition of *Leaves of Grass*, retained with minor changes in the final edition: "(Democracy—the destined conqueror—yet treacherous lip-smiles everywhere, / And Death and infidelity at every step.)" (TV, 1:190).

20. Jones, 107.

21. Ibid.

22. See, for example, HT, 1:25, where Traubel quotes from an undated Whitman holograph that at the time reflected the ideas informing *Democratic Vistas*: "Go on, my dear Americans, whip your horses to the utmost—Excitement; money! politics!—open all your valves and let her go—going, whirl with the rest—you will soon get under such momentum you can't stop if you would. Only make provisions betimes, old States and new States, for several thousand insane asylums. You are in a fair way to create a nation of lunatics." Whitman, upon hearing this early statement, said, "I don't know but it still holds good."

POLITICS AND SEXUALITY

*Besides, important as they are in my purpose as emotional expressions for human-
ity, the special meaning of the 'Calamus' cluster of LEAVES OF GRASS, (and more
or less running through that book, and cropping out in 'Drum-Taps,') mainly
resides in its Political significance.*

(1876 "Preface," LG, 751)

The Body Politic in *Democratic Vistas*

ESPITE WHITMAN'S disclaimer that *Democratic Vistas* is a casual collection of memoranda, "written at widely different times," rather than "the result of studying up in political economy" (PW, 2:362–363), the essay is the painstaking work of a writer who had been involved in political debate for more than a quarter of a century.[1] What H. L. Mencken called its "gnarled and gasping prose" testifies to the trouble Whitman had—and the trouble he took—in transforming the crude realities of his nation into a vision of a democratic community of self-reliant Americans.[2] Lacking the theoretical genius of Herbert Spencer and John Stuart Mill and without Henry George's keen insights into American capitalism as it evolved into its corporate phase, he nevertheless produced an astute, if idiosyncratic, analysis of the American scene. Apparently content to be a dreamer of the absolute and to subordinate sociological doctrine to poetic inspiration, he mingled fact, hope, and metaphor in his vital political essay.

Chief among his metaphors is that of the body politic. Although the precise phrase apparently never appears in Whitman's writings, throughout *Democratic Vistas* the body politic serves as a unifying structural metaphor, in terms of which the individual citizen becomes the prototype of the state and, conversely, the state is figured as the individual writ large. The body politic metaphor, employed by a broad range of social theorists, implied that biological laws were applicable to national development. The body personal was seen as a microcosm or analogue of the body politic, a concept that "linked man's view of the state to his most personal and indestructible source of identity, his body."³ Thus, Auguste Comte contended that "the whole social evolution of the race must proceed in entire accordance with biological laws; and the social phenomena must always be founded on the necessary invariableness of the human organism, the characteristics of which, physical, intellectual, and moral, are always found to be essentially the same, and related in the same manner, at every degree of the social scale."⁴ Utilizing a rich and daring "physiological" imagery throughout *Democratic Vistas*, Whitman, too, diagnoses American society as though it were a human patient and he were its physician, and he proposes a program of national eugenics to produce an inexhaustible supply of splendid individuals who would constitute the American body politic.

The closest precedent for Whitman's approach was Thomas Carlyle's lengthy essay "Characteristics" (1831). Carlyle's keynote, that "the healthy know not of their health, but only the sick," is said to be "an aphorism of the bodily physician" which "holds no less in moral, intellectual, political, than in merely corporeal therapeutics." To figure society as endowed with life is scarcely a metaphor, Carlyle said, "but rather the statement of a fact by such imperfect methods as language affords. . . . Society has its periods of sickness and vigor, of youth, manhood, decrepitude, dissolution and new birth. . . ." Anticipating Whitman's pose in *Democratic Vistas* as his nation's moral diagnostician, Carlyle diagnosed his own "spavined" dyspeptic society as suffering "constant grinding, internal pain" and "mad spasmodic throes"; "anatomically studied," he said, it appeared to lie "impotent," paralyzed with skepticism toward the existing social system and ailing "with a whole nosology of diseases." But despite "the whole tribe of social pestilences," he declared, the remedy "lies there clear, for whosoever will take the spectacles off his eyes and honestly look, to know."⁵

Like Whitman, whose references to an intuited natural law permeate *Leaves of Grass*, Carlyle proclaimed the concept that "every Society, every Polity, has a spiritual principle, is the embodiment, tentative and more less complete of a [governing subconscious] Idea" that "dwells vitally in every heart" as "something of a religion." "It is properly the Soul of the State."⁶ Rejecting the concept of progress, Carlyle located personal and societal wholeness in an imagined feudal past when "all men . . . were animated by one great Idea" and heroes inspired the diligent and pious masses, whereas Whitman projected such wholeness into a still uncharted and democratic future; but this premise of an inspirational national idea—acting as a vital intuitional law—animates and informs Whitman's essay.

The body politic metaphor was updated by a number of Whitman's contemporaries. Emerson spoke of "representative man" and of "the whole man;

of whom the existing government, it must be owned, is a shabby imitation."[7] Herbert Spencer held the body politic metaphor to be a "scientific truth," even to finding that the development of capitalism accords with evolutionary biological laws. He equated the laws of physiology with the functioning of the state, asserting that "the body politic . . . has a species of life, and conforms to the same laws of growth, organization, and sensibility that a being does. . . . one vitality circulates through it and him, and . . . his happiness depends on the normal action of every organ in the social body."[8] And the American scientist and historian John William Draper, whom Whitman apparently knew, declared that "social advancement is as completely under the control of natural law as is bodily growth. The life of an individual is a miniature of the life of a nation," the lives of both individual and nation progressing through analogous physical stages and both characterized at maturity by the attainment of personal freedom. Applying von Baer's law of cellular evolution to the development of nations, Draper concluded that applying "a physiological law holding good for the individual to this our social state" involves "no fictitious hypothesis. Society is only an aggregate of individuals; whatever affects, whatever regulates each of them, must affect it also. . . . we may therefore transfer from the individual to society all those phenomena of equilibrium and movement observed by the Physiologists."[9] Likewise, a very popular book by a conservative British physician, which Whitman apparently read, considered "society as the procession of the principles of the human frame," and drew analogies organ by organ. The author asserted that "*humanity is the greatest human body and the likest of all things to the least or individual body. . . .* its heart is the thousandfold love that carries the races to their goals, the poets whose bold blood licks up toward heaven, and talks in tongue-like alphabets of our own." He stated that "man in his body, equally as in his brain, is by nature a factory of Utopias."[10]

The twelve-hundred-word introduction to *Democratic Vistas*, with its dramatic use of the body politic trope, highlights the essay's principal themes and arguments. Whitman (who would one day honor Carlyle as a "first-class moral physician of our era"[11]) assumes the Carlylean stance of America's moral diagnostician, "like a physician diagnosing some deep disease." "Using the moral microscope upon humanity," he finds the American body politic in a sickly condition, its "moral conscience . . . the verteber to State and man, enfeebled or ungrown," and its men and women "canker'd, crude, superstitious, and rotten" and suffering from a "hollowness of heart" and a lack of democratic ideals. Beneath the "melodramatic screamings" and "all this hectic glow" (a phrase designating the feverish redness associated with tuberculosis), he finds corruption, lethargy, a profiteering business morality, and "weak infidelism." The sexual magnetism, which he had praised in many poems and prefaces, is rarely seen. Instead of athletic personalities who could endow a new race with manly and womanly qualities, he beholds sickly adults and youth who are "prematurely ripe" (a phrase implying the early onset of puberty, which one reformer called "a certain indication of a diseased state"[12]) and an "abnormal libidinousness"—all impediments to first-class parenthood (PW, 2:369–372).

Mixing physiological and agricultural imagery (a common practice among eugenic and medical reformers), Whitman proposes two basic strategies. First, he evokes the eugenic premise (often found in his writings) that the physiological upgrading and transformation of the American citizenry into "crops" of "athletes" and of "fine youths and majestic old persons" and of "perfect women, indispensable to endow the birth-stock of a New World" must precede, and form the basis for, the new democratic order.[13] Second, he insists that the development of full-fledged personalities and their integration into a new body politic ultimately depend on the catalyst of an inspirational democratic literature in order to "form the osseous structure" of the body politic, to permeate it "to the very marrow." For the American body politic, with its lack of a homogeneous culture ("a common skeleton, knitting all close"), only "something equivalent to [imaginative] creation" can provide the "spinal and essential attributes" required to form the "new blood, new frame of democracy." The American body politic, he maintains, must be integrated, and ultimately transformed—spiritualized—by "a cluster of mighty poets, artists, fit for us, national expressers," who will fire the American people, through their "vast, indefinite, spiritual, emotional power," with "a fervid and tremendous [democratic] IDEA." Such poets (in the imagery of breath therapy or mesmerism) can breathe into men and women "the breath recuperative of sane and heroic life," so vital to the coming era (PW, 2:364–372).

A democracy predicated on the existence of masses of superb individuals required a new definition of heroism. Four months after the *New York Herald* reprinted Carlyle's "Shooting Niagara," which ridiculed the "Swarmery" of mob rule, called for an intellectual elite to share the national leadership with the wealthy and titled, and demanded "heroes to govern you [the masses]," Whitman confronted the issue of heroism in his "Democracy" essay.[14] Mocking Carlyle's very language but adapting his concept of a governing national idea, he defined American democracy as an association of the "interminable swarms of alert, good-natured independent citizens," characterized by a powerful "central spirit" and independence (PW, 2:388). Responding to Carlyle's anti-American diatribe and his "comic-painful hullabaloo and vituperative cat-squalling" over extending the popular franchise, Whitman redefined the heroism appropriate to a democratic society with emphasis on "humanity it-self, and its own inherent, normal, full-grown qualities, without any super-stitious support whatever. The idea of perfect individualism it is indeed that deepest tinges and gives character to the idea of the aggregate" (374–375).[15]

Using the physiologically tinged language of muscular Christianity, Whit-man asserts that "political democracy, as it exists and practically works in America, with its threatening evils, supplies a training-school for making first-class men." "It is life's gymnasium, an arena fit for freedom's athletes." The Civil War, which Emerson had called "a potent alternative, tonic, magnetizer [that] reinforces manly power a hundred and a thousand times," had pro-duced the soldiers whom Whitman saw as his desired prototype of "a good stock . . . the first unquestioned and convincing western crop." Native born, "independent and intelligent," this eugenic vanguard of America's innumer-able "stock-personalities" emerging from the common folk was for Whitman the "plentifully-supplied, last-needed proof" that democracy could create vital new citizens "that never feudal lord, nor Greek, nor Roman breed yet rival'd" (PW, 2:377–379). Rather than training up a class of elite leaders for imperial capitalism, as Carlyle had urged in "The Nigger Question," his notorious apologia for British West Indian slavery (which Whitman had read), Whit-man affirmed that "real PEOPLE, worthy the name, and made up of heroic develop'd individuals, both sexes—is America's principal, perhaps only, reason for being."[16]

The distinction between Whitman's heroic masses and Carlyle's elitist heroes was voiced by Adam Gurowski, the Polish-born radical republican, whom Whitman called "sharp and severe and wise among men." Like Whitman, Gurowski maintained that "America personifies the [hitherto unknown] com-bination of free individuality with association in self-conscious democracy" (HT, 4:298).[17] His diary of the Civil War argued that, in the "onward march of peoples," this war marks the first instance in which "the whole people is inspired . . . a new era in the development and ascension of man." Feudal wars may have generated "a captain in the sense of Carlyle," but the war to pre-serve the American Union had created an entire heroic people, unlike those portrayed by "the Carlylian, erroneous, false, perverted comprehension of history" or by Emerson's "representative men." The American "scions of Car-lyle want a hero to sing, to lecture about; they cannot appreciate, compre-hend, nay, even feel that collective hero, THE PEOPLE!" But unlike these worshipers of false heroes, he asserts, "Walt Whitman, the incarnation of a genuine American, original genius, Walt alone in his mind and his heart has a shrine for the nameless, for the heroic people." [18]

But in the enthusiasm of wartime, Gurowski had oversimplified Whitman's agonized struggle to resolve the contradiction between the ubiquitous corruption of the American masses and his glowing vision of generations of splendid personalities springing from the loins of the "grand, common stock," who would constitute the new body politic. In an 1857 editorial deploring the "many evidences of corruption and decay" and "political atheism" in America, he had questioned whether the grand Jeffersonian ideal could be carried out by "the young men and women, who are growing up around us, soon to fill our places"—these "used up" males and "painted furbelowed animated balloons who are to be the future mothers of the Republic." [19] Whitman's difficulties in projecting real-life Americans into the desired body politic are reflected by some precautionary reminders that he jotted down among his welter of manuscript notes for *Democratic Vistas*:

> Offset the statement of depravity vulgarism &c, of the masses by a full acknowledgment of the latent heroism. . . .
> Beware of the too strong contradiction between the eulogiums [?] of the rank and file "the grand common stock" ¶'s, and the statement of depravity of the common classes—
> Put in such statement [even] when strongest, a parenthetical sentence or two, crediting the coarsest masses with the best qualities [?] eligibilities
> Say that the evils are mostly from foreign population. . . . Describe the effect of the Irish contribution to the breed in cities. [20]

Nor were Whitman's misgivings unique. In the postwar years, Henry George expressed the fear that "this crowding of people into immense cities, this aggregation of wealth into large lumps, this marshalling of men into big gangs under the control of the 'captains of industry'" jeopardized "personal independence—the basis of all virtues." And Henry Adams concluded that "the moral law had expired" here and that America's "moribund" society was undergoing a process of "devolution" ("Darwin ought to conclude that America was reverting to the stone age"). [21] However, to bridge the gap between an appalling social reality and the bright democratic future he desired, Whitman formulated not a political program but an intuitional faith—"sole worthiest elevator of man or state"—in the inevitability of democratic evolution. In this version of the Whig myth of history, Whitman insisted that democracy operates in conformity with the "strictest," unswervable natural law and that the most fundamental law "is the law of successions, that of the superior law, in time, gradually supplementing and overwhelming the inferior one" (PW,

2:381–382). Despite America's uneven development, "the People ever remain, tendencies continue, and all the idiocratic transfers in the unbroken chain go on" (384). Moreover, those "idiocratic transfers" of the democratic idea, presumably operating through a spiritual intuition in each self-reliant individual who is attuned to an influx of nature's evolutionary law, are the key element in the poetic-political theory underlying *Democratic Vistas.*[22]

The presumed powers of democracy to heal and spiritualize the body politic produced physiologically tinged tropes of social transformation. Humiliating class barriers are called "the curse and canker of Nations politically" (PW, 2:382n.); refined manners "threaten to eat us up like a cancer" (394); and "the extirpation of the [American] Slaveholding Class, (cut out and thrown away like a tumor by surgical operation,)" has proven to be "incomparably the largest advance for Radical Democracy" (756). During the Civil War, "Mother America" is said to be, "though only in her early youth, already to hospital brought" (378); in a related poem, she is said to be suffering from breast cancer, "moral corruption," and fevers, but she can predictably "surmount them all" and recover to enjoy a "beautiful world of new superber birth"—a "freer, vast, electric world to be constructed here," replete with "thy resplending coming literati—thy full-lung'd orators, thy sacerdotal bards, kosmic savans"— the very prophecy of *Democratic Vistas.*[23] And mixing imagery drawn from agriculture and the still-current theory of miasma, Whitman assures his "venerable friend" Carlyle that American democracy does indeed "expect to elevate and improve a nation's politics by absorbing such morbid collections" of ostensibly corrupt persons and by cultivating "all beneficent and manly outcroppage, and [the] aspiration for independence, and pride and self-respect, latent in all characters" (379). In a stunning simile, he compares nature's "antiseptic" purification of "morbific matter" (the organisms that cause disease, fermentation, and putrefaction) to the transformative power of democracy: "as, by virtue of its kosmical, antiseptic power, Nature's stomach is fully strong enough to digest the morbific matter always . . . intuitively gravitating thither—but even to change such contributions into nutrient for the highest uses of life—so American democracy's" (382). Similarly, "Song of the Universal" (1874) predicts that nature's "antiseptic" elements will eventually purify "the huge festering trunk" and "the morbid and shallow" elements in American society (LG, 227).[24]

Despite his faith in an inevitable evolution toward an American democracy, Whitman conceded that democracy meant to him only a word, "the real gist of which sleeps, quite unawaken'd" until the emergence of a culture which will favor "the formation of a typical personality of character." *Democratic*

Vistas, he said, focuses primarily on the forces that are needed to promote "co-pious supplies" of "healthy, acute, handsome individualities" (CORR, 2:18–19) suited to the new democracy—not refined and "well-wash'd" esthetes, but millions of "sane and generous and patriotic" farmers, workers, and small-holders, even if their grammar is faulty and their manners roughened by "a little healthy rudeness." In a figure that mixes agricultural and castration im-agery, he argued that refinement emasculates natural virtues, declaring that no person should so "lose himself in countless masses of adjustments . . . that the simply good and healthy and brave parts of him are reduced and clipp'd away, like the bordering of box in a garden" (PW, 2:393–395).[25] Instead, the "verte-bration of the manly and womanly personalism of our western world," which can "vitalize our country and our days," requires a culture based on "courageous instincts, and loving perceptions, and self-respect" and an "all-penetrating Re-ligion" that can free the individual to experience the natural law as a direct in-spiration or a felt need and thus to develop "the fresh eternal qualities of Being" (396, 398–399, 403). Eventually, millions of moral individualists, liber-ated from outworn modes of thinking, would assimilate into a new polity—a healthy body politic.

To achieve the longed-for transformation toward what Paschal Reeves has called "a luxuriant Democracy,"[26] Whitman does not outline a program of political and social changes. Instead—and not without a measure of personal mythmaking—he proposes two avenues by which the American body politic can be improved: a process of physiological upgrading and a poetic renais-sance that would inspire the masses with a renewed revolutionary spirit. *Democratic Vistas* proposes that the physiological upgrading of the individual citizen form the basis for the political and moral advancement of the state. "The metaphor of the body-politic," says Barker-Benfield, "linked man's view of the state to his most personal and indestructible source of identity, his body." The rise of eugenics in the latter half of the nineteenth century was a "procreative dream"—a "renewed and more desperate attempt to control and shape procreative powers as if the American body-politic were really a body." Eugenic reformers in Whitman's day "would have Anglo-American parents reproduce on stock breeding and stock raising principles" to preserve "the blood of strong races in our veins" and establish an improved "national physique." And "a concern for identity based on the body provided the au-thority for claims by doctors to be social engineers"—an authority which Whitman arrogates to himself in *Democratic Vistas*. Thus, typically, the famed gynecologist Augustus Kinsley Gardner maintained that national greatness would be achieved by the scientific management of copulation and nurture to produce superior offspring. Equating the soundness of the body personal with the health of the body politic, Gardner warned in 1872 that, unless America instituted physiological reforms, the nation's future looked glum, that neglecting the laws of scientific breeding would bring deterioration to America as it had to Rome, and that America, "careless of the rules of health may rapidly degenerate, or even disappear, as the poor Indians are doing."[27]

Democratic Vistas enunciates a comparable "procreative dream" of producing an ideal birthstock by encouraging the kind of genetic engineering advocated in the 1860s and 1870s by many physiologists and reformers. The Whitman persona in "Passage to India" (1871) is labeled an "ethnologist" (LG, 415–416), echoing *Democratic Vistas*, which presents Whitman's "democratic ethnology of the future"—"a science . . . the object of which should be to raise up and supply through the States a copious race of superb American men and women, cheerful, religious, ahead of any yet known" (PW, 2:395).[28] "Clear-blooded" parents capable of transmitting the best hereditary traits and imbued with the "noblest science" of motherhood and fatherhood would create dynamic offspring with the "best blood" to perfect America's Nordic masses and would lay the physiological groundwork for their moral perfection. And so *Democratic Vistas* outlines, "however crudely, a basic model or portrait of personality for general use for the manliness of the States"—"well-begotten" (that is, in accordance with what Whitman calls the "science" of parenthood), dynamic, and having "a general presence that holds its own in the company of the highest" (397). Such democratic prototypes, resembling Whitman's idealized self-portraits as a rosy-fleshed, "perceptive," musical-voiced athlete with a magnetic presence, function in the essay as Whitman's ethnological blueprints of the coming American citizen-heroes.

Similarly, *Democratic Vistas* also calls for an endless succession of "future first-class National Singers, Orators, Artists, and others creating in literature an *imaginative* New World, the correspondent and counterpart of the current Scientific and Political New Worlds."[29] Such a "literatus order" (PW, 2:423) would speed the transition to democracy by sweeping away nondemocratic superstitions and inspiring the vital ideas of selfhood, nationhood, and the "adhesiveness, or love, that fuses, ties, and aggregates, making the races comrades, and fraternizing all" (381)—what Emerson had called "the power of love, as the basis of a state."[30] By inspiring the people with visions of their personal and national greatness, Whitman hoped, the "literatus order" would help to resolve the contradictions between the crude American masses and the transcendental heroes of a future American body politic. The visions of poets—based on their intuition of nature's ameliorative law—underlie Whitman's body politic metaphor in *Democratic Vistas* and are a subtext throughout *Leaves of Grass*.

Confronting the postwar crises—"many a deep intestine difficulty, and human aggregate of cankerous imperfection" and "scrofulous wealth" that thwart America's "imperial destinies"—Whitman warns (in mixed physiological, sexual, and agricultural imagery) that America will never simply ripen "like a pear" into a democracy but will require "the ceaseless need of revolutions," the will to struggle, and constant "new projections and invigorations" of the democratic faith by inspired thinkers. From this viewpoint, the "great Ideal Nationality of the future" must first be imagined—experienced as an ever-renewed revelation—by prophetic poets who can then inject the citizenry with "a subtle and tremendous force-infusion for purposes of spiritualization, for the pure conscience, for genuine esthetics, and for absolute and primal manliness and womanliness" (PW, 2:422–424). Not "by paper and seal, or by compulsion" can "These States" be held together and "fused into the compact organism of one nation," says an 1860 poem, but by "living principles, as the hold of the limbs of the body, or the fibres of plants," and by poets who will be their "common referee." And of these bards, the poem makes clear, the vanguard poet is Whitman himself. "I lead them who plan, with decision and science . . . with friendly hand toward the future." [31]

In proposing to resolve the discrepant elements of the American democracy through the intervention of inspired poets like himself, Whitman transformed his political vision into personal mythmaking. His trope of an American body politic linked his real body and his mythic body to the collective and to the individual men and women in America's evolving future. In sexually charged but shifting imagery, in which the poet appears to be alternately Mother America's mate who begets an ideal "idiocratic" progeny upon her, or to be himself a nurturing Mother America, or to be the masterful poet who couples with his citizen-reader to instill in him or her a new consciousness, the conclusion of *Democratic Vistas* implies that Whitman himself may be the original begetter and conceiver of the new body politic. He undertakes to "fill the gross the torpid bulk [of Mother America] with vital religious fire," [32] "recruiting myriads of offspring" on the progenitress of a "democratic" and "popular" future (PW, 2:396, 425–426). The nation must remain crude and formless, he asserts, until inspired literati, such as he, can "endow a literature with grand and archetypal models" and *"put the nation in form"* (405; emphasis added). Only the true poet can inspire "a sense of matter, and of good animal health" and show Americans the path between their lives and their destinies and, by "the divine magic of his genius" and "image-making faculty," breathe "the breath of life" into poems in order to "free, arouse, dilate" the "intuition, faith, idiosyncrasy" of readers. Only the true poet attunes them to democracy, to the "throbbing . . . pulsations," "the eternal beats, eternal systole and diastole of life in things" (417, 419–420).

In addressing democratic personalities spirit to spirit, the poet "indirectly but surely" shapes individual and aggregate democracy by instilling "new law forces of written and spoken language." The poet's spermatic words thus become a generative force to beget spiritualized democrats and to instill "the lessons of the New World" by having the active reader absorb the poet's utterances in an embrace—"an exercise, a gymnast's struggle"—as a result of which the liberated mind is born. Thus, a "nation of supple and athletic minds, well-train'd, intuitive, used to depend on themselves, and not on a few coteries of writers" will learn to understand the "loftiest final meanings of history and man" and be able to translate poetry into politics and politics into poetry (PW, 2:424–425). Such a declaration recalls Whitman's statement that *Leaves of Grass* was "only a language experiment." In a poetic sense, of course, the experiment was Whitman's introduction of such things as a new cadence and a new diction. But in a political sense, it proposed to test whether the vatic creator of the new poetry could fashion a poetics effective enough to inspire and transform the American masses, whose crudity and corruption he deplores in *Democratic Vistas*. It was an experiment to determine whether words—his words—could attune Americans to nature's supposedly ameliorative laws, could develop them into "idiocratic"—transcendental and self-reliant—individuals and thereby usher in the wished-for democratic order. Of course, the language experiment involved more visionary thinking than it did practical politics. But without such visionary thinking, *Leaves of Grass* would have a certain hollowness at its core. And *Democratic Vistas* is Whitman's extension into often-inspired prose of that same language experiment.

Georg Lukàcs has criticized as quasi-scientific the practice of equating "the principle of harmony" governing societal development with the human "life-cycle" and "the human body," pointing out that the body politic metaphor is mechanistic, politically conservative, and romantic. To a degree Lukàcs's critique applies to Whitman, who often buttressed a good argument with bad science and who had earlier remarked that "we want no *reforms*, no *institutions*, no *parties*—We want a living principle as nature has, under which nothing can go wrong." Nevertheless, Whitman's honest appraisal of America's faults and his assumption that the state must undergo a qualitative transformation toward a free association of self-directed personalities endow the body politic metaphor with a progressive thrust. He wished not so much to reform the state—which Friedrich Engels called "double-edged, divided against itself, contradictory"—as to remove the institutionalized restraints that thwart personal development.[33] Citizens, not politics, were Whitman's measure of progress.

NOTES

1. On the history of *Democratic Vistas*, see PW, 2:361–362; CORR, 2; Edward F. Grier, "Walt Whitman, the *Galaxy*, and *Democratic Vistas*," *American Literature* 23 (November 1951): 332–350; Harold W. Blodgett, "Democratic Vistas—100 Years Later," in Karl Schubert and Ursula Müller-Richter, eds., *Geschichte und Gesellschaft in der amerikaner Literatur* (Heidelberg: Quelle and Meyer, 1975), 114–131; Scott Giantvalley, *Walt Whitman, 1838–1939: A Reference Guide* (Boston: G. K. Hall, 1981), 24, 26–27, 30, 34.

2. "The National Letters," in Alistair Cooke, ed., *The Vintage Mencken* (New York: Vintage, 1958), 86.

3. G. J. Barker-Benfield, *The Horrors of the Half-Known Life: Male Attitudes toward Women and Sexuality in Nineteenth-Century America* (New York: Harper and Row, 1976), 208.

4. Bruce Haley, *The Healthy Body and Victorian Culture* (Cambridge: Harvard University Press, 1978), 84.

5. Thomas Carlyle, "Characteristics," in *Critical and Miscellaneous Essays* (London: Chapman and Hill, 1899), 3:1, 4, 12–13, 18, 20–21; Carlyle, *Heroes and Hero-Worship* (New York: Thomas Y. Crowell, n.d.), 396–398. Whitman reviewed four of Carlyle's books in the 1840s, approving the "rich lore beyond the vague surface" and the "strangely agreeable" style; see Thomas L. Brasher, *Whitman as Editor of the "Brooklyn Daily Eagle"* (Detroit: Wayne State University Press, 1970), 224, 255.

6. Carlyle, "Characteristics," 356–357.

7. Ralph Waldo Emerson, "Politics," in *Essays: Second Series* (Boston: Houghton Mifflin, 1904), 224–226.

8. Haley, 86–87. See also Herbert Spencer, "Transcendental Physiology," in *Essays: Scientific, Political & Speculative* (Osnabrück: Otto Zeller, 1906), 1:101–107; Richard Hofstadter, "The Vogue of Spencer," in Philip Appleman, ed., *Darwin* (New York: Norton, 1979), 394–395.

9. John William Draper, *Thoughts on the Future Civil Policy of America* (New York: Harper and Brothers, 1865), 60, 159, 258–259. Several of Draper's essays appeared in the *Galaxy* during the period when portions of *Democratic Vistas* and some of Whitman's poems were published there. Whitman read a couple of Draper's scientific books and may have attended his lectures at New York's

Broadway Hospital; see Harold Aspiz, *Walt Whitman and the Beautiful* (Urbana: University of Illinois Press, 1980), 259. Karl Ernst von Baer, discoverer of the mammalian ovum, hypothesized that all organisms evolve from the simple to the complex.

10. James John Garth Wilkinson, *The Human Body and Its Connexion with Man* (Philadelphia: Lippincott, Grambo, 1851), 251 and passim; NUP, 1:246.

11. *Specimen Days* in PW, 1:261.

12. Henry C. Wright, *Marriage and Parentage; or, The Reproductive Element in Man* (1855; rpt., New York: Arno Press, 1974), 31n. On Whitman's interest in eugenics, see Aspiz, 183–209.

13. Compare Augustus Kinsley Gardner: "The right of woman 'to be free and equal' with man will come with a Declaration of Independence which shall strip off the fetters of petticoats and the gilded meshes of lace which have so long bound down the gentler sex" (*Conjugal Sins Against the Laws of Life and Health* [1870; rpt., New York: Arno Press, 1974], 208–209, 204).

14. Thomas Carlyle, "Shooting Niagara: and After?" in *Critical and Miscellaneous Essays*, 5:6, 30. *Democratic Vistas* replaced three harsh paragraphs included in the *Galaxy* version of "Democracy" with a note conceding that Carlyle's was the best opinion from a "feudal" viewpoint and that Whitman had often had some similar misgivings (PW, 2:375–376, 750). Whitman sent Carlyle a copy of *Democratic Vistas* (CORR, 2:174), and, unknown to him, Carlyle—who had compared Whitman to "a town-bull [that] had learned to hold a pen"—praised it "somewhat"; see David Alec Wilson and David Wilson McArthur, *Carlyle in Old Age (1865–1881)* (London: Kegan, Paul, Trench, Trubner, 1934), 240.

15. Compare the ideal city described in "Song of the Broad-Axe": "Where outside authority enters always after the precedence of inside authority, / Where the citizen is always the head and ideal . . . Where children are taught to be laws to themselves, and to depend on themselves" (LG, 190).

16. Edward Waldo Emerson and Waldo Emerson Forbes, ed., *Journals of Ralph Waldo Emerson* (Boston: Houghton Mifflin, 1913), 9:493–494; CORR, 1:69; "Emerson's Books, (The Shadows of Them)," in PW, 2:517; NUP, 6:2,171.

17. Adam Gurowski, *America and Europe* (New York: D. Appelton, 1857), 98, 126, and passim. Gurowski frequented Whitman's "Bohemia" at Pfaff's restaurant in Manhattan and sometimes joined Whitman's circle in wartime Washington, which included Northern radicals; see LeRoy Fisher, *Lincoln's Gadfly: Adam Gurowski* (Norman: University of Oklahoma Press, 1964), xx, 72, 235, 264–265, and passim.

18. Adam Gurowski, *Diary: 1863–'64–'65* (Washington: W. H. and O. H. Morrison, 1866), 127–128, 310. Gurowski mocked Jefferson Davis, Robert E. Lee, and many Northern generals as Carlylean heroes, that is, traitors (Fisher, 310,

330). On Whitman's similar view of the generals, see *Specimen Days* (PW, 1:28–29).

19. "What Are We Coming To?" *Brooklyn Daily Times*, August 5, 1857.

20. "Notes—Literary/Undated—'Depravity, Vulgarism, Greatness,'" Charles E. Feinberg Collection, Library of Congress; the bracketed "even" is canceled in the manuscript. If portions of the essay were drafted as early as 1863, as Grier conjectures (343–344), the anti-Irish sentiments may be a reaction to the New York anti-draft riots in July of that year.

21. Henry George, "What the Railroad Will Bring Us," *Overland Monthly* 1 (October 1868): 305; Henry Adams, *The Education of Henry Adams* (1907; rpt., New York: Time, 1964), 2:34, 46, 49.

22. Whitman's best nineteenth-century critic, Anne Gilchrist, phrased the concept: "CONTINUITY again is one of Nature's irrevocable words; everything the result and outcome of what went before; no gaps, no jumps; always a connecting principle which carries forward the great scheme of things as a related whole, which subtly links past and present, like and unlike. Nothing breaks with its past." Quoted in Marion Walker Alcaro, *Walt Whitman's Mrs. G.: A Biography of Anne Gilchrist* (Rutherford, N.J.: Fairleigh Dickinson University Press, 1991), 221.

23. "Thou Mother with Thy Equal Brood," LG, 458–460.

24. Compare "This Compost," LG, 369–370.

25. On the ruinous results of overrefinement and "delicatesse," see "By Blue Ontario's Shore," LG, 342. Excessive refinement is characterized by castration imagery in "Faces," LG, 464.

26. Paschal Reeves, "The Silhouette of the State in *Democratic Vistas*—Hegelian or Whitmanian?" *Personalist* 43 (Summer 1962): 375, 377, 382.

27. G. J. Barker-Benfield, "The Spermatic Economy: A Nineteenth-Century View of Sexuality," in Michael Gordon, ed., *The American Family in Social-Historical Perspective* (New York: St. Martin's Press, 1973), 351–353; Barker-Benfield, *The Horrors*, 222, 301, and passim.

28. On Whitman and eugenics, see Aspiz, 49–55. Gynecologists and other social "engineers" often advocated eugenic improvement through the control and limitation of women's sexuality. *Democratic Vistas*'s strong case for female sturdiness and economic independence is more in keeping with the sex radicals than with the conservative "engineers." But in addressing an elite audience in the *Galaxy*, Whitman may have chosen to mute the issue of female sexuality.

29. 1872 "Preface," LG, 741.

30. Emerson, "Politics," 219.

31. "By Blue Ontario's Shore," LG60, 114–115.

32. "Song of the Exposition," LG, 196.

33. Georg Lukàcs, *Studies in European Realism* (New York: Grosset and Dunlap, 1964), 86–87; Clifton Joseph Furness, ed., *Walt Whitman's Workshop* (Cambridge: Harvard University Press, 1962), 62; Friedrich Engels, *The Origin of the Family, Private Property, and the State* (New York: International Publishers, 1942), 59.

The Politics of Labor and the Poet's Work

A Reading of "A Song for Occupations"

THE CRUX of Whitman's politics lies in the formula he places at the opening of *Democratic Vistas*: "I shall use the words America and democracy as convertible terms" (PW, 2:363). Referring to an economic transaction, the exchange of money in a system of equivalence, convertible also refers to metaphor, an equivalence of two terms (the conversion of each into the other) by reference to an unspoken third. One term turns into another, or converts itself, because it already contains the other as a hidden, yet unrealized presence. America becomes democracy (or, the same thing, stands for it as its metaphor) because it already is democracy, though unconsciously so. The nation may not yet acknowledge its essence, not yet know that to be itself it must also be democracy, but in order for each, the nation and its political system, to be truly itself, they must become one, must come to realize their essential oneness.

To say that America and democracy are convertible words is to say that they are immanent to each other. But if they are already present to each other, if they already share an essence, what remains to be done to realize each term? What place is there for action, for politics, in this formula which grounds Whitman's vista upon his nation in the year 1870?

How labor figures in Whitman's work—his poetry and his political vision— can be made out against the light of this America/democracy conundrum and its implied process of conversion. There is always the question with Whitman about the status of his key terms. Is America a political word, the name of a political entity, or a metaphysical category? Is labor a social activity or a metaphor for an aesthetic state? By itself, to say that America converts to democracy is to say that the nation is already perfect yet infinitely perfectible, a paradox familiar to those who study American reformers throughout the nation's history.[1] Yet for much of its discourse, *Democratic Vistas* sounds not only like a political document but a fervent one, a militant call to arms. Clearly, the political arises for Whitman at that point where the two terms, America and democracy, approach and cross each other, where the latent convertibility demands an act, the performance of conversion: as William James might say, the cashing-in of America as democracy and vice versa. But convertibility implies that each term already contains its own perfection. The coexistence within both America and democracy of an ideal state and an imperfect state (the potential conversion remaining unrealized) produces Whitman's characteristic psychomachia, a conflict of soul between what already is and what might yet be. The two conditions, the history and, let us say, the myth, the society and its ideal, coexist for Whitman, and his turning over his hope for resolution to the work of poets, to makers of metaphor and turns of speech, suggests a vicious circularity deep within his political thought. Can America become democracy by means of metaphor, by a conversion of terms whose rapport with each other derives from the fact (hidden though it may be) that they are *already* one?

This may be no more than to say that for Whitman politics itself often seems a literary rather than a political activity, a trope for action rather than an action itself, except insofar as the utterance of a poem in public itself fulfills the requirements of an act. His poetry (and his prose) inspire political hopes, but do such hopes exceed the bounds of the poem itself? Does he imagine poets changing the world or the imagination of the world? What would the latter mean as politics? Did Whitman imagine the poet's work as political work?

How he figures labor in his poems, the figure labor makes, offers insight into the baffling issue of Whitman's politics, the place of democracy in his poetry. In *Democratic Vistas* he does not, for example, see America realizing or performing itself in unions of laborers. Poets, not organized industrial workers, are his political agents. His writings and recorded conversations show that he felt increasing unhappiness and anger with the economic system greedily taking charge of the country after the Civil War and producing among its negative effects what he called "the tramp and strike questions." In notes made in the late 1870s for a projected lecture on this subject, his remark that "the American revolution of 1776 was simply a great strike" alludes to the great railroad strike of 1877. But his tone is resigned; the militant labor movement held out, for him, no real hope for the conversion of America into democracy. And while he notes as "curious" the fact that "in what are called the poorest, lowest characters you will sometimes, nay generally, find glints of the most sublime virtues, eligibilities, heroisms," his political hope for actualizing America remained invested in poets, bards, literati. He remained suspicious of organized labor.[2]

Yet Whitman had a way of believing that his poetic persona was also a worker, one of the laboring classes. A third term figures among his convertibilities: labor. Not labor as such, but free labor, which meant not slave labor. His remarks on slavery show that he hated the system of bondage not mainly because it oppressed black people, though his few poetic portraits of enslaved blacks are sympathetic, but because it insulted and threatened white laborers. His view of blacks remained colored by their association with slavery, with coerced and debased labor. Comments on African Americans in his antebellum editorials and prose tracts and in later conversations recorded by Horace Traubel reveal surprising epithets. In 1890, for example, he said to Traubel:

> . . . the nigger would not turn—would not do anything for himself—he
> would only act when prompted to act. No! no! I should not like to see
> the nigger in the saddle—it seems unnatural; for he is only there when
> propped there, and propping don't civilize. I have always had a latent sym-
> pathy for the Southerner . . . from putting myself in a way in their shoes.
> Till the nigger can do something for himself, little can be done *for* him.
> (HT, 6:323)

There is no avoiding the unhappy truth about Whitman's theory of race present in such passages.

There is mitigation, to be sure, in the poetry, in stunning portraits of the runaway slave and of the black teamster in "Song of Myself." But even in the poetry the program does not change; free labor is always white labor. What needs underscoring is that Whitman's words to Traubel give away an unstated economic doctrine, not unlike Booker T. Washington's in the same years. Blacks don't deserve help because they don't help themselves. They supposedly are not self-motivating, not enterprising, not the kind of independent producers Whitman imagined free white laborers to be. His view of race was suffused with the economic doctrine he clung to from his early years as an ardent Jacksonian Democrat, a Loco-Foco and Free Soiler: the doctrine of laissez faire. "Democracy looks with suspicious, ill-satisfied eye," he would write in *Democratic Vistas*, "upon the very poor, the ignorant, and on those out of business. She asks for men and women with occupations, well-off, owners of houses and acres, and with cash in the bank—and with some craving for literature too" (PW, 2:384). Whitman comes to politics armed with an outlook shaped by antebellum entrepreneurial capitalist ideology. He gets his rousing antimonopoly and anti-banker/lawyer rhetoric from the same source, his populist tone and diction which are often taken for anticapitalist convictions.

The conviction that labor is the only authentic source of wealth, that free (nonslave) white laboring people are the true Americans (the "real America," he wrote in 1856 in "The Eighteenth Presidency!," is found among "the true people, the millions of white citizens" [NUP, 6:2,124]), does not by itself, however, explain the identity he claims between the poet and the laboring classes. Labor appears in the poems not out of a democratic need for inclusiveness. That's part of it, but in addition, labor provides a model for the poet's own work. What makes this rapport even more interesting is its reciprocity; the poet's work also provides a model for labor, teaches labor something about itself: not just that it is morally acceptable and valuable but "eligible," as Whitman often writes—eligible not for dignity and respect alone but for art, for representation within an art that has the conversion of those key terms— America, democracy, free labor—as its goal, the product of its own work. Whitman's laborer tends to be a person in the condition of potentiality: not so much a social figure but, like America and democracy, a literary figure, a trope of possibility.

Whitman remarked to Moncure Conway in 1855 that he "chose" to be one of the laboring class.[3] The chosen identity is registered in the fabricated pose of the 1855 frontispiece. That image of the poet as a freebooting worker declares that, along with making laborers eligible for poetry, the author would make a self-identified laborer eligible as poet: the singer as himself a laborer, heroic, lofty, and proud as the "god-like or lordly born characters" of "Greek and feudal poets" (LG, 571). This describes Whitman's most revisionary motive for poetry: to alter and enlarge the identity of the maker of poems. It entailed refiguring the worker-poet's work and simultaneously redefining the work of reading as something itself laborious and difficult. No wonder, as he admitted to Conway, his laboring friends love him but "cannot make head or tail of his book."[4]

The role of labor in Whitman's conception of the poet's work has something further to tell us about the poetics of Whitman's politics and the politics of his poetics. A rich source of insight, relatively untapped in criticism, is "A Song for Occupations," not one of Whitman's most brilliant poems but far from unworthy: a very creditable and important poem. It has a revealing history of revision, a history of internal changes, retitlings, and relocations within *Leaves of Grass*. Initially the second untitled poem of the 1855 edition, it was titled in 1856 "Poem of the Daily Work of The Workmen and Workwomen of These States"; in 1860, "Chants Democratic 3"; in 1867, "To

Workingmen"; in 1871, "Carol of Occupations"; and in the final edition in 1881, the title by which it is currently known (TV, 1:83–98). The Blue Book shows several other trial titles, including "Song of Trades and Implements" (BB, 2:143–144). In its 1855 place following "Song of Myself" (this title also first appeared in 1881), it can be read as a gloss of that poem, especially the passage which begins "A call in the midst of the crowd" (later Section 42). As "A Song of Occupations," the poem settled in 1881 into a cluster of declamatory verses, placed now between "Song of the Redwood-Tree" and "A Song of the Rolling Earth," lost between falling trees giving way to "the new society, at last, proportionate with Nature," and "Delve! mould! pile the words of the earth." Internal revisions correspond to the reconception of the poem implied by this odd repositioning, rendering it more programmatic, more declamatory than its original voice in 1855. The changes include improvements, to be sure: the cutting by more than half of the long catalog of trades and implements which makes up the penultimate section of the poem, and bringing that catalog up-to-date by replacing "the anvil and tongs and hammer" with "the blast-furnace and the puddling-furnace."

The changes are not so much ideological or political as formal; still, the history of the poem does cast light on Whitman's thinking about labor in the post–Civil War era. The poem's illumination is strongest, however, in its 1855 version. It lights up particularly well the correspondence between the poet's work and that of laborers, those in occupations.

It is noteworthy, in regard to its underlying theme of art as work and work as art, that "Occupations" shows not a single portrait of the working body of the sort which vivify "Song of Myself." The great catalog in Section 15 of "Song of Myself" weaves simple present-tense verbs into a tapestry or *tableau vivant* of gesture, motion, and sound:

> The pure contralto sings in the organ loft,
> The carpenter dresses his plank, the tongue of his foreplane whistles its wild
>   ascending lisp . . .
> The spinning-girl retreats and advances to the hum of the big wheel . . .
> The canal boy trots on the tow-path, the book-keeper counts at his desk, the
>   shoemaker waxes his thread,
> The conductor beats time for the band and all the performers follow him. (LG,
>   41–43)

The comparable long catalog of trades and crafts in "Occupations" uses gerundives and nouns, not actions but names of actions and of tools; it is a catalog of objects rather than actions, the names of things and of occupations in the form of atemporal verbal gerunds:

The awl and kneestrap the pint measure and quart measure . . the counter and
stool . . the writing pen o quill or metal . . .
Leatherdressing, coachmaking, boilermaking, ropetwisting, distilling, sign-
painting, limeburning, coopering, cottonpicking. (LG55, 95; the 1881 version
adds "electroplating, electrotyping, stereotyping")

Like that of the laborers it addresses, the poem's activity results in an object, a
printed page in a bound book, a reified version of its work. The work of reading results in a corresponding though intangible object, an event in the
reader's imagination. The reader's work is to imagine, by means of the printed
page, the sound of a living voice. That imagined voice and the printed page,
the poem argues, are mutually supporting and mutually constitutive: the
work as product and the work as process. The pun in the word *work*, activity
and object, process and product of that process, encapsulates Whitman's argument here. As he put it in a couplet he placed in 1867 just before the long catalog of names of acts and objects:

Strange and hard that paradox true I give,
Objects gross and the unseen soul are one. (TV, 1:93)

This strange and hard paradox is the nut which the pun in *work* cracks open.

Hannah Arendt writes that the products of work, the reified or thing-
character of objects, "guarantee the permanence and durability without which
a world would not be possible at all. . . . they give rise to the familiarity of the
world." If human life is "world-building," she notes, then it "is engaged in a
constant process of reification," the shaping of the "human artifice." In her
terminology, which accords nicely with this aspect of Whitman's argument
in "Occupations," labor, or "man" as *animal laborans*, only reproduces itself;
labor is a metabolic relation with nature and results in no permanent object.
This is Whitman's labor as pure act or motion, the lithesome beauty of his
teamsters and smithies and housebuilders in "Song of Myself" and elsewhere.
But work, the human as *homo faber*, brings objects into being, "fabricates the
sheer unending variety of things whose sum constitutes the human artifice."
This well describes the event of Whitman's catalog in "Occupations," where
tools predominate not simply as instruments of labor but more meaningfully
as products of labor, things produced, the objectification of the subjective experience of work. Whitman places tools securely among the works of civilization, sublime in their thinghood. Such objects establish for Arendt and also for
Whitman "a common world," "a home for men during their life on earth."[5]

Whitman's poem is a meditation on the common world of made things, the
collectivity of artifice arising by discrete acts of work. It is overtly an

argument which says that labor is work which produces *works*, the substance
of the common human life. Covertly, the poem has what John Hollander calls
in another connection "poetry's hidden, or derived, agenda—its concern with
itself."[6] That hidden agenda, the poem's reflection on itself, informs, compli-
cates, and infuses with energy the poem's argument about "occupations."

Like Section 42 of "Song of Myself," the untitled 1855 version of "Occupations" opens with a call:

> Come closer to me,
> Push close my lovers and take the best I possess,
> Yield closer and closer and give me the best you possess. (LG55, 87)

Poet and reader meet, in the guise of speaker and listener, in a space represented by measurable distances. Terms repeated throughout—nigh and
nighest, near and nearest, far and farther—recall the reader to this spatial condition, a condition defined by the physical fact of the book itself. Stanza two
explains:

> This is unfinished business with me . . . . how is it with you?
> I was chilled with the cold types and cylinder and wet paper between us.
> (LG55, 87)

The past tense can be taken as a reference to the preceding performance in
"Song of Myself." Now the same voice of the earlier poem reprises its argument that "what I assume you shall assume" by imploring closeness. But the
medium of the transaction between poet and reader, the book in our hands,
erects a barrier. Another pun further enacts the argument: the adverb *close*, by
a softening of the sibilant, becomes the verb *close*, to draw to an end, to finish,
to enclose in a closure, you and I in a single consummation. But how might
this happen if the printed book interrupts us, the very medium of our encounter interfering with its consummation?

Whitman counts on that question and the frustration it provokes to turn
the argument toward a meditation on thingness, on reified voices appearing as
pages of print. In a surprising but tactically effective move, he places official
"reports" and "census returns" (LG55, 90) among those printed documents
which include "this book," in which the reader will pointedly not find that
"something that comes home to one now and perpetually" (90), those official
reports and returns being precisely the instruments for reproducing the labor
process not as works but as "occupations," labor itself, its activity and process,
frozen into a classifiable social role.

By placing his own book among official reifying documents, does Whitman imply a difference in kinds of objectification, between tools and people?

And a difference in status between his own printed book and the others? If the poet's work requires him to print pages of type which silently represent uttered speech, how is closeness to occur? What is unfinished and can never be finished or closed is the separateness of reader and poet through the double-sided mediation of the opaque printed text. The conceptual problem the text poses for itself is to find a way to surpass this reification while acknowledging its necessity, the necessity of artifice for the sake of the common life. The printed poem stands for Whitman as "the 'dead letter' in which the 'living spirit' must survive," in Arendt's words: "a deadness from which it can be rescued only when the dead letter comes again into contact with a life willing to resurrect it."[7]

As the argument moves steadily toward the glacial catalog in the penultimate section, Whitman introduces two keywords, terms or tropes, which illuminate the process of resurrecting the living spirit from the dead letter, the laboring life from the finished work. They are "exurge," to rise up from, and "tally."

All doctrines, all politics and civilization exurge from you,
All sculpture and monuments and anything inscribed anywhere are tallied in
   you. (LG55, 92)

The next stanza, leading to the catalog, continues in this declamatory mode:

All architecture is what you do to it when you look upon it. . . .
All music is what awakens from you when you are reminded by the
   instruments. (LG55, 92)

Exurge and tally are the presiding figures here, through which the poem completes its preparation for the catalog, before the consummation of the final stanza.

Harold Bloom calls tally Whitman's "most crucial trope or image of voice." He traces the word back to the name of a stick on which an account is kept by making notches, and notes that this looks suspiciously like a phallus, but he overlooks the economic meaning of keeping an accounting.[8] The *OED* reveals that tally meant a rod notched with a record of debt or payment, then "being cleft lengthwise across the notches, the debtor and creditor each retained one of the halves, the tallying of which constituted legal proof of the debt." Even as late as the 1860s the term meant "any tangible means of recording a payment or amount," or figuratively, a correspondence, or as a verb, "to cause [things] to correspond or agree." Whitman's tally explicates the poet's work by means of a figure which represents simple economic exchange, this for that, give and take—an exchange or conversion serving in lieu of physical money. His tally conforms to the exchange of the two halves of the marked and riven stick to establish or cancel a debt, to reach the sum of zero, of equality.

Throughout the poem Whitman deploys commonplace terms of economic life: possess, give and take, business, price, value, rate, sum, rent, savings-bank, accounts of stock. The last two items suggest that "yield" in the opening stanza—"Yield closer and closer"—can be read as a pun which proclaims Whitman's use of economic terminology to be ironic. The yield of profit or unearned increment gives way to, is subsumed under, or better, is transumed into the yield of the lover's surrender. So with "value" in "I . . . offer no representative of value—but offer the value itself," which echoes Emerson's wise man in "Politics," who needs "no money, for he is value."[9] When Whitman's poet offers value itself rather than its representative, it is not only the scorned paper money of Jacksonian demonology he rejects but any abstraction which leeches away the life embodied in the act and the object of labor. Irony governs his use of conventional economic fictions, an irony which inverts market practices and prepares for the reassertion of "the value itself" in the laboring act.

The terms Whitman ironizes, however, also shape his alternative vision. The alternative restates the economic terms as aesthetic terms; exchange of labor for money is simply awed by the give and take of the opening stanza: "take the best I possess . . . give me the best you possess." The give and take of love is reciprocity or barter, a mode of marketing which presumes equality, presumes "I will be even with you, and you shall be even with me."

Can we avoid noting that the poem speaks nowhere of wages, takes no notice of capital, of money in its fictive guise as producer of wealth—and that the poet does not wonder who owns the tools and products so magnificently chanted in the catalog? Money in the poem means false values, abstraction, representation in place of the thing itself—no more. Whitman doesn't imagine the abolition of money, he only subsumes it under "the value itself," as if values might be intrinsic, wholly private, free of exchange.

The closing stanza of "Occupations" calls upon the concluding stanza of Section 42 of "Song of Myself": "My words are words of a questioning, and to indicate reality" (LG55, 74)—later revised to "Not words of routine this song of mine, / But abruptly to question, to leap beyond yet nearer bring" (LG, 77). To tally is at once to make a notch, cleave the stick, divide the parts, and to return the separated halves to each other, assuring equity and equality. Thus, in Section 42: "This printed and bound book . . . but the printer and the printing-office boy? / . . . The well-taken photographs . . . . but your wife or friend close and solid in your arms?" (LG55, 74). The final stanza of "Occupations" echoes this with supremely controlled sarcasm:

> When the psalm sings instead of the singer,
> When the script preaches instead of the preacher,
> When the pulpit descends and goes instead of the carver that carved the
>   supporting desk,
> When the sacred vessels or bits of the eucharist, or the lath and plast,
>   procreate as effectually as the young silversmiths or bakers, or the masons
>   in their overalls,
> When a university course convinces like a slumbering woman and child
>   convince,
> When the minted gold in the vault smiles like the nightwatchman's daughter,
> When the warrantee deeds loafe in chairs opposite and are my friendly
>   companions,
> I intend to reach them my hand and make as much of them as I do of men
>   and women. (96–97)

The procreating silversmiths and bakers and masons equal the most sacred of reified vessels, and that recognition itself performs a resurrection of life without loss of object, the psalm or script, the printed poem itself.

The poet's work within this paean to work is to retrieve occupation from the cold type of official lists and classifications, to return it to living praxis, the activity of labor and production, of which the poet's own work provides the exemplary model. Tally is the method, and the result, the close and consummation, a restoration of something, a condition Whitman names in a line added just before the concluding stanza in 1860 and dropped in the next edition: "All I love America for, is contained in men and women like you" (TV, 1:98).

"In the beginning," wrote John Locke, "all the world was America, and more so than it is now; for no such thing as money was anywhere known."[10] Whitman reimagines America as the space in which the encounter between poet and reader occurs on the surface of a page whose very thingness excites the desire and need for a closeness attainable only by tallying this for that, the thing or object for the price paid for it in living labor. Here lies the utopian politics of the poem, its tallying of America with an economy of aesthetic exchange, a bartering of being for being. It is not coincidental that by 1867 Whitman had purged the poem of its few original allusions to nonwhites, thus relieving the poem of the burden of any labor less free than that of free white Americans.

Whitman's declamatory song of labor has seemed so sincerely an expression of politics, of his radical egalitarianism, that readers often find in "A Song of Occupations" little more than a populist confirmation. But the poem has less to say about politics, narrowly construed, than political economy, and with political economy as it bears on aesthetic theory, as it might be tallied into a theory of creative use, of work as art. "A Song for Occupations" registers pressures on the poet's thought from market relations which by 1855 had transformed society in the United States, transformed not only relations but the terms for thinking about persons and groups, about categories of being. The term "occupations" itself indicates the change, the categorical definitions based on social role and status by which market society had restructured the public realm and public discourse, had introduced systems of measuring and identifying persons by their roles within a rapidly proliferating division of labor. "Occupations" signifies a system already in place, a cognitive as well as social term for labor already transformed into something else, a reduction of one's cognizable and cognitive identity to the name of a job.

Whitman follows in a tradition of deriving tropes for poiesis from such crafts or labors as weaving and mowing and leech gathering. He shares the obsession with labor in the fiction and verse of antebellum America but differs in certain regards. His poetry does not picture social conditions, overworked and underpaid and angry wage laborers, degraded laborers like Thoreau's teamster: "Talk of a divinity in man! Look at the teamster on the highway, wending to market by day or night; does any divinity stir within him? His highest duty to fodder and water his horses! What is his destiny to him compared with the shipping interests?" [11]

Whitman gives us no shipping interests; the aesthetics and erotics of the working body excite him more than the economics of the laboring condition. The marketplace seems only passingly present in Whitman's poetry and then as something to be avoided, a place of trippers and askers, where people walk "with dimes on the eyes." But in fact the market does play a more subtle, positive, and constructive role in Whitman's verse; through a laissez faire theory of labor he arrives at a theory of the poet's work which applies terms from the fictions of political economy to the larger, embracing fiction which he understands it to be the poet's work to produce and promulgate: his supreme fiction of an autonomous self whose essential labor is the exchange of creative being with others. It is this figure, his "one's self," who tallies America with democracy, performs the conversion of each into the other.

Occupation belongs to the system of thought of laissez faire, and Whitman is less its critic than its great poet. Capitalism emancipated labor, the great historic feat which Karl Marx believed would eventually undo the system—emancipated labor into the system of wages. Whitman's guise as one of the laboring class he consistently mythologized as America's middle class swept him up in contradiction, the paradox of an emancipation which leads to a new, less visible or tangible enslavement, an enslavement disguised by the American theory of race: white is free, black is not. Whitman subscribed to the racialist theory; he celebrated the liberatory effects of capitalism and closed his eyes to the rest. The social logic of the wage system escaped him, though he registered its effects fitfully during the Gilded Age. Still, he grasped the difference, if not its cause, between use-value (the value itself) and exchange-value, and he joined in powerful tropes and a music of amalgamation, use with being, work with art. From the contradiction between use and exchange he extracted a heroic celebration of labor as life, work as art. He asks, what does it mean to be occupied, to possess an occupation, to repossess oneself within an occupation? He does not ask how labor, property, and society might otherwise look, does not imagine the overthrow of the system of occupations or the social relations of labor but subsumes that system by singing it, subsumes it to an ideal version, a convertible America the poet's work might bring about. Readers today may want to define their own work as the refiguring of that America with all its historical contradictions intact, retrieving it, with the aid as much of Whitman's blindness as his insight, from the clutch of the White Republic.

NOTES

1. See, for example, Warren Susman, *Culture as History* (New York: Pantheon Books, 1984), 86–97.

2. On the complications and shifts of viewpoint in Whitman's attitudes toward trade unions, see Newton Arvin, *Whitman* (New York: Macmillan, 1938), especially 83–149. On his view of slavery and of blacks, see p. 32 and passim.

3. Milton Hindus, ed., *Walt Whitman: The Critical Heritage* (London: Routledge and Kegan Paul, 1971), 29.

4. Hindus, 29.

5. Hannah Arendt, *The Human Condition* (Chicago: University of Chicago Press, 1958), 94, 96, 136, 173.

6. John Hollander, *Melodious Guile: Fictive Pattern in Poetic Language* (New Haven: Yale University Press, 1988), 86.

7. Arendt, 169.

8. Harold Bloom, "Whitman's Image of Voice: To the Tally of My Soul," in Harold Bloom, ed., *Modern Critical Views of Walt Whitman* (New York: Chelsea House, 1985), 127–142.

9. Stephen E. Whicher, ed., *Selections from Ralph Waldo Emerson* (Boston: Houghton Mifflin, 1960), 249.

10. John Locke, *Of Civil Government* (New York: E. P. Dutton, 1924), 140.

11. Henry David Thoreau, *Walden and Civil Disobedience* (Boston: Houghton Mifflin, 1960), 4.

Whitman and the Dreams of Labor

T HERE HAS been, and I hope there will always be, a fertile quarrel in Whitman criticism between those who seek, by various means, to historicize him and those who are inspired, by his poetic presence, to leap out of place and beyond time and soar into the never-never land of forever. Those of the latter inclination used to be expert at a move that involved elevating Whitman the poet above history, while leaving his alter ego, Whitman the journalist, firmly embedded in his period, regrettably timebound and embarrassingly dated. Of course, Whitman the poet is himself partly responsible for this cult of suprahistoricism—his is, after all, one of the best self-levitation acts in the whole poetic business. He was not a rogue disciple of the free-floating transcendentalists for nothing. Moreover, up to a point it's certainly important for a reader to be caught up with him and to be carried away by him. But there are also occasions when it is advisable, not least for the sake of the poetry, to repatriate the writing by returning it to its place and period of origin. And that, I take it, is what many recent scholars, including those who have repoliticized Whitman's mature poetry, have attempted to do.

Included in the title of my essay—but hideously mangled, I must admit, beyond recognition—is a phrase from Robert Frost's sonnet "Mowing": "The fact is the sweetest dream that labor knows. / My long scythe whispered and left the hay to make."[1] Typical of Frost's best work in being cunningly innocent of its potential for larger meanings, the poem is about making poetry precisely to the extent that the speaker insists it is simply about mowing grass to make hay. And, for my present purposes, I am happy to take him at his word, because the sonnet then becomes a twentieth-century example of what Irving Howe has called "the literature of work." This, he claims, represents an interesting segment of American writing in the nineteenth century, and he acknowledges Whitman to be a major author in this minor genre.[2] My aim, however, will not be to examine the ways in which Whitman actually depicts work in his writings; instead, it will be to consider just a few of the ways in which both the dreams and the realities of the nineteenth-century world of labor crucially influenced, in different ways at different times, his reading of American political affairs.

Since I have elsewhere attempted to examine aspects of the first two editions of *Leaves of Grass* from this frankly limited point of view,[3] I shall turn here for a change to the 1860 edition. As Fredson Bowers painstakingly demonstrated, Whitman began to prepare material for this third edition as early as 1856—a conclusion Bowers safely based on the discovery of a notebook containing both an early draft of the 1860 poem "Proto-Leaf" (later "Starting from Paumanok") and the following extract from the *New York Express*, October 21, 1856, carefully copied out in Whitman's own hand: "But for the American party, the Northern, sectional, geographical party of Wm H. Seward and Co. would, under Fremont, have swept the whole Northern country" (MLG, xxxv, n2). We may, then, note that politics is there at the very start of what became the 1860 edition of *Leaves of Grass*, sharing a notebook with the embryonic poetry.

Less than a year before the *Express* report appeared, Whitman had actually written to William Henry Seward, requesting such items as copies of "public documents, your speeches." He closed the letter by explaining: "I am a writer, for the press and otherwise. I too have at heart Freedom, and the amelioration of the people."[4] Seward, of New York, had been an antislavery Whig, but in the run-up to the 1856 election he joined the newly established Republican party and supported its candidate for the presidency, John C. Frémont. That party's campaign song was written to be sung to *"La Marseillaise"*: "Arise, arise ye brave / And let your war-cry be, / Free speech, free press, free soil, free men—Frémont and liberty."[5] As Whitman's letter implies, these were freedoms that mattered passionately to him also in 1855 and 1856, even if he was reluctant to couple the name of Frémont so glibly with that of liberty and correspondingly unwilling to declare himself an out-and-out Republican.

"Free soil, free men": this was close to what, for Whitman, American democracy essentially stood for. To realize this is to notice anew and to appreciate the way the 1860 edition of *Leaves of Grass* actually opens: "Free, fresh, savage . . ." (TV, 2:273). It is a very politically pointed beginning, and by the end of the first verse paragraph Whitman has made his political position even more uncompromisingly clear: "Solitary, singing in the west, I strike up for a new world." Slightly later he refers, with deceptive casualness, to his "programme of chants" as "Inland chants—chants of Kansas" (275). When it was first written, sometime in late 1856, this phrase was political dynamite. After all, the Republicans had fought the recent election on the issue of Bleeding Kansas. The West was the great contemporary arena of political conflict, and it was obvious to all that the increasingly bloody dispute between the America of slavery and the America of "freedom" would be decided there. By "singing in the west" and "striking up for a new world," Whitman was also striking a blow for that freedom. His "Proto-Leaf," like several of the other 1860 poems, was a considered political act. He was using his poetry to claim disputed territory and to occupy it in his imagination. He was out to preempt history and to secure the future of America as a democracy of "free men" living on "free soil."[6]

As "The Eighteenth Presidency!," the unpublished personal manifesto he produced for the 1856 presidential election, shows, Whitman was an unwavering supporter of the campaign for a "democratic" new West: "not one square mile of continental territory shall henceforward be given to slavery, to slaves, to the masters of slaves—not one square foot" (NUP, 6:2,134). Instead, the new territories shall be filled, not with financiers, entrepreneurs, and assorted "yuppies" who were the real leaders and beneficiaries of the new enterprise culture of America in the 1850s, but with the numberless members of the wage-earning underclass, who appear in Whitman's anachronistic imagination still to be the independent artisans, mechanics, and sturdy yeomen of a romanticized bygone age. It is they who shall be given the freedom of the West.

In actual historical fact, the eastern capitalists had, up to the end of the 1840s, opposed every attempt to provide workers with cheap western lands, as demanded by the labor leader George Henry Evans, because they feared it would mean the end of an abundant supply of cheap labor in the East. By the late 1850s a wave of new immigrants guaranteeing low eastern wages, combined with a realization that western settlement meant new markets for eastern goods, caused industrialists to change their minds and raise their voices, too, in favor of homestead legislation. In his interest in such an issue Whitman was, then, in the mainstream of northern political thinking during the 1850s. But his distinctive version of "the imagined West" was surely a result of his early education in what Eric Foner has called "the central ideas and values of artisanal radicalism." This shows in particular in his use of poetry to call into existence a western society that will be simultaneously individualistic and cooperative.[7]

"Workmen! Workwomen!" Whitman declaimed in "The Eighteenth Presidency!," "Those immense national American tracts belong to you; they are in trust with you" (NUP, 6:2,128). And the backbone of this vision is a straight line of thought linking the promise of the West with the repressed, authentically democratic underlife of the great northern cities: "From my mouth hear the will of These States taking form in the great cities" (2,134). And how does the opening poem of the 1860 *Leaves of Grass* begin? With a verse paragraph in which the visionary speaker who was once a "Boy of the Mannahatta, the city of ships, my city," ends up, after a mental journey that embraces the whole continent, "Solitary, singing in the west," where he can "strike up for a new world" (TV, 2:273–274).

So wearily familiar are we by now with the tireless continental perambulations of Whitman's imagination in his poetry that we may, understandably, scarcely bother to listen when, in "Proto-Leaf," he once more rhapsodizes over his lands: "Land of wheat, beef, pork! Land of wool and hemp! Land of the potato, the apple, and the grape! / Land of the pastoral plains, the grass-fields of the world! . . . / Lands where the northwest Columbia winds, and where the southwest Colorado winds!" (TV, 2:285). Such a numbingly predictable invocation can, however, take on a rather different complexion when it is placed in the context of the furious political debates of the day. The Republican party, which Whitman was broadly inclined to favor, was routinely described by its opponents as the "northern, geographical, sectional party," in the words of that passage from the *New York Express* included in the original "Proto-Leaf" notebook. In its ostentatious embrace of the whole continent, "Proto-Leaf" therefore constitutes a poetic rebuttal of such an accusation. Moreover, during the course of his famous debates with Douglas in 1858, Lincoln was forced to answer his opponent's charge that in wishing to see a westward extension of the northern sociopolitical system he was really wanting to reduce all the states in the union to a single, dull, uniform pattern of life. "[Douglas] argues erroneously," Lincoln replied, "the great variety of the local institutions in the States, springing from differences in the soil, differences in the face of the country, and in the climate, are bonds of union."[8]

In "Proto-Leaf" Whitman, too, shows regional differences as underlining rather than undermining the union between the states. "If they produce in one section of the country what is called for by the wants of another section, and this other section can supply the wants of the first," argued Lincoln, "they are not matters of discord but bonds of union, true bonds of union."[9] "Interlinked, food-yielding lands!" writes Whitman, "Land of coal and iron! Land of gold! Lands of cotton, sugar, rice!" A few lines later, in the original draft, he adds, "Full-draped land, tied at the breast, with the belt stringing the oval lakes" (MLG, 26). It is a fine illustration of one of the fundamental terms of his thinking—the belief that nature itself has destined these states, and eventually the whole of America, both North and South—to be a single vast country. Whereas conventional maps are concerned only to show the political geography of a continent, Whitman's poetic map is carefully drawn to illustrate what he regards as the predestined geographical politics of the Americas. He adopts a geopolitical outlook that may eventually derive from the work of the great geographer Alexander von Humboldt via the ecstatic political rhetoric of William Gilpin, the onetime friend of Jackson who was in 1861 to be one of the handful of men accompanying Lincoln on his journey from Springfield to Washington.[10]

As the first draft of "Proto-Leaf" shows, Whitman's dream of labor was at the literal center of his geopolitical system: "The Kentuckian, Mississippian, Arkansian—the workwoman and workman of Iowa, Illinois, Indiana, Michigan" (MLG, 28). But in the published version he substituted "woman and man" for "workwoman and workman," possibly because he realized that in its original form the politically loaded phrase might jar on the ears of the "Louisianian, the Georgian" who, he claims, are "as near to me, and I as near to him and her" (TV, 2:286). It is a small example of what I take to be a large concern in the 1860 edition—Whitman's intermittent wish to conciliate southern opinion without compromising his "free soil" and "free men" principles. And it is, I believe, this genuine, if confused, concern that caused him in "Proto-Leaf" to exploit to the full the potential for ambiguity in the prophetic mode of utterance he carefully cultivated.

The ambiguity arises from uncertainties regarding time. When is the poetry referring to the present, when to the future; how distant is that future, and in what relation, precisely, does it stand to the present? It may be worth recalling that similar questions haunted, and bedeviled, the real, fateful political debates of the time—so much so that the Civil War itself could almost be said to have been precipitated by a confusion of tenses. It was on June 16, 1858, that Lincoln declared: "A house divided against itself cannot stand. I believe this government cannot endure permanently half slave and half free. I do not expect the Union to be dissolved—I do not expect the house to fall—but I do expect it will cease to be divided. It will become all one thing, or all the other."[11] It was in vain that he later protested that his belligerent-sounding remarks applied not to the present or to the immediate future but to the predicted state of affairs a whole century hence.

If Lincoln was the victim of his ambiguous tenses, then in "Proto-Leaf" Whitman seeks to be the beneficiary of his. He defuses the bitter sectional conflicts of his time by gently imagining an indeterminate future when, by natural processes antithetical in spirit to the violent events of actual recent history, an America shall have emerged in which differences are honored but harmonized. Not only does he consistently go out of his way to include the southern states in this prospectus, he diplomatically avoids indicating the precise terms on which they have been admitted to his visionary union. Have they been accepted just as, in 1860, they stand, with all their sins still upon them? Or have they undergone extensive social and political reconstruction? Whitman's mode of writing ensures, of course, that such questions do not arise. Indeed, his poetic discourse is a medium in which the various, sometimes conflicting opinions Whitman had on the southern slavery question can be held in fluid suspension.

These opinions are clear enough in the prose and have a common origin in Whitman's belief that slavery is primarily to be judged—and condemned—with reference to its threats to the interests of free white labor throughout the states.[12] For this reason its western spread cannot ever be countenanced, but its persistence in the South must be accepted, until the mass of whites there realize both that they are being ruled by a tiny, powerful, slave-owning white elite and that slavery is damaging to white workers: "once get the slavery question to be argued on, as a question of White workingmen's Labor against the Servile Labor of the Blacks, and how many years would slavery stand in two-thirds of the present slave-states?"[13] In fact, Whitman foresaw a common "democratic" front eventually forming between the exploited and oppressed workers of both the northern and the southern states—a dream of labor which emerges in "Proto-Leaf," with all its frailty exposed. There Whitman finds in the Alabaman mockingbird, whose song is "A charge transmitted, and gift occult, for those being born," a tender secret analogue for himself: "Democracy! Near at hand to you a throat is now inflating itself and joyfully singing" (TV, 2:282). That the choice of Alabama is not merely coincidental seems to be confirmed by the evidence of the earliest extant version of this line, where the unspecified locale is vaguely northern in character: "As I have walked my walk through the rows of orchard trees, I have seen where the she-bird faithfully sat on her nest" (MLG, 18).

The South again seems the "natural" setting for an experience of lonely, secret joy, in the famous "Calamus" poem "I Saw in Louisiana a Live-Oak Growing." It would be transparently silly to read this simply as a political allegory, but Whitman's political sense of the South as a land where feelings of democratic comradeship were slowly cohering, visible as yet only in isolated cases, may have influenced his choice of Louisiana as the home of the live oak growing "without any companion": "I wondered how it could utter joyous leaves, standing alone there, without its friend, its lover near—for I knew I could not" (TV, 2:390). One's mind is, in fact, turned in the direction of the contemporary sociopolitical milieu by the poem which in the 1860 "Calamus" sequence immediately precedes "I Saw in Louisiana," since that is a piece in which Whitman presents himself as an isolated northerner—a dweller in populous Manhattan who is out of step with the "timid" life around him because he follows a different model which he offers to his lands. In spite of his unprepossessing outward appearance, there "comes one, a Manhattanese, and ever at parting, kisses me lightly on the lips with robust love, / And I, in the public room, or on the crossing of the street, or on the ship's deck, kiss him in return" (389). In other words, as Whitman affirms more explicitly elsewhere, there exists in the cities of the North a rudimentary, fugitive feeling of "brotherhood" among workers, out of which a new, extended American society of "comrades" will duly develop. Contrasted with this is the solitary, yet wondrously self-sufficient, state of the live oak in the Louisiana of the South.

On occasions, though, the South appears in the 1860 edition in a carefully neutral, vaguely benign, or quietly conciliatory light. This response to rising political tensions is consistent with several aspects of Whitman's complicated position on slavery in the South: his paramount concern with preserving the Union;[14] his perhaps exaggerated respect for states' rights; his rooted dislike of abolitionism; his belief in the inevitable but gradual decay of the institution of slavery; his liking for the supposed openness of the white southern character; his contempt for politicians and trust in the long-term triumph of working people, north and south, over a system that was inimical to their vital interests; and, of course, his fierce conviction that the situation of workers in the North urgently required as much remedial attention as the plight of the slaves— the nightmare of slavery was for him always inseparable from the dream of labor. At the same time, many of these publicly pronounced certainties were shadowed by corresponding private doubts—hence the presence in the 1860 edition of signs of disillusionment, distress, and confusion and the poetic evidence of a personal disintegration which obviously had its political dimensions. But as these features of the 1860 edition are already well known and have been extensively discussed,[15] I would prefer to concentrate briefly instead on what I would like to call "the rhetoric of conciliation" in some of the poems.

Whitman's hatred of slavery is repeatedly and openly declared in 1860, most vociferously in the 1856 "Poem of the Many in One," a work, mostly consisting of phrases from the 1855 Preface, which was pointedly made the first poem proper of "Chants Democratic." But historical hindsight has perhaps rather blinded us to the fact that he also needed somehow to develop a conciliatory discourse, the poetical equivalent, as it were, of his states' rights philosophy. The strangest and most blatant attempt to achieve this is the 1860 poem "Longings for Home," where Whitman unconvincingly impersonates a southerner nostalgically recalling the beautiful, colorful, faintly exotic land-scape of the South. Needless to say, there are no great plantations to be seen, and the only black mentioned is carefully set in a picturesque context de-signed to counteract and neutralize the political significance of the descrip-tion: "The piney odor and the gloom—the awful natural stillness, (Here in these dense swamps the freebooter carries his gun, and the fugitive slave has his concealed hut)" (TV, 2:409). Since the fugitive slave figures so often in Whitman's work—most famously in "Song of Myself"—it may be worth suggesting that the appeal of the figure to him lay partly (though only partly) in the ambivalence of its political signification.[16] It immediately brought the Fugitive Slave Act of 1850 to mind—an act to which Whitman was opposed on the grounds of states' rights, while willingly conceding (on the same grounds) that once the act was repealed then northern states should readily undertake to return escaped slaves to their southern masters. In this context, to picture a fugitive slave was therefore less to indict the South than to raise, by implication, the whole issue of the invasive powers of the federal govern-ment, as of course Whitman does directly in his "A Boston Ballad."

A more interesting, extended example of his unionist strategy of political quietism is to be found in the important poem later called "Our Old Feuil-lage." As published for the first time in the 1860 edition ("Chants Democratic" 4), this poem consists of a captivating series of word pictures depicting the beau-ties of the American natural and social landscape throughout the geographi-cally diverse states of the Union. It includes several references to the South:

> There are the negroes at work, in good health—the ground in all directions is
>   covered with pine straw;
> In Tennessee and Kentucky, slaves busy in the coalings, at the forge, by the
>   furnace-blaze, or at the corn-shucking;
> In Virginia, the planter's son returning after a long absence, joyfully welcomed
>   and kissed by the aged mulatto nurse. (TV, 2:295)

It is a recognition of the established facts of life in the South that amounts to a conditional, provisional endorsement of them. The earlier notebook version of the poem shows how Whitman eventually chose to print a highly selective, deliberately uncontroversial picture of slavery, because originally "Feuillage" (as it was then called) included the following three lines, only the first of which was published (in modified form) in 1860:

> The Texas cotton-field and the negro-cabins—drivers driving mules or oxen
>   before rude carts—cotton bales piled on rude wharves,
> A slave approaching sulkily—he wears an iron necklace and prong—he has
>   raw sores on his shoulders,

> The runaway, steering his course by the north star—the pack of negro-dogs
>   chained in couples pursuing. (MLG, 130)

Had these lines been included they would have shattered the decorum of a poem specifically intended to promote harmony between the states on existing, rather than on some distant future, terms.

There is even evidence, in the form of some of the earliest lines he wrote for the 1860 edition, that Whitman intended from the very beginning to build this conciliatory discourse into the fabric of his third collection. Originally "Proto-Leaf" (then entitled "Premonition") represented the composite speaker as "Boy of the Mannahatta—boy of the prairies, Boy of the southern savannahs / Looking friendlily southward . . ." (MLG, 36). As well as reproducing with revelatory clarity the tripartite structure of Whitman's political thinking in "The Eighteenth Presidency!" (northern cities—the West—the South), these lines also illustrate his sporadic policy of appeasement. Yet his feelings about the South were at best equivocal, and nothing illustrates this better than the line he penciled in some time later as a substitute for "Looking friendlily southward": "Looking and longing southward" he wrote at the second attempt, revealing in the process how his affection for the contemporary South was really in anticipation of its emancipation from its enslavement to slavery. Indeed, as I have already suggested, he frequently confuses the present with the future, conflating the two until they are indistinguishable: "Still the Present I raise aloft—Still the Future of the States I harbinge, glad and sublime," as he exclaims in what is, perhaps, the key declaration and declamation of the whole poem (TV, 2:287). The present takes on the welcome attributes of the future, and the future is seen as a natural, easy extension of the present—which allows Whitman to minimize, to the point of ignoring, the trauma of revolutionary historical change that will be required if his vision of a thoroughgoing union is ever to become reality.

Conciliatory equivocations of this sort also appear in "Calamus." Take the well-known piece ("Calamus" 5) where Whitman proffers a love which is superior to the legal contracts which bind the states into mere nominal union:

> States!
> Were you looking to be held together by the lawyers?
> By an agreement on a paper? Or by arms?
> Away!
> I arrive, bringing these, beyond all the forces of courts and arms.
> These! to hold you together as firmly as the earth itself is held together.
> . . . Affection shall solve every one of the problems of freedom. (TV, 2:371–372)

The radical fervor of these lines is what is generally appreciated. Whitman is clearly anticipating a time when all the states, without exception, will be united by a common, comradely passion for freedom. But "The Eighteenth Presidency!" allows us to see the latent conservatism of these lines, by showing that they apply not only to the utopian future but also—in the unsatisfactory meantime—to the pragmatics of the present. In the 1855 pamphlet Whitman had invited people to disobey the Fugitive Slave Law on the grounds that good faith and "friendship," rather than the crude compulsion of law, should require the free states to "deliver back" runaway slaves: "I had quite as lief depend on the good faith of any of These States, as on the laws of Congress and the President. Good faith is irresistible among men, and friendship is" (NUP, 6:2,132). Read with this in mind, the "Calamus" poem speaks with two voices. In the name of "friendship" it announces a future union of free states in which everyone will be joined in a glorious "companionship." But also in the name of "friendship" it persuades contemporaries that slave and free states should continue to coexist amicably, free of the coercion of federal law. In other words, Whitman is a conservative among radicals, the impetuous abolitionists who wanted federal action to dispose of slavery. But he is also a radical among conservatives, who were happy to see the Union continue half-slave and half-free indefinitely. In this "Calamus" poem, he uses his determinedly confident vision of the future not only to predict change but also paradoxically to promote tolerance of what, in the perspective he offers, seems to be only a temporary difference between North and South.

What needs to be emphasized here, however, in the light of my present concerns, is that both Whitman's radicalism and his conservatism on the slavery issue were the direct result of his dreams of labor. "All attempts to discuss the evils of slavery in its relations to the whites," he insisted in "The Eighteenth Presidency!," had been deliberately sabotaged in the South, where "the three hundred and fifty thousand masters keep down the true people, the millions of white citizens, mechanics, farmers, boatmen, manufacturers and the like" (NUP, 6:2,124). But at least in the South, leading politicians openly declared that "the workingmen of a state are unsafe depositories of political power and rights, and that a republic can not permanently exist unless those who ply the mechanical trades and attend to the farm-work are slaves, subordinated by strict laws to their masters" (2,129). Whereas in the North, leading political figures concealed similar beliefs under a "fog of prevarications." And it is at this point that we come to the very heart of Whitman's fears. Sensing that northern society had recently suffered a great sea-change, that economic power was being concentrated in the hands of a new class, that his beloved working masses had been almost imperceptibly degraded into wage-slaves, and that politics had become the monopoly of cynical party professionals, Whitman looked for a simple dramatic explanation of what were, in fact, complex by-products of the advance of capitalism. He found it in his comprehensive theory of the leading political issue of the day: the issue of slavery. According to him, northern monopolists, who wanted to enslave the democratic masses, were conspiring with southern slave-owners, with a view to taking the country over by political stealth.

In the Civil War, Whitman, of course, claimed to find confirmation of everything he had believed about the plight and the heroic potential of the northern worker. In the peace that followed, he overloudly asserted that the dreams of labor were well on their way to becoming reality. Yet, in *Democratic Vistas*, he faced up to a very different truth and heroically struggled to reconcile the facts of postwar society with his great expectations. The effort involved in this attempt was altogether too much for his poetry, and such as his later poems as are interesting are so only when the full social and political pathos of their weakness is recognized. Betsy Erkkila has written well about the artisanal nostalgia in "Song of the Exposition," and Alan Trachtenberg has shown how "Passage to India" is "a poem of 'progress' [which] reverts obsessively to the 'past.'" [17]

These, then, are all matters which have already been so thoroughly discussed by recent criticism as to seem self-evident truths. Let me therefore concentrate, in conclusion, on what seem to me to be neglected examples of Whitman's postwar disorientation. The bewildered state of mind which he generally took pains to conceal is conveyed with touching indirectness in two consecutive sections of *Specimen Days*. The first originated as a public lecture to commemorate Thomas Paine, the great hero of his working-class father. In it, Whitman casts his mind back thirty-five years to a time when he used to meet "Thomas Paine's most intimate chum" in the back parlor of Tammany Hall (PW, 1:140–142). The image is such a politically suggestive one—Tom Paine's surrogate, as it were, symbolically attached to the Democratic party. Those indeed were the days—the long dead days of the 1840s, before Tammany had become synonymous with the politics of cynicism, when Whitman was still an idealistic young Democrat and the party seemed to him to be instilled with a Painite passion for the rights of workers. Yet by 1877 (the date of the lecture), Paine had long since been shown the door, ejected from political memory.

There then follows in *Specimen Days* a section that describes Whitman's return home to Camden across the frozen Delaware River on a winter evening:

> unable to make our landing, through the ice; our boat stanch and strong
> and skillfully piloted, but old and sulky, and poorly minding her helm.

(Power, so important in poetry and war, is also first point of all in a winter steamboat, with long stretches of ice packs to tackle.) For over two hours we bump'd and beat about, the invisible ebb, sluggish but irresistible, often carrying us long distances against our will. In the first tinge of dusk, as I look'd around, I thought there could not be presented a more chilling, arctic, grim-extended, depressing scene. (PW, 1:142)

Anyone who has read his old-age poems will instantly realize that this scene is partly a trope for the aging Whitman's own crippled condition, but behind that, in turn, given the case made out in the preceding section in *Specimen Days* for Paine as the kind of political figure "the season demands," may be a carefully occluded image of Whitman's powerlessness in the face of the socio-economic currents of his age. If so, it wouldn't be the first time that Whitman had deliberately displaced his feelings of political impotence, placing the blame for his social despair instead on his physically shattered state: "I shall only be too happy," he had written earlier, "if these black prophecies and fears can be attributed, (as of course they will be,) to my old age and sickness and growling temper" (NUP, 3:1,152).

That remark appears in the extensive notes he prepared for a piece provisionally entitled "The Tramp and Strike Questions," and in the fragment published in *Specimen Days & Collect* (1882) he offered an incisive and nowadays well-known analysis of the "grim and spectral dangers" facing his society. Scorning euphemistic references to "the Science of wealth," he bluntly raised "the Poverty question" and proceeded to conclude that "beneath the whole political world, what most presses and perplexes today, sending vastest results affecting the future, is not the abstraction question of democracy, but of social and economic organization, the treatment of working-people by employers, and all that goes along with it" (PW, 2:527–529). In his notebook entry on the same subject, he succinctly observes "that humanity in the US is being divided merged more and more definitely into two marked divisions, the vast masses of employed persons, poor, ignorant, desperate, & dissatisfied / & the luxurious rich" (NUP, 3:1,154).

There was, of course, nothing particularly remarkable about this analysis—indeed, it was the conclusion forced on many thinking people both inside and outside the labor movement by a complex series of developments that began in the early 1870s as the states entered what Trachtenberg has called "the age of incorporation." It was the end of the old republican dream of labor getting its just rewards and of *everyone* enjoying modest comforts—a dream which, incidentally, Trachtenberg specifically associates with Whitman. The mass of the people found themselves fixed immovably in their place as meager wage-earners, helplessly dependent on large, impersonal business organizations. As

Trachtenberg explains, "They tended to view wage labor as another form of slavery, of life-long dependency, and the monied classes as usurpers."[18] The narrative of these times, from labor's point of view, can be simplistically summarized as follows. After the severe depression of 1873 had shaken everyone, the public euphoria associated with the centennial exposition of 1876 was ironically followed by the strikes of 1877, a year of labor violence which spurred the middle-class to efforts of organized charity and cultural enlightenment. In spite of these ameliorative measures, the 1880s brought further unrest, culminating in the Great Upheaval of 1886. This was the year of the Knights of Labor's great strike against Jay Gould's railroad in the Southwest, of peak agitation for an eight-hour day, and of the Haymarket riot in Chicago. It was the shape of things to come: between 1881 and 1905 there were to be 37,000 strikes involving 7 million workers—"dramatic indices of turmoil," indeed, as Trachtenberg says,[19] and incontrovertible evidence of a widening class rift. For most of the 1880s, Whitman's anachronistic dream of labor was shared to a significant extent by the Knights of Labor, who refused to accept the new economic order dividing owners from workers and strove to establish a single, classless society. Out of the wreckage of that dream there arose the Amalgamated Union of Labor, which fatalistically accepted the status quo and was concerned only to defend the interests of its members.

Since scholars have traditionally been rather slow to consider the implications of these momentous developments for Whitman's later writings, it was pleasing recently to see the subject receive illuminating attention from Betsy Erkkila and Robert Schulman.[20] It was not only through his writings, though, that Whitman struggled to come to terms with all this turmoil, and the story of one of his most interesting attempts to find an image to focus his confusion of feelings begins with him boarding a train in April 1881 to travel to Boston. It was an overnight sleeper which carried him in speed and in comfort—the very image, in fact, of modern progress, as indeed was the Boston in which he arrived early the next morning. Whitman marveled at its "immense material growth," seeing in it "the wand of future prosperity," and he registered with vivid appreciation the difference between the old part of the city and the new: "Old Boston with its zigzag streets and multitudinous angles (crush up a sheet of letter paper in your hand, throw it down, stamp it flat, and that is a map of old Boston)—new Boston with its miles upon miles of large and costly houses—Beacon Street, Commonwealth Avenue, and a hundred others" (PW, 1:274–275).

Carefully overlooking the North End of Boston, already crammed with Irish immigrants, Whitman concentrated on the magnificent middle-class metropolis that had arisen from the ashes of the great 1872 fire and had been partly built on public lands created by the filling in, over a twenty-year period, of the marshes and bogs of the Back Bay. This elegant new Boston, with its handsome five-story brownstone houses in the French Second Empire style, intermixed with brick houses, Victorian Gothic mansions, and buildings in the Romanesque style, had been laid out by Arthur Gilman on the Paris model, an attractive feature of which was the wide, tree-lined boulevards.[21] Farther out from the city center were new affluent suburbs like Brookline, Roxbury, and Dedham, and it was to the similar district of Jamaica Plain that Whitman traveled to visit "a home full of treasures: Japanese ware—laces—decorations—the most incredible mass—the finest, rarest" (HT, 6:181).

This was the home of one of the wealthiest men in New England, Quincy Adams Shaw, and Whitman was later to doubt "that he has any deep artistic, aesthetic appreciation of the things he has collected there—doubt very much if he has" (HT, 6:181). Indeed, Shaw, a retiring man, seems to have been quietly and decently dedicated to a view of culture perilously similar to the one Whitman had savagely attacked fifteen years earlier in *Democratic Vistas*. Thirty years ago, in his classic study of nineteenth-century Bostonian culture, Martin Green accused people of Shaw's class of supporting a genteel kind of culture that cocooned them from the disturbing downtown realities of their city. More recently, Trachtenberg has seen them as steering an ineffectual middle-way between the philistine plutocrats and the immigrant masses.[22]

Be that as it may, Whitman was to remember for the rest of his life what he saw in Shaw's house that day—and that memory became his precious stay in old age:

> "I was there with others," [he told Traubel seven years later]: "I wanted to
> be alone: I waved them all off"—here he gestured—threw his head back—
> "'Here you fellows,' I said, or something in that manner: 'I want you to all
> go out—to leave me alone: I want to be alone here': they went: and so I got
> an hour or two to myself—the sweetest, fullest, peaceablest: then I saw
> Millet." He ceased talking. I didn't break in. (HT, 3:89)

Earlier, in *Specimen Days*, he had given an equally moving account of the experience of seeing Millet's work: "Two rapt hours. Never before have I been so penetrated by this kind of expression" (PW, 1:267).

Over the decade that followed this extraordinary shock of recognition, Whitman was to elaborate his sense of Millet's significance for himself into an ever more complex myth of the mystic union of the souls of two democratic artists. In this he was unhealthily encouraged by his coterie of cronies. And a bizarre apotheosis was surely reached when Richard Maurice Bucke produced an eleven-point checklist triumphantly proving that Millet was indeed

Whitman's French alter ego or spiritual twin (HT, 3:93–94). This, however, is not the place to probe that particular phenomenon. Instead, I want to suggest that at least part of Millet's attraction for Whitman lay in the prominent attention Millet gave to "work" in powerful pictures that allowed Whitman to focus his hopelessly confused feelings about labor in a single imperceptibly ambivalent image.

The frequent commentaries on Millet that appeared in American magazines in the late 1880s invariably praised him as "the Apostle of Work" [23] and, as was pointed out recently in the introduction to the catalog of the great Millet exhibition at Boston's Museum of Fine Arts, Shaw himself may well have been encouraged to collect Millet by his wife's passionate interest in this very aspect of the paintings. Pauline Agassiz Shaw (daughter of Louis Agassiz, the great zoologist and geologist) used to hang the pictures in the kindergartens and nurseries she ran in Boston, believing that they were useful for teaching children the dignity of labor. [24] This was very much in line with what has been called the "romantic capitalism" of the time—the assiduously cultivated belief that the lords of industry, the captains of commerce, and the kings of corporations during the Gilded Age were really genuine aristocrats of labor and had achieved success through hard, physical work. The corollary of this view was, of course, the belief that restless, dissatisfied members of the workforce should cease their envious agitation and obediently strive instead to emulate those who had risen through their own efforts.

There is plenty of evidence that Whitman was not immune to this kind of propaganda—the most nauseous example of it being, perhaps, the mutual admiration that developed between him and Andrew Carnegie. Or, to put the matter more kindly, it is probable that in the sentimentalization of labor Whitman found both relief from the real intractable labor problems of the day and grounds for a continuing belief in a "single society" theory of American life. Millet's paintings may, then, have appealed to him in much the same way that they did to the Shaws. But that is by no means the whole picture, so to speak. In order to see that, one needs to reexamine the passage in which Whitman recorded his first experience of seeing Millet's paintings:

> I stood long and long before "The Sower." . . . There is something in this
> that could hardly be caught again—a sublime murkiness and original pent
> fury. Besides this masterpiece, there were many others, (I shall never forget
> the simple evening scene, "Watering the Cow,") all inimitable, all perfect as
> pictures, works of mere art; and then it seem'd to me, with that last impal-
> pable ethic purpose from the artist (most likely unconscious to himself)
> which I am always looking for. To me all of them told the full story of
> what went before and necessitated the great French Revolution—the long

precedent crushing of the masses of a heroic people into the earth, in abject poverty, hunger—every right denied, humanity attempted to be put back for generations—yet Nature's force, titanic here, the stronger and hardier for that repression—waiting terribly to break forth, revengeful—the pressure on the dykes and the bursting at last—the storming of the Bastile— the execution of the king and queen—the tempest of massacres and blood. Yet who can wonder? (PW, 1:268)

This is one of those studied compositions, complete with a high-gloss finish, which Whitman went in for in his overelaborate postwar prose. My interest, however, is in the three different coats of paint which give the passage its rich emotional color. Two of these coats are easily discernible and have perhaps been too consciously applied. First, there is the ethereal hue of pathos in his treatment of "Watering the Cow," a painting regarded as a solemnizing example of art hallowing the work of the poor. Second, there is the dark color associated with "The Sower" and the other paintings which Whitman sees as representing the life of the oppressed, repressed peasantry of prerevolutionary France. To the extent that Whitman believed the United States of the 1880s still to be a guiding light for corrupt, reactionary Europe, then implicit in this interpretation of Millet's paintings is Whitman's pride in his own politically emancipated and progressive society.

The third coat of paint, or level of feeling, in the passage seems to me, however, to be one which Whitman would probably not care to acknowledge, even to himself. One notices it only if one has other passages in mind which Whitman wrote around the same time, of which the following is the best example:

Two grim and spectral dangers—dangerous to peace, to health, to social security, to progress—long known in concrete to the governments of the Old World, and there eventuating, more than once or twice, in dynastic overturns, bloodshed, days, months, of terror—seem of late years to be nearing the New World, nay, to be gradually establishing themselves among us. . . . Curious as it may seem, it is in what are call'd the poorest, lowest characters you will sometimes, nay generally, find glints of the most sublime virtues, eligibilities, heroisms. Then it is doubtful whether the state is to be saved, either in the monotonous long run, or in tremendous special crises, by its good people only. . . . The American Revolution of 1776 was simply a great strike, successful for its immediate object—but whether a real success judged by the scale of the centuries, and the long-striking balance of Time, yet remains to be settled. The French Revolution was absolutely a strike, and a very terrible and relentless one, against ages of bad pay, unjust division of wealth-products and the hoggish monopoly of a few, rolling in superfluity, against the vast bulk of the work-people, living in squalor. (PW, 2:527–528)

That is Whitman's attempt, in "The Tramp and Strike Questions," to come to terms with the labor unrest of the late 1870s; it turns on the painful parallels he uneasily draws between conditions in contemporary America and conditions in prerevolutionary France. His first reaction, on entertaining this comparison, is to be terrified by the specter of unbridled violence it releases. His second reaction is to discover, in the comparison of the French Revolution with the very different American Revolution, a hope that American labor will produce "heroic" leaders who will bloodlessly rectify the infamous inequities of American society. It is surely this volatile mixture of unacknowledged feelings that lends disturbing intensity to his description of Millet's "The Sower" as full of "a sublime murkiness and pent fury."

I have, then, tried to distinguish between three different layers of paint, or levels of feeling, in the "picture" Whitman offers of his response to the Millet paintings. At two of these levels he echoes the contemporary ruling-class view by officially affirming that labor is assured of a central place in existing American society. But at the third level he expresses an unacknowledged, uneasy, and guilty wish to see labor reclaiming its redeeming place at the center of a society corrupted and distorted by wealth. Needless to say, this last attitude directly contradicts the previous two, and the three taken together expose the deep confusion of mind and of feeling that characterized Whitman's attitude toward labor during his final years.[25]

For final, comical, and pathetic proof of this, one need only turn to Sidney Morse's account of a visit paid to the sick Whitman by a labor agitator who

... was the happy possessor of a loud voice and in manner was quite imperious. The conversation ran somewhat like this: "I have solved the problem, Mr. Whitman." "Ah!" "In my own mind." "The right spot to begin." "I believe, in fact, I've settled the matter." "Oh!" "Now to convince the world. You yourself have struck the key-note." "Thanks." "Your words are a great reinforcement to the cause." "Thanks." And so on for ten minutes or more, the man standing with hat in hand orating, Whitman when there came a lull, looking up from perusal of his letters, interposing his "thanks." Finally, the man, grown weary or perceiving he was making little, if any, progress, suddenly brought up with: "Well, Mr. Whitman, I think I'll take my leave." "Thanks." Not until after he had departed did the inopportuneness of his response become manifest. He was not, however, greatly disturbed in consequence. . . . [Whitman felt that] the labor problem, as a practical question, belonged to younger heads than his, if there really was anything to be said or done about it. He was not sure but things were working well enough as they were, evolving in their natural course for better results than any theory of socialism could promise. . . . so far as he could see there was as much "cussed selfishness" on the one side as the other. It was a question of manhood, if anything. Workingmen's strikes were apt to develop little of that. They would set on their fellow-workingmen who didn't belong to their "union" like tigers or other beasts of prey. It was their "union" against the world. The spectacle was not pleasing. . . . At other times he betrayed an anxiety in behalf of the "masses driven to the wall," and felt that somehow the Republic was not safe while "anybody was being so driven." He commended and gave me Carnegie's book on "Triumphant Democracy," as containing much that was "about so and gratifying." [26]

It is a commonplace of recent scholarship that, after the Civil War, prose replaced poetry as Whitman's chief medium for bringing his visions into living, mutually restorative contact with his times. In its turn, his prose also failed to cope with the economic facts and altered social mentality of a new age; Whitman's exhausted, superannuated imagination, the ideological product of an earlier period, was forced to look to art, specifically to Millet, for reinforcement and reinvigoration. We can thus usefully reverse Whitman's familiar remark and say that for him Millet's paintings were really only *Leaves of Grass* in another form. In those pictures the dreams of labor, which had necessitated and sponsored so much of Whitman's mature work, found their final artistic image; the paintings were, rather poignantly I feel, the *Leaves* that the dying, politically disorientated Whitman had failed in putting into words. [27]

NOTES

1. Robert Frost, *Selected Poems* (Harmondsworth, England: Penguin, 1955), 24–25.

2. Irving Howe, *The American Newness* (Cambridge: Harvard University Press, 1986), 65–70.

3. See M. Wynn Thomas, *The Lunar Light of Whitman's Poetry* (Cambridge: Harvard University Press, 1987).

4. Walt Whitman to William Henry Seward, December 7, 1855, CORR, 1:41–42.

5. Quoted in R. B. Nye and J. P. Morpurgo, *A History of the United States* (Harmondsworth, England: Penguin, 1965), 2:442.

6. Whitman repeatedly discussed Kansas and other issues relating to the slavery question in his editorials for the *Brooklyn Daily Times* (1857–1859). See Emory Holloway and Vernolian Schwarz, eds., *I Sit and Look Out: Editorials from the*

"Brooklyn Daily Times" (New York: Columbia University Press, 1932), particularly the sections on "Slavery" and "National Politics."

7. For the contributions of Evans, the Free Soil movement, and the political parties to these debates, see Eric Foner, *Politics and Ideology in the Age of the Civil War* (New York: Oxford University Press, 1980). Ray Allen Billington, *Westward Expansion: A History of the American Frontier* (New York: Macmillan, 1974), provides a full history of the homesteading movement. Various versions of "the imagined West" are usefully summarized in Rush Welter, *The Mind of America: 1820–1860* (New York: Columbia University Press, 1975), 298.

8. Philip Van Doren Stern, ed., *The Life and Writings of Abraham Lincoln* (New York: Modern Library, 1940), 463. Interesting comparisons are made between poetry and politics in Allen Grossman, "The Poetics of Union in Whitman and Lincoln," in Walter Benn Michaels and Donald E. Pease, eds., *The American Renaissance Reconsidered* (Baltimore: Johns Hopkins University Press, 1985), 183–208.

9. Stern, 463.

10. See Henry Nash Smith, *Virgin Land* (New York: Vintage Books, 1950).

11. Stern, 429.

12. Whitman's position on these matters is succinctly summarized in Daniel Aaron, *The Unwritten War* (Madison: University of Wisconsin Press, 1987), 59–62.

13. Editorial, May 6, 1858, in Holloway and Schwartz, 90.

14. Herbert J. Levine, "Union and Disunion in 'Song of Myself,'" *American Literature* 59 (December 1987): 570–589. See also Jerome Loving, "Whitman's Democratic Vision in the First *Leaves of Grass*," in Joann P. Krieg, ed., *Walt Whitman, Here and Now* (Westport, Conn.: Greenwood Press, 1985), 139–146; George B. Hutchinson, *The Ecstatic Whitman: Literary Shamanism and the Crisis of the Union* (Columbus: Ohio State University Press, 1986).

15. See, for example, Betsy Erkkila, *Whitman the Political Poet* (New York: Oxford University Press, 1989); Dennis K. Renner, "Lear and the *Leaves of Grass* Poet," in Krieg, 185–191.

16. For thoughtful discussions of the subtle implications of Whitman's treatment of slavery in key passages in his poetry, such as the "Lucifer" passage from "The Sleepers" and the slave auction passage in "I Sing the Body Electric," see Kerry C. Larson, *Whitman's Drama of Consensus* (Chicago: University of Chicago Press, 1988).

17. Erkkila, 274–276; Alan Trachtenberg, *The Incorporation of America* (New York: Hill and Wang, 1982), 61.

18. Trachtenberg, 73, 72.

19. Ibid., 79.

20. Erkkila, passim; Robert Schulman, *Social Criticism and Nineteenth Century American Fictions* (Columbus: University of Missouri Press, 1987).

21. For the growth of Boston, see Sam Bass Warner, *Street Car Suburbs: The Process of Growth in Boston, 1870–1900* (Cambridge: Harvard University Press, 1978); Stephen Thernstrom, *The Other Bostonians: Poverty and Progress in the American Metropolis, 1880–1970* (Cambridge: Harvard University Press, 1973); Marjorie Drake Ross, *The Book of Boston: The Victorian Period, 1837–1901* (New York: Hastings House, 1964); Andrew Burni and Alan Rogers, *Boston: City on a Hill* (Boston: Windsor Publications, 1984).

22. Martin Green, *The Problem of Boston: Some Readings in Cultural History* (New York: Norton, 1966); Trachtenberg, 142ff. For a thoughtful defense of Boston's cultural elite, see Neil Harris, "The Gilded Age Revisited: Boston and the Museum Movement," *American Quarterly* 14 (Winter 1962): 545–566.

23. The phrase is used by Mrs. Henry Ady in "Jean Francois Millet," *Nineteenth Century* 137 (July 1888): 419–438. The view expressed was commonplace—see, for example, the comments of William Morris Hunt, as reported in Helen M. Knowles, *The Life of William Morris Hunt* (Boston: Little, Brown, 1899), 12; Wyatt Eaton, "Remembrances of Jean Francois Millet," *Century* (May 1889): 100.

24. Susan Fleming, "The Boston Patrons of Jean-Francois Millet," in Alexandra R. Murphy, *Jean-Francois Millet* (Boston: Museum of Fine Arts, 1984), xiii. Of the fifty paintings in Shaw's possession, twenty-one pastels were exhibited in the schoolroom. After 1883, Pauline Agassiz Shaw "supported children's classes of manual arts in the public schools as well as in her North Bennet-Street Industrial School" (Dumas Malone, ed., *The Dictionary of American Biography*, vol. 17 [New York: Charles Scribner's Sons, 1935]).

25. From the very beginning, Millet's work had lent itself to widely different political interpretations: "Left-wing writers claimed him as the painter of the 'Modern Demos,' while conservatives decried the brutal picture of bestial humanity painted with what Theophile Gautier called 'masonries of paint.' Against both interpretations Millet was defended by Alfred Sensier, who offered instead a picture of a man of deep piety and filial duty, more dedicated to the representation of the biblical injunction to Adam and Eve to 'earn their bread by the sweat of their brow' than concerned with attempts to order more egalitarian distribution of both bread and sweat" (Griselda Pollock, *Millet* [London: Oresko Books, 1977], 7).

26. Horace L. Traubel, Richard Maurice Bucke, and Thomas B. Harned, eds., *In Re Walt Whitman* (Philadelphia: David Mackay, 1893), 378–380.

27. "The *Leaves* are really only Millet in another form—they are the Millet that Walt Whitman has succeeded in putting into words. . . . Millet is my painter: he belongs to me: I have written Walt Whitman all over him. How about that? or is it the other way about? Has he written Millet all over me?" (HT, 1:7, 62).

Whitman and the Homosexual Republic

I N A LETTER dated March 13, 1946, Malcolm Cowley wrote to Kenneth Burke: "I'm working on Whitman, the old cocksucker. Very strange amalgam he made between cocksucking and democracy."[1] The letter itself seems strange coming from Malcolm Cowley, who in his famous 1959 introduction to the Viking edition of the 1855 *Leaves of Grass* became instrumental in the critical construction of Whitman as neither cocksucker nor democratic poet but as an essentially spiritual poet who had been miraculously transformed from hack political journalist to prophetic poet by a "mystical experience."[2] But Cowley's private and public comments are characteristic of a critical tradition that has insisted on silencing, spiritualizing, heterosexualizing, or marginalizing Whitman's sexual feeling for men.[3] Recent works on Whitman by gay critics and others have sought to name the sexual love of men that earlier critics insisted on silencing, but while these approaches have emphasized the centrality of Whitman's sexuality and homosexuality to his work, they have also tended to maintain a distinction between Whitman the private poet and Whitman the public poet, Whitman the homosexual poet and Whitman the poet of democracy, that unduly privatizes and totalizes Whitman's sexual feeling for men.[4] It is this distinction between private and public, homosexuality and democracy, that I would like to question and problematize in this essay by exploring what Cowley very aptly called the "very strange amalgam" of "cocksucking and democracy" in Whitman's work.

I would like to begin by describing a brief public service announcement produced by the Philadelphia Lesbian and Gay Task Force as a means of reflecting on the uses to which Whitman may and may not be put in contemporary American culture. A young man stands at the Delaware River's edge, with the Walt Whitman Bridge in the background, and says:

> Hey, I just found out Walt Whitman was gay . . . you know the guy
> they named the bridge after. I wish I had known that when I was in high
> school. Back then, I got hassled all the time by the other kids, 'cause I'm
> gay—and the teachers—they didn't say anything. Why didn't they tell me
> Walt Whitman was gay?

All six television stations in the Philadelphia market refused to air this public service announcement, arguing that it was too "controversial" and that it "advocated a particular lifestyle." When two of the stations called the Walt Whitman Poetry Center, the director said that to tell the world that Whitman was gay "would really be detrimental to the Center. A lot of our programming is geared to teens. Kids don't need a lot to scare them off."[5] At issue in this controversy was not the question of whether Whitman was gay; there seemed to be widespread if covert agreement that he was. At issue was the idea that Whitman's gayness must not be aired publicly and the belief that such public airing would be detrimental to the American public and "scare" young kids. What the controversy suggests, finally, is the extent to which Whitman as the poet of the people, the poet of democracy, and the American poet, has also become an American public property whose image is bound up with the maintenance of American public health and American national policy. It is not only the academic and critical establishment but those in positions of social and cultural power and, I would add, the national government itself, that are heavily invested in keeping Whitman's sexuality, and specifically his sexual love for men, out of any discussion of his role as the poet of democracy, and the American poet.[6] In other words, if we can control Whitman's sexuality, we can also control the sexuality of the nation.

Against those who insist on separating Whitman's work into an either/or proposition—either Whitman the private poet or Whitman the public poet, Whitman the poet of gay men or Whitman the democratic poet, Whitman the homosexual or Whitman the poet of the American republic—I would like to argue that we take Whitman seriously when, in the preface to the 1876 centennial edition of *Leaves of Grass*, he says of the "ever new-interchange of adhesiveness, so fitly emblematic of America" that "the special meaning of the 'Calamus' cluster of 'Leaves of Grass' (and *more or less running through the book*, and cropping out in 'Drum-Taps,') mainly resides in its *political significance*." "It is," Whitman goes on to say, "by a fervent, accepted development of comradeship, the beautiful and sane affection of man for man, latent in all the young fellows, north and south, east and west—it is by this, I say, and by what goes directly and indirectly along with it, that the United States of the future, (I cannot too often repeat,) are to be most effectually welded together, intercalated, anneal'd into a living union" (PW, 2:471, emphasis added).

In arguing for the political significance of adhesiveness as a fervent passion among and between men in the "Calamus" poems, *Drum-Taps*, and throughout *Leaves of Grass*, I do not mean to return to older interpretations of Whitman's love poems to men as allegories of American democracy. Rather, I mean to argue the centrality of Whitman's sexual love of men to the democratic vision and experimental poetics of *Leaves of Grass* and to Whitman's hopes for welding the American republic into a "living union," especially in the post–Civil War period. In making this argument, I want to explore the ways the discourse of democracy intersects with material transformations in labor, industry, and social relations in the nineteenth century in the United States to construct homosexuality as a type and a pathology.[7] But in exploring the emergence of homosexuality as a modern type and sensibility in nineteenth-century America, and in Whitman's work in particular, I want to try to avoid the tendency among recent critics, despite their distinction between what Jeffrey Weeks calls "homosexual behavior, which is universal, and a homosexual identity, which is historically specific," to construct both homosexual behavior and homosexual identity as transhistorical and monolithic categories.[8] I want to insist, that is, on the fact that the word and the category *homosexual* did not exist when Whitman began writing. As he himself put it in *An American Primer*: "The lack of any words . . . is as historical as the existence of words. As for me, I feel a hundred realities, clearly determined in me, that words are not yet formed to represent" (AP, 21). The words Whitman did use to articulate and name his erotic feeling for men were the words of democracy—of comradeship, brotherhood, equality, social union, and the glories of the laborer and the common people. But Whitman also used other languages. And thus, against those who tend to treat homosexuality as an a priori or monolithic given in Whitman's work, I want to argue the fluidity of Whitman's articulation of same-sex love among men as the language of democracy intersects with other languages, including the languages of temperance, sexual reform, artisan republicanism, labor radicalism, phrenology, heterosexual love, familial and specifically father-son relationships, and spirituality in Whitman's attempt, as he says, to express "a hundred realities, clearly determined in me, that words are not yet formed to represent."

In past approaches to Whitman's work, there has been a tendency to discuss the arc of Whitman's poetic development as if he emerged miraculously as a "homosexual poet" in the 1860 *Leaves of Grass* and then disappeared or was sublimated just as miraculously during the Civil War and in the post–Civil War period. As Charley Shively and Michael Moon have pointed out, however, Whitman's desire to name his erotic attraction to men is already evident in his early story "The Child's Champion" (1841, later entitled "The Child and the Profligate") and in his temperance novel *Franklin Evans; or the Inebriate* (1842), both published by the *New World*, a popular and widely circulated workingman's magazine.[9] But while these stories name a kind of sexual cruising among men in the city, to which youths newly arrived from the country are particularly prone, they also locate physical relations among men under the sign of intemperance, thus rendering them potentially dangerous to the healthy and virtuous personal relationships and republican body the stories advocate. While the profligate is transformed into a provider by his erotic attraction to the child, and while he sleeps that night with the young boy folded in his arms, the narrator makes it clear that this is not a totally "unsullied affection": "Fair were those two creatures in their unconscious beauty— glorious, but yet how differently glorious! One of them was innocent and sinless of all wrong: the other—O to that other, what evil had not been present, either in action or to his desires!" (EPF, 76).

Similarly, while *Franklin Evans* seems driven by a narrative urge to kill off women and heterosexual marriage in the interest of affirming the primacy of social and erotic bonding among men, these relationships are associated with intemperance as a sign of drinking, carousing, and other forms of bodily excess and therefore ultimately at odds with the temperance and virtue necessary for a healthy republican body politic. When Franklin Evans is transformed from inebriate into advocate of temperance, the transformation is figured in the political language of republican regeneration and manifest destiny: "Now man is free! He walks upon the earth, worthy the name of one whose prototype is God! We hear the mighty victory chorus sounding loud and long. Regenerated! Regenerated! . . . Victory! Victory! The Last Slave of Appetite is free, and the people are regenerated!" (EPF, 223).

Sometime in the 1840s this apparent antithesis between unhealthy sexuality among men and a healthy republican body politic begins to shift in Whitman's work, as he begins to articulate a position different from but often expressed in the same language as such popular male purity and antimasturbation tracts as Sylvester Graham's *Lecture to Young Men on Chastity* (1834) and Orson Fowler's *Amativeness: Or Evils and Remedies of Excessive and Perverted Sexuality* (1844), in which masturbation and sexual play among men are presented as destructive to the physical and moral health of a productive, reproductive, and ultimately heterosexual American republic.[10] In Whitman's notebook dated 1847, in which he begins working toward the experimental language and form of *Leaves of Grass*, he insists on locating the soul and vision in the body and matter. And in an early version of the famous touch sequence in "Song of Myself," he represents masturbation, which also doubled in the nineteenth century as a code word for sexuality among and between men, as a source at once of sexual ecstasy, mystical vision, and poetic utterance.

> I do not wonder that one feeling now does so much for me,
> He is free of all the rest,—and swiftly begets offspring of them, better than
>   the dams.
> A touch now reads me a library of knowledge in an instant.
> It smells for me the fragrance of wine and lemon-blows.
> It tastes for me ripe strawberries and melons,—
> It talks for me with a tongue of its own,
> It finds an ear wherever it rests or taps. (UPP, 2:72)

Just as in "Song of Myself," where the pleasures of touching, either oneself or "what is hardly different from myself," and the orgasmic spilling of male seed give rise to the nationalist vision of "Landscapes projected masculine full-sized and golden" (LG55, 53, 54), so in his notebook entry Whitman reverses the nonreproductive figurations of masturbation and same-sex touching in the male purity tracts, associating the sexual pleasure of "He" who "is free of all the rest" and "better than the dams" with the "offspring" of vision, voice, poetic utterance, and a gloriously reproductive image of nature and nation.

This figuration of the body, sexuality, and same-sex love among men as the site of ecstasy, vision, and poetic utterance becomes even more emphatic in the first edition of *Leaves of Grass*. In his long opening poem, later entitled "Song of Myself," the poet describes the "sexual experience" that is at the origins of his democratic voice and vision.

> I believe in you my soul . . . . the other I am must not abase itself to you,
> And you must not be abased to the other.
>
> Loafe with me on the grass . . . . loose the stop from your throat,
> Not words, not music or rhyme I want . . . . not custom or lecture, not even
>   the best,
> Only the lull I like, the hum of your valved voice.
>
> I mind how we lay in June, such a transparent summer morning;
> You settled your head athwart my hips and gently turned over upon me,
> And parted the shirt from my bosom-bone, and plunged your tongue to my
>   barestript heart,

And reached till you felt my beard, and reached till you held my feet. (LG55,
28–29)

"Isn't this cocksucking plain and simple?" Charley Shively asks, arguing that
in this passage "Whitman demonstrates part of his Americanness by placing
cocksucking at the center of *Leaves of Grass*."[11] But before we completely liter-
alize this passage as a direct transcription of cocksucking among men, it is important to recognize that the "I" and "you" are unspecified and ungendered in
the passage and that the passage has also been read as the transcription of what
James E. Miller calls an "inverted mystical experience."[12]

Rather than posing cocksucking and mysticism as antithetical readings,
however, or arguing that Whitman seeks consciously to disguise his homosexuality through the language of the soul, I would like to suggest that this passage is paradigmatic of the ways the languages of sexuality and spirituality,
same-sex love and love between men and women, private and public, intersect
and flow into each other in Whitman's work. It is unclear finally whether
Whitman is describing sexuality in the language of spiritual ecstasy or a mystical experience in the language of sexual ecstasy, for he seems to be doing
both at once. What is clear is that the democratic knowledge the poet receives
of an entire universe bathed in an erotic force that links men, women, God,
and the natural world in a vision of mystic unity is associated with sexual and
bodily ecstasy, an ecstasy that includes but is not limited to the pleasures of
cocksucking between men. In other words, here we have precisely Malcolm
Cowley's strange amalgam "between cocksucking and democracy" in Whitman's work. Giving tongue is associated at once with sexuality, including sexuality between men, democracy, spiritual vision, and poetic utterance.

This amalgam between men loving men and democracy would become
even more emphatic in Whitman's work as the actual political union—on
which Whitman had staked his identity and faith as a democratic poet—
began to dissolve. In traditional readings of Whitman's life and work, it is
argued that at some time in the late 1850s Whitman had a love affair that
caused him to turn away from his public role as the poet of democracy toward
the privacy of love. To disguise the real "homosexual" content of his "Calamus" poems in the 1860 edition of *Leaves of Grass*, it is argued, Whitman
interspersed more public poems of democracy, such as "For You O Democracy," with more private and personal poems of homosexual love. Joseph Cady
argues that Whitman's attempt to invent a "new order based on his private experience as a homosexual" was only partially successful because in the "least
satisfying" strain of "Calamus," Whitman does not sustain his separation and
conflict but seeks to "translate" his experience into the language of common
culture.[13]

But this notion of a neat division between the more revolutionary impulses of the private poet of homosexual love and the more conventional impulses of the public poet of democracy is not born out by a close reading of the "Live Oak with Moss" sequence, the original sheaf of twelve love poems of "manly love" out of which the "Calamus" poems emerged. In this sequence, it is precisely in and through rather than against the more conventional language of democratic comradeship, phrenological adhesiveness, and brotherly love that the poet articulates his feelings for men.[14] "I dreamed in a dream of a city where all men were like brothers," Whitman writes in the poem that would later become "Calamus" 34:

> O I saw them tenderly love each other—I often saw them, in numbers, walking hand in hand;
> I dreamed that was the city of robust friends—Nothing was greater there than manly love—it led the rest,
> It was seen every hour in the actions of the men of that city, and in all their looks and words. (MLG, 114)

What this poem suggests is that, in its most visionary realization, the dream of democracy will give rise to a city—and ultimately an American republic—in which men loving men can live and love and touch openly—a dream city, I might add, that we are still very far from achieving despite the fact that the first lines of "Calamus" 34 ("I dreamed in a dream, I saw a city invincible," LG60, 373) are now inscribed on the Camden city hall. Although the "Live Oak With Moss" sequence and the "Calamus" sequence bear the traces of a rather appealing crisis of representation in which Whitman realizes that he may not speak for everybody, there is no distinct separation between the poet of democracy and the poet of "manly love." Like other poems in the "Live Oak" sequence and in the "Calamus" sequence, "I Dream'd in a Dream" marks not so much a conflict between Whitman the democratic poet and Whitman the lover of men but a shift in Whitman's conceptualization of his role as democratic poet that locates his personal and sexual love for men at the very center of his vision, role, and faith as the poet of democracy. Thus, in the opening poem of "Calamus," "In Paths Untrodden," the poet avows his desire "To tell the secret of my nights and days, / To celebrate the need of comrades" (342). While these lines might be read as a sign of the separation and conflict between private and public poet, they might also be read paratactically as an example of the ways Whitman's "secret" love of men is articulated together with, in the same language as and as the very condition of, his celebration of democratic comrades in the "Calamus" poems.

"Ah lover and perfect equal," Whitman writes in "Calamus" 41 ("Among the Multitude"), suggesting the ways the proliferation of the eighteenth-century natural law philosophies of equality and natural rights come to underwrite and in some sense produce the emergence of homosexuality simultaneously with the emergence and spread of democracy in the United States. It is no co-incidence that the proliferation of the rhetoric (if not the reality) of democra-tic equality during the Age of Jackson corresponded with the emergence of the temperance movement, the male purity crusade, and an increasing cultural anxiety about drinking, masturbation, same-sex sexuality, and other forms of bodily excess and indulgence among and between men. In other words, democracy, particularly in its more egalitarian and fraternal forms, might be said to have simultaneously produced, affirmed, and demonized the modern homosexual as a distinct identity and role.

In *Whitman the Political Poet*, I argued that the "Calamus" sequence was Whitman's most radical sequence of poems both personally and politically.[15] But in this essay, I would like to revise that reading to suggest that the "Chil-dren of Adam" poems (originally entitled "Enfans d'Adam") may indeed be the more sexually radical sequence that Emerson and the censors who banned *Leaves of Grass* in Boston in 1882 always believed it to be. In traditional ac-counts of Whitman's poetic development, "Children of Adam" is represented as an afterthought, a sequence of poems that Whitman added to the 1860 edi-tion of *Leaves of Grass* in order to provide a legitimizing heterosexual context for the actually more radical personal love poems to men in the "Calamus" se-quence. A notebook entry suggests that Whitman initially conceptualized "Children of Adam" as a companion piece to his "Calamus" poems: "A string of Poems (short etc.), embodying the amative love of woman—the same as Live Oak Leaves do the passion of friendship for man" (NF, 169). But whatever Whitman's initial intentions, the "Children of Adam" poems do not read as a neatly heterosexual counterpart to his poems of passion for men in the "Cala-mus" sequence. (And here it is perhaps important to remember that the term *heterosexual* actually came later than the term *homosexual* in the construction of modern sexuality.) While the "Children of Adam" poem "A Woman Waits for Me" consistently provoked nineteenth-century censorship for its represen-tation of an athletic, sexually charged, and desiring female body, the poem is in fact atypical in its emphasis on the amative, and ultimately procreative and eugenically productive, love between men and women.

"Singing the phallus" and the "bedfellow's song," many of the "Children of Adam" poems are not about women or procreation or progeny at all but about amativeness as a burning, aching, "resistless," emphatically physical "yearning" for young men (see "From Pent-Up Aching Rivers"). Whereas in the "Calamus" poems physical love among men is limited to touching and kissing, in the "Children of Adam" poems Whitman, in the figure of a "lusty," "tremulous," and insistently "phallic" Adam, names and bathes his songs in an active, orgiastic, and physical sexuality among men. "Give me now libidinous joys only!" the poet exclaims in "Enfans d'Adam" 8 ("Native Moments"), evoking scenes of nonreproductive sexual play and pleasure among men:

> I am for those who believe in loose delights—I share the midnight orgies of
>   young men,
> I dance with the dancers, and drink with the drinkers,
> The echoes ring with our indecent calls,
> I take for my love some prostitute—I pick out some low person for my dearest
>   friend,
> He shall be lawless, rude, illiterate—he shall be one condemned by others for
>   deeds done;
> I will play a part no longer—Why should I exile myself from my companions?
> (LG60, 311)

Even the poem "A Woman Waits for Me" is as much a celebration of a deliciously phallic male sexuality as it is a celebration of sexual love between men and women. Associating the "woman" of the title with traditionally masculine activities, the language of the poem slips ambiguously between a celebration of same-sex and opposite-sex love. Moreover, in later revisions of the "Enfans d'Adam" poems, Whitman actually edited out several of the more explicit "heterosexual" references while retaining the emphasis on an insistently phallic and physical male sexuality. Thus, Whitman's later deletion of the phrase "I take for my love some prostitute" in the above passage from "Native Moments" ends up underscoring the "libidinous joys" and "loose delights" of an explicitly same-sex sexuality among and between men.[16]

Whereas in the 1860 *Leaves of Grass* the "Enfans d'Adam" poems are immediately followed by "Poem of the Road" ("Song of the Open Road"), "To the Sayers of Words" ("A Song of the Rolling Earth"), "A Boston Ballad," and then the "Calamus" sequence, in the final edition of *Leaves of Grass*, the "Calamus" poems immediately follow the "Children of Adam" poems. Rather than suggesting a neatly "heterosexual" and "homosexual" pairing, however, this final arrangement further underscores the fluid relationship between the "lusty, phallic" and ultimately nonreproductive and nonmonogamous sexual play and pleasure among men in the "Children of Adam" poems and the less insistently phallic but nonetheless explicitly physical lover and democrat of the "Calamus" poems. "Touch me, touch the palm of your hand to my body as I pass, / Be not afraid of my body," says the naked Adamic speaker in the final poem of the "Children of Adam" sequence, as he passes and steps quite imperceptibly into the "paths untrodden" and more emphatically (but not exclusively) male contexts of the "Calamus" poems (LG, III).

Against popular associations of masturbation and excessive adhesiveness among men with solitude, impotence, and emasculation, it was Whitman's invention not only to extend the meaning of adhesiveness, the phrenological term for friendship, to same-sex love among men as a virile and socially productive force for urban, national, and international community, but also to extend amativeness, the phrenological term for procreative love between men and women, to include physical and procreative love among men. Implicit in the sexual and social vision of "Children of Adam" is a new world garden and a new American republic ordered not by the marital, procreative, familial, and monogamous bonds between men and women but by the sexually and socially productive and non-monogamous relations among men. While the "Children of Adam" appear to refer to *all* the children produced presumably by Adam and Eve, as the exclusive emphasis on Adam in the title suggests, these children are also the male children produced and "prepared for" by the "act divine" and "stalwart loins" of a phallic and virile Adam, whose sexual union with men bears the creative and procreative seeds of both his poetry and the ultimate realization of the American republic and the American race.

In his important article "'Here is Adhesiveness': From Friendship to Homosexuality," Michael Lynch argues that when in the 1856 edition of *Leaves of Grass* Whitman wrote "Here is adhesiveness, it is not previously fashioned—it is apropos" in reference to exclusively same-sex relationships among men, his words marked an important shift toward a definition of the homosexual and heterosexual as distinct types. "Whitman's restriction of Adhesiveness to male-male relationships opened the way for an understanding of same-sex expression of a sexual instinct that was polar to an opposite-sex expression of it." Rather than representing the emergence of what Lynch calls "a distinct 'homosexual identity' and 'homosexual role,'"[17] I would argue that Whitman's "Calamus" and "Children of Adam" poems imply just the opposite. By conceptualizing and articulating his love for men in the language of democratic comradeship and by celebrating physical pleasure among men in the context of male and female amativeness and procreation, Whitman in fact suggests the extent to which the bounds between private and public, male and female, heterosexual and homosexual, are still indistinct, permeable, and fluid in his work.

In most critical discussions of Whitman's life and work, it has become almost axiomatic to argue that Whitman's "homosexual" love crisis of the late 1850s was sublimated in the figure of the "wound-dresser" during the Civil War and ultimately silenced and suppressed in the "good gray" politics and poetics of the post–Civil War period. Here, again, however, a close reading of Whitman's Civil War writings suggests that just the opposite may be the case: that in fact the discourses of desire among men and the occasions and contexts for their expression in Whitman's work actually proliferated during the Civil War.[18] "How I love them! how I could hug them, with their brown faces, and their clothes and knapsacks cover'd with dust!" Whitman exclaims in the opening poem of *Drum-Taps*, "First O Songs for a Prelude," as the fire of his passion for men bursts forth along with and in the same language as the "torrents of men" and "the pent fire" of the Civil War ("Rise O Days from Your Fathomless Deeps," (DT, 6, 37). Rather than sublimating his feelings for men, the historical role Whitman played in visiting thousands of soldiers in the Washington hospitals and the poetic role he played as the "wound-dresser" actually enabled a range of socially prohibited physical contacts and emotional exchanges among men. Soothing, touching, hugging, and kissing the sick and dying soldiers, the private poet merges with the public, female with male, "wound-dresser" with soldier, lover with democratic patriot, in Whitman's poems of the Civil War. "Many a soldier's loving arms about this neck have cross'd and rested, / Many a soldier's kiss dwells on these bearded lips" ("The Dresser," 34).

The intensity of Whitman's passion for men, released and allowed by the "manly" context of war, is particularly evident in "Vigil Strange I Kept on the Field One Night," which along with "When I Heard at the Close of the Day" is perhaps Whitman's most intense and lyrically moving expression of same-sex love. But having said this, it is also important to recognize the ways the languages of manly love, paternity, military comradeship, and maternal care intermix and mingle in the poem.

> Vigil strange I kept on the field one night,
> When you, my son and my comrade, dropt at my side that day,
> One look I but gave, which your dear eyes return'd, with a look I shall never
>   forget;
> One touch of your hand to mine, O boy, reach'd up as you lay on the ground;
> Then onward I sped in the battle, the even-contested battle;
> Till late in the night reliev'd, to the place at last again I made my way;
> Found you in death so cold, dear comrade—found your body, son of
>   responding kisses, (never again on earth responding). (DT, 42)[19]

As the poet carefully envelopes his "dearest comrade," his "son" and "soldier," and his "boy of responding kisses" in a blanket and buries him "where he fell," he, in effect, prepares the ground which, as in "A March in the Ranks Hard-Prest, and the Road Unknown," "A Sight in Camp in the Daybreak Gray and

Dim," and "As I Toilsome Wander'd Virginia's Woods," will enable him to carry on amid what he called the "malignancy," butchery, and surrounding darkness of the war.

The centrality of the Civil War in testing and affirming not only the American union but a range of physical and emotional bonds of affection and intimacy among men as the foundation of the future American republic is most explicitly expressed in "Over the Carnage Rose Prophetic a Voice," which, with the exception of the opening and closing lines, was transferred from the "Calamus" sequence into *Drum-Taps and Sequel* (1865):

> Over the carnage rose prophetic a voice,
> Be not dishearten'd—Affection shall solve the problems of Freedom yet;
> Those who love each other shall become invincible—they shall yet make
>   Columbia victorious.

As in "I Dream'd in a Dream," the poet affirms the relation between "manly affection," physical touching among men across state and class bounds, and the dreams of democracy:

> It shall be customary in the houses and streets to see manly affection;
> The most dauntless and rude shall touch face to face lightly;
> The dependence of Liberty shall be lovers,
> The continuance of Equality shall be comrades.
>
> These shall tie you and band you stronger than hoops of iron;
> I, extatic, O partners! O lands! with the love of lovers tie you. (DT, 50)

Rather than representing a retreat from the privacy of same-sex love, in Whitman's writings of the post–Civil War period this love actually proliferates, even in the most public context of Whitman's famous wartime elegy for Abraham Lincoln, "When Lilacs Last in the Dooryard Bloom'd," where the poet mourns the death of Lincoln as "lustrous" comrade and lover.

The Civil War not only affirmed "manly affection" as the ground of a new democratic order, it also gave Whitman a more militant and combative language in which to affirm his commitment to the ongoing struggle for this order in the post–Civil War period. "I know my words are weapons, full of danger, full of death," the poet declares in "As I Lay with My Head in Your Lap, Camerado," urging his readers to join him in the democratic struggle:

> For I confront peace, security, and all the settled laws, to unsettle them;
> I am more resolute because all have denied me, than I could ever have been
>   had all accepted me;
> I heed not, and have never heeded, either experience, cautions, majorities, nor
>   ridicule;

And the threat of what is call'd hell is little or nothing to me;
And the lure of what is call'd heaven is little or nothing to me;
. . . Dear camerado! I confess I have urged you onward with me, and still urge
    you, without the least idea what is our destination,
Or whether we shall be victorious, or utterly quell'd and defeated. (*Sequel*,
    DT, 19)

Ironically, it was in the fields and hospitals of the Civil War that Whitman came closest to realizing his democratic and homosexual dream of a "new City of Friends." Included among the poems of demobilization, "As I Lay with My Head in Your Lap, Camerado" registers uneasiness as the poet moves away from the true democracy of wartime comradeship toward the potentially oppressive structures of a peacetime—and heterosexual—economy. Addressing a "you" who is, as in "Calamus," both personal lover and democratic comrade, the poet expresses renewed dedication to a boundless democratic "destination" that will include and indeed be grounded in same-sex love among men.[20]

It is ironic that the iconography of the good gray poet came to dominate Whitman's public image and later critical treatments of his life and work at the very time that we have the most specific historical documentation in Whitman's notebooks and in his correspondence with Peter Doyle and Harry Stafford of his emotional and loving attachments to young working-class men.[21] In a notebook entry that apparently refers to the "*enormous* PERTURBATION" of his "FEVERISH, FLUCTUATING" emotional attachment to Peter Doyle, Whitman writes:

Depress the adhesive nature
It is in excess—making life a torment
All this diseased, feverish disproportionate *adhesiveness*. (UPP, 2:96)

In Whitman criticism, this entry is usually cited as an instance of the poet's attempt to suppress his sexual desire for men in order to transform himself into the safer and more publicly acceptable image of the good gray poet. But at no place in his notebooks does Whitman suggest that "adhesiveness" is itself "diseased." Rather, like the male purity tracts, what Whitman suggests is that it is "adhesiveness" in excess that makes "life a torment" and must be brought under control. "PURSUE HER NO MORE," Whitman writes, coyly changing the object of his passion from him to her. But the change once again suggests the extent to which the languages of male and female love and male/male love intersect and are articulated together in Whitman's work. What is important for my point is the fact that the poet's perception of his "adhesiveness" as "diseased" and "disproportionate" and in excess does not change even if the object of his excessive attachment is a woman.

In support of the idea of the increasing split between private and public in Whitman's works in the postwar years, as Whitman the lover of men gives way to the iconography of the good gray poet, many emphasize the changes that Whitman made in his "Calamus" poems after he was fired from his job at the Department of the Interior for moral turpitude.[22] But here again, a close study of the changes that Whitman made in future editions of *Leaves of Grass* reveals no clear pattern of suppressing or even toning down his love poems to men. In fact, Whitman's decision to delete three poems from "Calamus"—"Who Is Now Reading This?," "I Thought That Knowledge Alone Would Suffice," and "Hours Continuing Long"—suggests that he sought not to tone down or suppress his expression of "manly love" but rather to suppress the more negative dimensions of his love for men and to blur the distinction between public poet and private lover he set forth in "I Thought That Knowledge Alone Would Suffice." Moreover, in "The Base of All Metaphysics," the one poem he added to the "Calamus" sequence in 1871, Whitman represents "The dear love of man for his comrade, the attraction of friend to friend" as the "base and finale too for all metaphysics," underlying the philosophies of Plato, Socrates, and Christ and the systems of German philosophy represented by Fichte, Schelling, and Hegel (LG, 121).

This representation of same-sex love between men as the base of a new social order underlies the visionary democracy of *Democratic Vistas* (1871). In this important and wide-ranging attempt to come to terms with the problems of democracy in America, Whitman concludes that "intense and loving comradeship, the personal and passionate attachment of man to man," represents "the most substantial hope and safety of the future of these States." "It is to the development, identification, and general prevalence of that fervid comradeship, (the adhesive love, at least rivaling amative love hitherto possessing imaginative literature, if not going beyond it)," Whitman explains in a footnote, "that I look for the counterbalance and offset of our materialistic and vulgar American democracy, and for the spiritualization thereof." Amid what he called the aggressive selfism, vulgar materialism, and widespread corruption of the Gilded Age, Whitman looked not to marriage or to the traditional family but to "the personal and passionate attachment of man to man" as the social base and future hope of the American republic. "I say democracy infers such loving comradeship as its most inevitable twin or counterpart, without which it will be incomplete, in vain, and incapable of perpetuating itself" (PW, 2:414–415).[23]

So, if what I have been arguing is correct, why did Whitman not just come out with it in his famous exchange with John Addington Symonds in 1890, when Symonds asked him outright if his "conception of Comradeship" included the possibility of "semi-sexual emotions & actions" between men? Whitman could have said, "Yes, John, *Leaves of Grass* is, indeed, about cock-sucking and democracy. You found me out." Instead, he disavowed Symonds's "morbid inferences" about the "Calamus" poems as "undream'd," "unreck'd," and "damnable" and cautioned him about the necessity of construing "all parts & pages" of *Leaves of Grass* "by their own ensemble, spirit & atmosphere" (CORR, 5:72–73). Although Whitman's response is coy, it also seems right to me for all the reasons I have been trying to suggest. Whitman and Symonds were speaking two different, not entirely separable languages. Whereas Havelock Ellis and John Addington Symonds were central in the process of medicalizing and singling out the homosexual as abnormal and pathological,[24] Whitman was talking about physical and emotional love between men as the basis for a new social and religious order. Given his representation of male sexual love as the source of spiritual and poetic vision and the ground for a new democratic social order and given Ellis's and Symonds's medicalization of physical love between men as "sexual inversion" and "abnormal instinct," it makes sense that Whitman would disavow Symonds's attempt to medicalize and sexually categorize the "Calamus" poems as "morbid inferences" contrary to the "ensemble, spirit & atmosphere" of *Leaves of Grass* (73).

Whitman's famous assertion, in this same letter to Symonds, that he had fathered six children is, to say the least, disingenuous. But it is not wholly at odds with the amative, reproductive, and familial languages and contexts in which he expressed the loving relationships among and between men. In fact, given the languages of paternal, maternal, and familial affection in which Whitman carried on his relationships and correspondence with Peter Doyle, Harry Stafford, and some of the soldiers he met during the war, one might argue that Whitman was thinking of some of the "illegitimate sons" he adopted, fathered, and mothered over the course of his life.

In his attempt to give Whitman's conception of comradeship and his "Calamus" poems only one reading, Symonds in some sense anticipates the tendency among recent Whitman critics to treat Whitman's homosexuality as a single, transhistorical monolith. Against those who see in Whitman's work an instance of what Symonds would have called "sexual inversion" or what Michael Lynch has recently called "a distinct 'homosexual identity' or 'homosexual role,'"[25] I have been arguing that we read Whitman's expression of sexual, emotional, and social intimacy among men not as a monolithic homosexual presence but as the complex, multiply located, and historically embedded sexual, social, and discursive phenomenon it was. To those who insist on dividing Whitman the private poet and Whitman the public poet, Whitman the lover of men and Whitman the poet of democracy, or in Malcolm Cowley's apt phrase, "cocksucking and democracy," I have been trying to suggest that read within what Whitman calls the "ensemble, spirit & atmosphere" of his work the homosexual poet and the American republic refuse any neat division; they intersect, flow into each other, and continually break bounds. "Who need be afraid of the merge?" Whitman asked in "Song of Myself." The answer to that question is still, in this centennial year, we all are.

NOTES

1. Paul Jay, ed., *Selected Correspondence of Kenneth Burke and Malcolm Cowley* (New York: Viking, 1988), 273.

2. Cowley, "Introduction," LG55, xii.

3. In letters to his lover, Russell Cheyney, F. O. Matthiessen had also drawn sympathetic attention to Whitman's erotic attachments to men, but in his influential book *American Renaissance: Art and Expression in the Age of Emerson and Whitman* (New York: Oxford University Press, 1941), he dismissed the "vaguely pathological and homosexual" quality of Whitman's work and sought to reclaim him for serious national and international attention by an insistently formalist approach to *Leaves of Grass* as a "language experiment" with analogues in oratory, opera, the ocean, and the visual arts (517–625). For a review of Whitman criticism and homosexuality, see Robert K. Martin, *The Homosexual Tradition in American Poetry* (Austin: University of Texas Press, 1979), 3–8; Scott Giantvalley, "Recent Whitman Studies and Homosexuality," *Cabirion and Gay Books Bulletin* 12 (Spring/Summer 1985): 14–16. Justin Kaplan, in "The Biographer's Problem," *Mickle Street Review* 11 (1989): 80–88, begins by observing that "the history of over a century of Whitman biography is to a large extent the history of a pussyfooting accommodation to the issue of sexuality, more specifically, homosexuality. One sees biography being skewed in the interests of literary public relations" (83–84). But he concludes by reconsigning the "issue" of Whitman's homosexuality to the margins when he notes that "perhaps it's time to move on to a broader focus" (88).

4. Robert K. Martin pioneered in the field of gay studies and in the study of Whitman and homosexuality in his groundbreaking article "Whitman's *Song of Myself*: Homosexual Dream and Vision," *Partisan Review* 42 (1975): 80–96. See also Martin's chapter on Whitman in *The Homosexual Tradition*, 3–89; Joseph Cady, "Not Happy in the Capitol: Homosexuality and the Calamus Poems," *American Studies* 19 (Fall 1978): 5–22; Cady, "*Drum-Taps* and Nineteenth-Century Male Homosexual Literature," in Joann P. Krieg, ed., *Walt Whitman: Here and Now* (Westport, Conn.: Greenwood Press, 1985), 49–60; Charley

Shively, ed., *Calamus Lovers: Walt Whitman's Working Class Camerados* (San Francisco: Gay Sunshine Press, 1987). M. Jimmie Killingsworth, *Whitman's Poetry of the Body: Sexuality, Politics, and the Text* (Chapel Hill: University of North Carolina Press, 1989), and Michael Moon, *Disseminating Whitman: Revision and Corporeality in Leaves of Grass* (Cambridge: Harvard University Press, 1991), both focus on Whitman's "sexual politics," but in emphasizing the split between the corporeal and the social self in Whitman's work, they tend to maintain the bounds between private and public, sexuality and politics, homosexuality and democracy, as separate and relatively distinct realms. Killingsworth, for example, notes: "Two voices predominate in Whitman's poetry of the body. One is private—confessional, inward, at times self-indulgent and sentimental. The other is public—the voice of the orator and journalist" (46). For a recent attempt to problematize the private/public binary in critical interpretations of Whitman's work, see Jay Grossman, "'The Evangel-Poem of Comrades and of Love': Revising Whitman's Republicanism," *American Transcendental Quarterly* 4 (September 1990): 201–218. See also Betsy Erkkila, "Democracy and (Homo)Sexual Desire," in *Whitman the Political Poet* (New York: Oxford University Press, 1989), 155–189.

5. David Warner, "The Good G(r)ay Poet," *Philadelphia City Paper*, January 12–19, 1990.

6. Given the controversy surrounding the National Endowment for the Arts and homosexuality, it cannot be entirely coincidental that the Library of Congress, which holds the largest and most substantial collection of Whitman materials in the world, sponsored no exhibit or other series of events in commemoration of the centennial of the poet's death.

7. For a study of the relation between between capitalist transformation and the male purity movement, see Carroll Smith-Rosenberg, "Sex as Symbol in Victorian Purity: An Ethnohistorical Analysis of Jacksonian America," *American Journal of Sociology* 84 (Supplement 1978): 5,212–5,247.

8. Jeffrey Weeks, *Sexuality and Its Discontents: Meanings, Myths, and Modern Sexualities* (London: Routledge & Kegan Paul, 1985), 6. See also Michel Foucault's comment on the emergence of the homosexual as a distinct personage in the nineteenth century: "The sodomite had been a temporary aberration; the homosexual was now a species" in *The History of Sexuality: An Introduction*, trans. Robert Hurley (New York: Random House, 1978), 43.

9. Shively; Moon.

10. Sylvester Graham, *Lecture to Young Men on Chastity* (Boston: Light and Stearns, 1834); Oscar Fowler, *Amativeness: Or Evils and Remedies of Excessive and Perverted Sexuality Including Warning and Advice to the Married and Single* (New York: Fowler and Wells, 1844).

11. Shively, 21.

12. James E. Miller, Jr., "'Song of Myself' as Inverted Mystical Experience," *PMLA* 70 (September 1955): 636–661.

13. Cady, "Not Happy," 15; Killingsworth (99) makes a similar distinction between sentimental rhetoric and homoerotic love in Whitman's *Calamus* poems.

14. For studies of Whitman and phrenology, see Edward Hungerford, "Walt Whitman and His Chart of Bumps," *American Literature* 2 (1931): 350–384; Harold Aspiz, *Walt Whitman and the Body Beautiful* (Urbana: University of Illinois Press, 1980); Michael Lynch, "'Here is Adhesiveness': From Friendship to Homosexuality," *Victorian Studies* 29 (Autumn 1985): 67–96.

15. Erkkila, 183.

16. See also Whitman's deletion of the reference to "the perfect girl" in "Enfans" 2 ("From Pent-Up Aching Rivers") and the explicit references to the female in "Enfans" 6 ("One Hour to Madness and Joy").

17. Lynch, 91, 67.

18. Cady makes a similar point in "Male Homosexual Literature," but he continues to insist on a neat division between the private poet of homosexual love and the more public figure of the soldier-comrade through whom Whitman self-protectively masks his homosexual desire. What I want to stress is the inseparability of the private discourses of male homosexual desire from the more public discourses of combat and democratic nationalism in Whitman's poems of the Civil War.

19. The language of paternal and familiar care is so marked in "Vigil Strange I Kept on the Field One Night" that M. Wynn Thomas, in *The Lunar Light of Whitman's Poetry* (Cambridge: Harvard University Press, 1987), actually reads the poem as literally about a father mourning the loss of his son during the war (208).

20. As I argue in *Whitman the Political Poet*, this representation of same-sex love between men as the ground of democracy is accompanied by an increased emphasis on the feminine and the maternal in Whitman's post–Civil War writings (261–262).

21. For a study of the erotic bonds Whitman formed with soldiers during the Civil War, see Charley Shively, ed., *Drum-Beats: Walt Whitman's Civil War Boy Lovers* (San Francisco: Gay Sunshine Press, 1989). Killingsworth and Moon both argue for a clear division between what Moon (11) calls the "visionary and utopian project" of the pre–Civil War Whitman and the Whitman of the post–Civil War years.

22. For a recent version of this argument, see Killingsworth: "Propriety had become a central tenet for the postwar Whitman" (148).

23. See also *Specimen Days* (1882), where Whitman finds among the workers and crowded city streets of "Human and Heroic New York" "a palpable outcropping

of that personal comradeship I look forward to as the subtlest, strongest future hold of this many-item'd Union" (PW, 1:172).

24. See Havelock Ellis and John Addington Symonds, *Sexual Inversion* (London: Wilson and Macmillan, 1897).

25. Lynch, 67.

Whitman and the Politics of Identity

F OR TWENTY years John Addington Symonds had been pestering Whitman. What does the "Love of Friends" mean, he asked repeatedly, suggesting that he knew what it had "been in the Past" and what it "alas!" meant "here now," but he was uncertain as to what it "can and shall be" in Whitman's vision. No doubt put off by Symonds's insistence, and, as others have pointed out, their class differences, Symonds's continued use of the Greek model, and the need for a written reply, Whitman invented his whopper about the six children. But before he wrote that famous letter in August 1890 he commented about Symonds, "I doubt whether he has gripped 'democratic art' by the nuts, or L of G either."[1] This remark seems to have attracted surprisingly little critical attention. What it importantly suggests, though, is that Whitman's distancing of himself from Symonds is not designed to assert his "purity" but rather his "impurity."

Whitman's reproach to Symonds implies, of course, the physically sexual basis of his politics and poetics. He at least has balls, and so do his poems, whereas Symonds, well . . . Symonds is still in his letter to Whitman talking about "semi-sexual emotions" and pussyfooting around the question, daring only to suggest that he does "not agree" with those who argue that "ardent and physical intimacies . . . would absolutely be prejudicial to social interests."[2] Not agreeing with those who think such relations "*absolutely* prejudicial" is hardly the same thing as thinking them beneficial, as, say, Whitman writes in "Calamus" 5:

These shall tie and band stronger than hoops of iron,
I, extatic, O partners! O lands! henceforth with the love of lovers tie you.

I will make the continent indissoluble,
I will make the most splendid race the sun ever yet shone upon,
I will make divine magnetic lands.   ＇

I will plant companionship thick as trees along all the rivers of America, and
    along the shores of the great lakes, and all over the prairies,
I will make inseparable cities, with their arms about each other's necks.
    (LG60, 351)

Whitman found no response to this enthusiasm in the timid teasing of
Symonds, who remained too Greek, too English, too upper class. Symonds
not only, by implication, didn't have balls, he also never grabbed anybody
else's. Whitman even in his old age refused to accept a sublimated or transcendentalized version of his athletic love. He was not about to be enlisted for
that kind of politics.

The manner of Whitman's reply to Symonds is deliciously ambiguous. It
hardly answers Symonds's question, although it does set Whitman off against
Symonds and his "morbid inferences," even as it asserts that "I wholly stand
by L of G as it is, long as all parts & pages are construed as I said by their own
ensemble, spirit & atmosphere" (CORR, 5:73). Whitman is not denying the
sexual in *Leaves of Grass* but the morbid—an important clue to understanding
Whitman's reticence at being associated with Symonds. The sexual is indeed
what is missing in Symonds, and so Whitman provides it, in spades.

My life, young manhood, mid-age, times South, &c: have all been jolly,
bodily, and probably open to criticism—
    Tho' always unmarried I have had six children—two are dead—One liv-
ing Southern grandchild, fine boy, who writes to me occasionally. Circumstances connected with their benefit and fortune have separated me from
intimate relations. (73)

Whitman parades his physicality, dilates as it were, and gives birth to an entire
fantasy brood—not merely one child who might have done to prove his heterosexual credentials but *six*, thereby topping Symonds's own four daughters.
He will not be outdone. At the same time, the very audacity of his lie makes it
almost transparent, except to those poor literal souls who actually went looking for the missing children. Whitman's story of his six children is on the one
hand a defensive response and assertion of "breeder" credentials; on the other
hand, it is by its very manner a case of camping, or, as they say in black studies, signifying.[3] Whitman is putting Symonds on by "yessing" him to death, as

Ralph Ellison's *Invisible Man*'s grandfather suggests: "overcome 'em with yeses, undermine 'em with grins, agree 'em to death and destruction, let 'em swoller you till they vomit or bust wide open."[4]

The context for reading the difference between Whitman's exuberance in the early editions of *Leaves of Grass* and his duplicitousness in 1890 is a major shift in the conceptualization of sexual identity. In Michel Foucault's famous formulation, the homosexual has been invented as a "species" and hence subject to the disciplinary power of discourses of medicine and psychiatry, as well as of the "liberatory" discourses of sexual politics. Symonds himself was about to publish privately *A Problem in Modern Ethics*, and the Wilde trial was only a few years away (it had been prepared for by the Cleveland Street scandal of 1884, focusing on a male brothel). On the continent, Gide was about to meet Wilde and embark on his journey to self-discovery in Tunisia, Richard von Krafft-Ebing had just published his *Psychopathia Sexualis*, and the first German gay periodicals were only a few years away. The situation was vastly different from that Whitman had known in the America of the 1840s and 1850s.

Historians still quarrel over a precise date when the modern homosexual emerged (a few see a continuous line back to ancient Greece), but it seems evident that there is a radical break between Byron and Whitman or even between Tennyson and Whitman. The pre–Civil War years, a time of remarkable political and social dissent and experimentation, encouraged the exploration of issues of gender and sexuality in a way and to a degree that would not be seen again in America at least until the early twentieth century. Much of the response can be described as paranoid or panicked: for example, in James's portrait of the lesbian women's rights advocate Olive Chancellor in *The Bostonians*, a portrait that is itself a rewriting of Hawthorne's almost lifelong obsession with the threatening figure of Margaret Fuller. For James it is the war that has made the difference, as if Hawthorne's world of the 1840s can remain innocent in a way that is now impossible: Olive is now a "case." Something of the same shift seems to occur in Whitman, where the war at the very least tempers the enthusiasm for the social possibility of male friendship. In his early poems, at least (those of the first three editions), the "nuts" are visible and ready for gripping,

> Root of washed sweet-flag, timorous pond-snipe, nest of guarded duplicate
>   eggs, it shall be you,
> Mixed tussled hay of head and beard and brawn it shall be you,
> Trickling sap of maple, fibre of manly wheat, it shall be you. (LG55, 49)

Having "nuts," or gripping them, does not prove homosexual identity, of course. No one suggests that homosexual conduct did not exist before the last 100 or 150 years; the question is when it comes to determine an identity.

As I have said elsewhere,[5] that identity is established in Whitman's work in the "Calamus" poems. The fact that several of the poems record doubts and anguish hardly serves as a counterargument. The existence of homophobia ensures that any claim for a homosexual identity, and particularly one with relatively little social support, will be fraught with terror. What I think I must acknowledge as a weakness of my earlier argument is a tendency to see homosexual identity as both univocal and in some sense "natural"—that is, that we "know" what it means to be a homosexual—although I do make a clear distinction between homosexual acts and homosexual identity. Let me here look at a particular site for the statement of what I will no longer call homosexual identity but rather the construction of a particular gay identity in "Calamus" 19. This nine-line poem (in the original version) is, I believe, strategically located between two poems offering quite different views of relationships between men. In "Calamus" 18, Whitman employs one of his frequent instances of negation. After two lines of apostrophe to the "City of my walks and joys!," there are five lines beginning "Not" or "Nor," finally broken by the "but" of line seven (LG60, 363). Rejecting the "pageants" of the city, its material riches, and its "learned persons," the poem turns instead to the "frequent and swift flash of eyes offering me love" (363). As the later title and altered first line of 1867 would suggest, Manhattan is a "City of Orgies," proposing an apparently boundless source of erotic energy. "Lovers, continual lovers, only repay me," the poem concludes in its tribute to cruising (363). However much he may have done for the city by offering it a kind of poetic immortality, the city offers him in return "continual lovers."

The remapping of the city, in which a cartography is constructed out of a series of random sexual encounters, or intersections, is directly linked to an aesthetic of the multiple and quotidian, to the technique of enumeration (or what is frequently called the "catalog"). Like the democratic refusal of hierarchy and the poetic use of metonymy instead of metaphor, Whitman's city lacks public monuments, substituting for them a dynamics of erotic possibility signaled by the "flash of eyes."

The pendant to this view of the city, in the triptych I am constructing, is "Calamus" 20's celebration of friendship. Indeed, this poem, with its setting of Louisiana, evokes a natural world whose emblems of male love can be harnessed along with the new pleasures of the metropolis. (The analogies to Baudelaire here are very striking, although there is no evidence that Whitman had actually read Baudelaire;[6] both poets create urban tableaux that are filled with sexual promise and threat alongside a more distant remembered world of erotic pleasure in an exotic setting.) "I Saw in Louisiana a Live-Oak Growing" was apparently intended to be the second poem of a sequence of poems called

"Live Oak with Moss" which ultimately was reworked and enlarged into the "Calamus" sequence.[7] If "Calamus" 18 records the rejection of personal meaning for a diffused self-consciousness of repeated sensual and erotic stimulation, "Calamus" 20 records the abandonment of a figure of self-sufficiency (the live oak) which is content to utter its own "joyous leaves" (of grass?) while the poet, although acknowledging that it "made me think of myself," nonetheless feels that he "could not" continue without the presence of "a friend, a lover" (LG60, 364–365). Twining the moss around the twig, Whitman creates "a curious token" of "manly love" that would obviously have provided a very different center to this collection of poems from that offered by the calamus root (365). In the 1860 arrangement of the poems, the assertion of lasting affection and friendship serves as a counterweight to the vision of the erogenous city.

Between "Calamus" 18 and "Calamus" 20 is Whitman's "Behold This Swarthy Face," originally entitled "Mind You the Timid Models of the Rest, the Majority?" Even after the elimination of the first stanza, termed by Bradley and Blodgett an "improve[ment]" (LG, 126n), the poem remains one of the sequence's most politically charged. Still, in my view, the opening belongs with the poem, since it provides an explicit political context in the opposition of the two "models," those of "the rest, the majority" and those "adopted . . . for myself" and now "offer[ed] . . . to The Lands" (LG60, 364). Whitman's proposal here, for a "salute of American comrades," is grounded in a conception of the minority while simultaneously implying an at least potential future majority or unanimity (364). Although the majority would hardly dare the public kiss on the lips, it is seen as an "American" gesture, one that is ultimately democratic—it is directly related to the "nuts" that Symonds will not grip. If the two side panels of this triptych offer, as it were, promiscuity and fidelity, the central panel offers a democratic public affection that is neither promiscuous nor faithful. It is, in terms of Whitman's analysis, "natural and nonchalant" (364). The very writing of the poem, with its reenactment of the coming out of the public gesture it records, is more daring than nonchalant. The "natural" is, as always, Whitman's trope for the fulfillment of desire and the breakdown of class boundaries. It is a utopian appeal to a world that he is simultaneously constructing.

Whitman's self-presentation in the poem is a crucial part of that process of construction. Echoing the portrait of himself that serves as the frontispiece, Whitman claims for himself the status of the "natural" bearded man, which is to say the construction of the self as democratic and masculine. Whitman goes so far as to suggest an identification with a black slave—a remarkable act in 1860. He has a "swarthy and unrefined face" ("unrefined" was removed in

later editions), a beard of "white wool," and "brown hands." "Swarthy" con-
notes both blackness and dirtiness, and while it is undoubtedly used here in its
modern meaning of dark or sunburnt—a condition that obviously had clear
class implications in the nineteenth century—it still carries some traces of its
etymological origins. Whitman is constructing himself as the outsider, the
outlaw, the blackguard, at the very same moment that he is asserting his assumption of that role as fundamentally American. (It's a little bit like the Village People, in their demonstration that it is the very heart of patriotic
America that is most gay.) Whitman's strategies here are of significance to us
not only for the place they occupy in his construction of his own sexuality and
its relation to the culture but also for the role they play in determining a modern gay male urban identity.

Poem 19 is a crucial moment in "Calamus" because it attempts to mediate
between two models of gay male sexuality, one based on ideal friendship and
one based on repeated anonymous encounters, because it locates a public act
of affection between men as a political act in America, as such an act remains
even today, and because it attempts to construct a model of the self that will
be adequate to a new sense of identity. There is, despite Whitman's rhetoric,
nothing "natural" about the comradely image he seeks to create. After all, part
of the reason, I have suggested, for Whitman's distancing himself from
Symonds is Symonds's affiliation to another model of male homosexuality,
one that we can call the aristocratic or connoisseur or feminized model.[8] Despite Whitman's attempt to develop a "masculine" model of the male homosexual, and its influence on Edward Carpenter, that model was largely
supplanted by the end of the nineteenth century by a contesting image of the
homosexual as aesthete, which came to dominate Anglo-American culture
until the period of Stonewall.

Whitman's "worker" image of himself is, of course, a pose (although this is
often said as if some alternate self-formulation would be less of a pose), but it
is one that has enormous cultural resonance. Two particular textual sites, one
prior to the 1860 "Calamus" poems, may draw our attention. In the 1855
"Song of Myself" (as it would later be called), after celebrating his sexual encounter with the sea, Whitman declares, a bit oddly, "Washes and razors for
foofoos . . . for me freckles and a bristling beard" (LG55, 46). Against the signs
of effeminacy ("washes and razors," associated with grooming and the "artificial"), Whitman employs the signs of masculinity, a masculinity that is largely
inseparable from class. For someone who grew up in the 1950s, as I did, it is
necessary to imaginatively recall a time, later to return in the 1960s, when
grooming, perfume, and the like were signs of heterosexuality, when homosexuality was, in Luce Irigaray's pun, *homm*osexuality. One can almost see at

work here the cultural transformation of the figure of the overdressed and coiffed fop from a sign of a dangerous heterosexuality to that of a dangerous homosexuality. Whitman's gesture distinguishes him from the "foofoos," those who apply aristocratic principles to self-presentation. But by the introduction of a term such as "foofoos," with its connotations of madness and effeminacy ("*fou*," "*fol/le*") and its aural links to "*frou-frou*," Whitman begins the process of establishing the "true" homosexual self. Homosexuality is the space where men are men. The portrait in the 1860 edition is ample evidence that the process of construction is not complete. Whitman there appears carefully coiffed if bearded, and his open neck is counteracted by a loose tie. The iconographic evidence accords with the contrasts between the typographical flourishes and the plain speech of the poems and with Whitman's textual tensions between the available models for the construction of a homosexual male self.

Similarly, in "Proto-Leaf," later "Starting from Paumanok," a key poem in the 1860 *Leaves of Grass*, Whitman creates a double sense of himself as the liberator of self and the forger of a new homosexual consciousness:

> I will therefore let flame from me the burning fires that were threatening to
> consume me,
> I will lift what has too long kept down those smouldering fires,
> I will give them complete abandonment,
> I will write the evangel-poem of comrades and of love. (MLG, 13)

If I were to revise my comments of almost a generation ago, it would be toward less willingness to accept Whitman's role on his own terms. Although these metaphors of "fire" and "smoldering" indeed suggest repression, I would want to clarify that the act of liberation from repression is always far less total than one imagines, for there is no position from which one can speak other than somewhere already within the relations of power, as Foucault often argued. Thus, for instance, Whitman's desire to free himself from what he sees as conventional models of heterosexual behavior leads him to stress his role as pure male, unsullied by the "feminine" or degenerate, and hence to replicate the regime of surveillance from which he sought to escape. Whitman wants to see himself as a "new man," and so he announces,

> No dainty dolce affettuoso I;
> Bearded, sunburnt, gray-necked, forbidding, I have arrived,
> To be wrestled with as I pass. . . . (29–31)

But the definition of self apparently must pass through the repudiation of other. Whitman cannot say what he is without first saying what he is not. In his first line here, the alliterative *d* and the Italian serve as signs once again of the "artificial" and "unmanly." The fastidious, the sweet, the affectionate[9] must be eliminated in the name of a new muscular identity that challenges the other to wrestle. Whitman in fact signals the importance of this shift, and of his renunciation of the European models, not merely by the language he employs but even more by his rhythms, since "No dainty dolce affettuoso I" not only has an absurd inversion of syntax but is couched in perfect iambic pentameter. The problem is that Whitman apparently sees these signs of rebellion as timeless markers rather than as culturally embedded signifiers. If for Whitman it is necessary to refuse the Italian as the effeminate, it will be necessary for a later generation to claim its "Italianate" qualities against what it sees as a drab conformity, whether of dress or of meter. Things, after all, have meaning only in context.

Whitman's conflation of his poetic nationalism with his sexual politics creates a complex and troubled heritage. On the one hand, modern nationalism is regularly imagined, as in Whitman, as a revolt against the "effeminate," the European colonizer, and the collaborating colonized. But what then can be the place of a woman? Can she, as in Whitman, be only the mother of men? And indeed what of gay men whose very sexuality may locate them as "feminine," whatever Whitman's efforts to separate these terms? Is Whitman paradoxically the father of abstract expressionism and its painting with the penis as of a beat aesthetic of the phallic?[10] Recent attempts to complicate the study of gay identity by shifting to a term such as "queer" seek to address some of the problems and to avoid the reification that is the danger of a complacent and increasingly visible gay community. No one is, of course, born gay—in the same way that Simone de Beauvoir explained that "one is not born a woman, one becomes one." That does not mean that there is no identity but simply that identity cannot be seen as something entirely subjective, transhistorical, and transcultural. It is important to remember that, and for me to be reminded that, I cannot write the history of *the* homosexual tradition but only of *a* homosexual tradition. What being a woman, or a black, or a homosexual means varies enormously according to class, place, ethnicity, and so forth. But within a given cultural community, identities do exist and are constructed, deconstructed, and fought over.

Saying that a category is not natural is not the same as saying it does not exist, as David Halperin has usefully reminded us.[11] Identity means both sameness (identical to) and difference (my identity is different from yours). Every creation of an identity, every claim of a space from which to speak, is purchased at the price of participation in some larger whole. But for those for whom that right to speak and participate has been at best illusory, the price may seem well worth paying. Without identity—whether it is an American identity of the early nineteenth century or a gay identity post-Stonewall—there can be no political action. One may hope that the creation of multiple, specific identities is a strategic move from which one may eventually return to claim one's place in a larger world that is not simply a tolerated anteroom off the great hall of hegemony. But let there be no mistake about it: that return cannot take place on the old terms; the terms must be redrawn in the name of a true diversity and difference, a metonymy that can never allow any of its parts to stand singly for the whole.

Categories are arbitrary, as Foucault shows, and there is no reason why the sex of one's object of desire should be more important than age, color, taste, size, or any other imaginable category. But homosexuality in its modern sense is the product of homophobia, which is in turn the result of a homosocial system and its inherent misogyny. Queer culture in the 1990s attempts to reinvigorate a gay movement that it sees as both too complicit, in its concentration on integrationist goals, and too debilitated by the effect of AIDS to offer the kind of hard-edged challenge that is necessary. The "foofoos" will, I suppose, feel more at home at Queer Nation than at a traditional gay gathering, but once again they may be judged lacking in balls. Whitman's reproach to Symonds, funny and accurate as it may be, is also a sign of a failure of communication, indicating Whitman's inability to grasp the new homosexuality of the fin de siècle and his desire to preserve the model he had so carefully constructed. Can one not imagine a gay identity, or simply an antihomophobic discourse, as Eve Sedgwick puts it, that will have room for both Symonds and Whitman, that will not continue to inquire about "nuts"?

Such an identity would see its own contemporary pose of hypermasculinity as a form of signifying. Gay macho style may indeed always be accompanied by a wink; as always with irony, the power of that wink to unwrite the cultural text it signals its distance from is uncertain. Even when the wink is clearly visible in the original, will it survive its translation into mass culture? Whitman's signifying on the gay male culture of the 1890s poses problems of reading and writing the self that still perplex us.

NOTES

1. Quoted in Justin Kaplan, *Walt Whitman: A Life* (New York: Simon and Schuster, 1980), 46. See CORR, 5:72–73, for Whitman's letter of August 19, 1890, to Symonds.

2. For Symonds's letters to Whitman (August 3 and September 5, 1890), see the Charles E. Feinberg Collection, Library of Congress; excerpts from his correspondence are provided in CORR, 5:72n.

3. For this form of "critical parody," see the famous essay by Henry Louis Gates Jr., "The Blackness of Blackness: A Critique of the Sign and the Signifying Monkey," in Gates, ed., *Black Literature and Literary Theory* (New York: Methuen, 1984), 285–321.

4. Ralph Ellison, *Invisible Man* (New York: Vintage Books, 1972), 16. .

5. Robert K. Martin, *The Homosexual Tradition in American Poetry* (Austin: University of Texas Press, 1979), 50–57 and passim; Martin, "Conversion and Identity: The Calamus Poems," *Walt Whitman Review* 25 (June 1979): 59–66.

6. Betsy Erkkila, *Walt Whitman among the French* (Princeton: Princeton University Press, 1980), 53–54.

7. MLG, lxiv–lxvii; Alan Helms, "Whitman's Live Oak with Moss," in Robert K. Martin, ed., *The Continuing Presence of Walt Whitman: The Life after the Life* (Iowa City: University of Iowa Press, 1992), 185–205.

8. For more on the English rejection of the implications of a more socialist and feminist model of the male homosexual, see Eve Kosofsky Sedgwick, "Whitman's Transatlantic Context: Class, Gender and Male Homosexual Style," *Delta* 16 (May 1983): 111–122. See also my "Edward Carpenter and the Double Structure of *Maurice*," *Journal of Homosexuality* 8 (Spring/Summer 1983): 35–46.

9. It seems quite possible that Whitman associated "affettuoso" with the English "affected."

10. The implications of these associations in a Canadian and Québécois context have been studied, for instance, by Robert Schwartzwald in "Fear of Federasty: Québec's Inverted Fictions," in Hortense J. Spillers, ed., *Comparative American Identities: Race, Sex, and Nationality in the Modern Text* (New York: Routledge, 1991), 175–195, and by me in "Sex and Politics in Wartime Canada: The Attack on Patrick Anderson," *Essays on Canadian Writing* 44 (Fall 1991), 110–125.

11. David Halperin, *One Hundred Years of Homosexuality* (New York: Routledge, 1989), 28.

THE INFLUENCE

WHITMAN AMONG OTHERS

Poets to come! . . .

. . .

I am a man who, sauntering along without fully stopping,
* turns a casual look upon you and then averts his face,*
Leaving it to you to prove and define it,
Expecting the main things from you.

("Poets to Come," LG, 14)

Whitman's Multitudinous Poetic Progeny
Particular and Puzzling Instances

F ROM THE TIME I first began to read Whitman as an undergraduate, I
have had great curiosity as to the nature and measure of his influence on
me and other common readers, as well as on successor poets. Back in
1960, Karl Shapiro, Bernice Slote, and I published a wild and "anti-new critical" book entitled *Start with the Sun: Studies in Cosmic Poetry*, focusing on
Whitman's complex connections with D. H. Lawrence, Hart Crane, and
Dylan Thomas. I launched out on my own some twenty years later with *The
American Quest for a Supreme Fiction: Whitman's Legacy in the Personal Epic*,
tracing the Whitman lineage through many twentieth-century poets, including
Ezra Pound, T. S. Eliot, Wallace Stevens, William Carlos Williams, Hart Crane
again (the easy one), Charles Olson, John Berryman, and Allen Ginsberg.

In 1991, I wrote a review for the *Walt Whitman Quarterly Review* and discussed four recent books, each of which made some kind of case for a vital
Whitman connection—sometimes positive, often negative—with modern
poets. The four books together covered, without duplication, a total of
twenty-two poets—many well known, others lesser known—whose work revealed Whitman's influence. It seems that time has indeed proved Whitman
to be what the British poet Donald Davie in 1976 called "that inescapable
figure in every American poet's heritage."[1] What I would like to do now is en-
gage in some wide-ranging and perhaps eccentric speculation about the puzzling nature of Whitman's often startling, even baffling impact on his readers.

I open with some lines from the end of "Song of Myself" (Section 52) in
which, seeming to anticipate such an impact of his poetry, Whitman said to

the reader: "You will hardly know who I am or what I mean, / But I shall be good health to you nevertheless, / And filter and fibre your blood" (LG, 89). I would like to examine the claims of Whitman's words in these lines as they might characterize his "influence" on his readers: that they have "hardly" known what he is or means, that he has proved to be "good health" to them "nevertheless," and that he has indeed been able to "filter and fibre" their "blood." I take it that such influence as Whitman is getting at in these lines is of a kind so direct and deep that it enters the emotional bloodstream immediately without passing through understanding or intellect—those faculties of the mind that tend to screen, moderate, or suppress. I wish to explore some tentative answers to two questions raised by these observations: does the recorded history of Whitman's influence tend to support the poet's claim to—so to speak—get under the skin of his readers, including successor poets, in spite of themselves? And if so, what was the nature of Whitman's strategy in Leaves of Grass that enabled him to "filter and fibre" his readers' "blood"?

Ralph Waldo Emerson's overall ambivalent response to Whitman may be taken as the prototype of the kind of response relevant to the first question. Emerson's famous letter, written immediately upon reading the first edition of Leaves of Grass, contained some of the warmest, most enthusiastic sentences endorsing the book ever written: "I am very happy in reading it, as great power makes us happy. . . . I give you joy of your free and brave thought. I have great joy in it. I find incomparable things said incomparably well, as they must be. I find the courage of treatment which so delights us, and which large perception only can inspire."[2] Whitman's use—or misuse—of Emerson's letter in and on the 1856 edition of Leaves is well known. But in itself, it cannot explain why Emerson never again expressed himself so passionately or openly about Whitman's work and passed it by completely when he compiled and published Parnassus, his 1874 anthology of British and American poetry.[3]

Henry David Thoreau showed a similar ambivalence in his reaction to Whitman. His long comment on Whitman, made in a letter to Harrison Blake (December 7, 1856) after a visit to Whitman and after reading the second edition of Leaves of Grass, is full of contradictory impulses to praise and condemn. Thoreau confesses that reading the new edition "has done [him] more good than any reading for a long time," and he cites the two poems he remembers best: "Song of Myself" and "Crossing Brooklyn Ferry" (then called, respectively, "Poem of Walt Whitman, an American" and "Sun-Down Poem"). Immediately after this opening praise, Thoreau adds: "There are 2 or 3 pieces in the book which are disagreeable to say the least, simply sensual. He does not celebrate love at all. It is as if the beasts spoke. I think men have not been ashamed of themselves without reason."

Following this moral charge, Thoreau seems on the point of refuting it: "But even on this side, he has spoken more truth than any American or modern that I know. I have found his poem exhilarating, encouraging. As for its sensuality,—& it may turn out to be less sensual than it appears—I do not so much wish that those parts were not written, as that men & women were so pure that they could read them without harm, that is, without understanding them." Here Thoreau seems to be obliquely endorsing Whitman's intention to so "filter and fibre" the blood of his readers as to give them not some definable meaning or truth but the "good health" of an "exhilarating" or "encouraging" experience of the kind Thoreau seems to have had. Thoreau concluded his evaluation: "On the whole, it [Whitman's poetry] sounds to me very brave & American after whatever deductions. I do not believe that all the sermons so called that have been preached in this land put together are equal to it for preaching. We ought to rejoice greatly in him."[4]

Sidney Lanier and Algernon Swinburne were similar to Emerson and Thoreau in their ambivalent responses to Whitman's book. They endorsed it with extravagant praise at first, but then drew back from it later and, in effect, rejected it. Here, for example, is a passage from the letter Lanier wrote to Whitman in 1878, shortly after encountering *Leaves* for the first time: "It is not known to me where I can find another modern song at once so large and so naive; and the time needs to be told few things so much as the absolute personality of the person, the sufficiency of the man's manhood *to* the man, which you have propounded in such strong and beautiful rhythms. I beg you to count me among your most earnest lovers. . . ."[5] And here, three years later, is one of the most delightfully convoluted and weirdly contorted passages in all of Whitman criticism from Lanier's largely condemnatory lecture-essay:

> While I am immeasurably shocked at the sweeping invasions of those reserves which depend on the very personality I have so much insisted upon, and which the whole consensus of the ages has considered more and more sacred with every year of growth in delicacy; yet, after all these prodigious allowances, I owe some keen delights to a certain combination of bigness and naïvity which make some of Whitman's passages so strong and taking, and indeed, on the one occasion when Whitman has abandoned his theory of formlessness and written in form he has made "My Captain, O my Captain" surely one of the most tender and beautiful poems in any language.[6]

The misquotation of the title of one of Whitman's most mediocre poems is perhaps oddly revealing.

Swinburne first expressed his warm feelings about Whitman's poetry in a twenty-two-stanza poem entitled "To Walt Whitman in America," written in 1871. The third stanza is typical:

O strong-winged soul with prophetic
  Lips hot with the bloodbeats of song,
With tremor of heartstrings magnetic,
  With thoughts as thunders in throng,
With consonant ardours of chords
That pierce men's souls as with swords
  And hale them hearing along.[7]

In his essay entitled "Whitmania," published sixteen years later (1887), Swinburne startles the reader with a first sentence of such scorn that it overpowers the second sentence, which attempts to undo what cannot be undone:

> The remarkable American rhapsodist who has inoculated a certain number of English readers and writers with the singular form of ethical and aesthetic rabies for which his name supplies the proper medical term of definition is usually regarded by others than Whitmaniacs as simply a blatant quack—a vehement and emphatic dunce, of incomparable vanity and volubility, inconceivable pretensions, and incompetence. That such is by no means altogether my own view I need scarcely take the trouble to protest.[8]

Such ambivalent or ambiguous responses to Whitman have occurred frequently enough in the history of his reputation to suggest that he has indeed been able through his book to "filter and fibre" the blood of many of his sensitive readers—and their initial emotional embrace of the poet dissolves later in an intellectual or analytical distancing or even rejection. Moreover, their attempts to identify the source of Whitman's power are frequently expressed in a critical vocabulary that seems unequal to the task: Emerson's "great power" and "free and brave thought"; Thoreau's "It is as if the beasts spoke"; Lanier's "the sufficiency of the man's manhood *to* the man . . . propounded in such strong and beautiful rhythms"; Swinburne's "prophetic / Lips hot with the bloodbeats of song." Many distinguished readers have left behind the tracks of their complex and shifting reactions to Whitman, including, among others, Henry James, Gerard Manley Hopkins, Ezra Pound, D. H. Lawrence, T. S. Eliot, and William Carlos Williams. Some of these writers (Henry James is a prominent example) reversed the pattern established by Emerson of first endorsing and then rejecting Whitman by first rejecting and then embracing him. There are, of course, many readers who have left no record of their responses to reading Whitman, but we may reasonably assume that a number of them had similar experiences of mixed, shifting, or inexplicable feelings.

Accepting for the moment these reactions to Whitman as in some sense typical, we might at this point venture a series of propositions: that Whitman's greatest poetic power strikes the reader at the subconscious level; that his political-sexual-spiritual themes are so inextricably interwoven that the reader feels the power of the whole but often concludes (usually later) that the power comes from an individual part and is contaminated by the intermixture of undesirable elements that should be rejected; that Whitman is best experienced by comprehending the interrelatedness—and the necessity of such interrelatedness—of his major political-sexual-spiritual themes. Thus, the first of the "hot little prophets," W. D. O'Connor, focused in *The Good Gray Poet* (1866) on the spiritual themes in *Leaves of Grass* and trivialized the sexual themes; in his tale "The Carpenter" (1892), he turned Whitman into a Christ figure. D. H. Lawrence, in *Studies in Classic American Literature* (1923), while celebrating Whitman's omnisexual affirmations, showed great disdain as well as distaste for Whitman's comprehensive democratic embrace, failing to see that neither of the themes as developed by Whitman could stand without the other. And Carl Sandburg, in setting aside Whitman's sexual themes and taking over his indiscriminate democratic celebration of the multitudes, as in *The People, Yes* (1936), never achieved Whitman's power because he, too, failed to perceive the vital linkage Whitman made between his political and sexual themes.

Allied to this set of propositions is my belief that the "central" theme uniting the political theme on one side with the spiritual theme on the other is the straddling (or binding) omnisexual theme in the center. In a metaphorical sense, the omnisexual theme stands in the middle holding the hands of its comrade themes—very much as Whitman, when he finally follows the call of the hermit thrush in "When Lilacs Last in the Dooryard Bloom'd," retreats to the "swamp cedars" accompanied by two comrades, the three holding hands: on one side the "thought of death," on the other the "sacred knowledge of death"; the one caught up in grief for the dead Lincoln, the other bringing reconciliation to death through the spiritual insight bestowed by the bird.

Near the beginning of his career, in his long letter to Emerson in the 1856 edition of *Leaves of Grass*, Whitman defined his sexual themes as both programmatic and, in some sense, "cosmic," in this way: "Of bards for These States, if it come to a question, it is whether they shall celebrate in poems the eternal decency of the amativeness of Nature, the motherhood of all, or whether they shall be the bards of the fashionable delusion of the inherent nastiness of sex, and of the feeble and querulous modesty of deprivation."[9] Near the end of his career, in "A Backward Glance O'er Travel'd Roads," Whitman said of his sexual themes (his terms are "Amativeness, and even animality"):

> I shall only say the espousing principle of those lines [of *Leaves of Grass*] so gives breath of life to my whole scheme that the bulk of the pieces might as

well have been left unwritten were those lines omitted. . . . I am not going to argue the question by itself; it does not stand by itself. The vitality of it is altogether in its relations, bearings, significance—like the clef of a symphony. At last analogy the lines I allude to, and the spirit in which they are spoken, permeate all "Leaves of Grass," and the work must stand or fall with them, as the human body and soul must remain as an entirety. (PW, 2:727–728)

My understanding of Whitman's comments and my reading of the whole of *Leaves of Grass* lead me to the conclusion that the sexual themes were at the beginning and remained throughout central and essential, giving the book (as Whitman says) its "breath of life." If this is true, then it is interesting to contemplate the mutilation of Whitman's book when it was edited in 1868 by William Michael Rossetti for publication in Great Britain and to wonder about those readers who first encountered Whitman's work in this bowdlerized version. Opening the book is a cluster of poems called "Chants Democratic," with "Starting from Paumanok" placed in first position. Next comes "Drum-Taps." We search in vain for the "Children of Adam" and "Calamus" clusters, but some of the poems of the latter are placed in a grouping entitled "Walt Whitman." It is in this section that we might expect to find "Song of Myself"; but the poem most vital to the experiencing of the whole of *Leaves of Grass* has been expurgated. Rossetti no doubt understood that, among other things, "Song of Myself" is Whitman's most powerful celebration of sex in all its manifestations in human experience. The comprehensive omnisexual vision places sexuality at the center of individual identity and portrays it as pivotal in all human relationships, from the bonding of two people to the forming of communities and nations. This latter theme is elaborated, of course, in the two clusters that follow it in *Leaves of Grass*, "Children of Adam" and "Calamus," both of which are missing in the British volume.[10]

To explore the generalizations or propositions ventured so far, I turn to the poem I consider the "founding" poem of *Leaves of Grass*, "Song of Myself." It appeared as the lead poem of the work's first edition in 1855 and assumed the key opening position in the basic structure as finally shaped in the 1881 edition. In its scope it elaborates and weaves together in a complex pattern the major themes of the book—political (or democratic), sexual (or physical), spiritual (or religious). I shall attempt no comprehensive examination of the poem here but will make a few forays into it for illustrative purposes.

"Song of Myself" opens with a political—or democratic—accent: "I celebrate myself, and sing myself, / And what I assume you shall assume, / For every atom belonging to me as good belongs to you" (LG, 28). Here and throughout, the poet includes the reader, by the recurring intimacy of

"private" direct address and in his celebration of individuality; the reader becomes a character at one with the poet, a companion on his journey, an equal
sharer of his experiences: individuality and equality are dramatically affirmed.
The opening sections of "Song of Myself" lead step by step to the poem's first
and surely most brilliant climax in Section 5, representing an intertwining of
the poem's political themes (with which the poem began), its sexual themes
(which have already been introduced), and its spiritual themes (which move
front and center here).

In Section 5, the poet's body seems to be embraced by his soul, both sexually and mystically:

> I believe in you my soul, the other I am must not abase itself to you,
> And you must not be abased to the other
>
> Loafe with me on the grass, loose the stop from your throat,
> Not words, not music or rhyme I want, not custom or lecture, not even the
>   best,
> Only the lull I like, the hum of your valvèd voice.
>
> I mind how once we lay such a transparent summer morning,
> How you settled your head athwart my hips and gently turn'd over upon me,
> And parted the shirt from my bosom-bone, and plunged your tongue to my
>   bare-stript heart,
> And reach'd till you felt my beard, and reach'd till you held my feet.
>
> Swiftly arose and spread around me the peace and knowledge that pass all the
>   argument of the earth,
> And I know that the hand of God is the promise of my own,
> And I know that the spirit of God is the brother of my own,
> And that all the men ever born are also my brothers, and the women my sis-
>   ters and lovers,
> And that a kelson of the creation is love,
> And limitless are leaves stiff or drooping in the fields,
> And brown ants in the little wells beneath them,
> And mossy scabs of the worm fence, heap'd stones, elder, mullein and poke-
>   weed. (LG, 32–33)

This is the moment of greatest concentration and tension in the first part of
"Song of Myself." Before this we have seen the poet, with whom we have been
asked to identify, abandoning his civilized encumbrances and retreating to the
woods to become "undisguised and naked" and there to invite the experience
that will bring comprehension of the mysteries that swarm through the poet's
consciousness (and unconscious), including the role of sex in the evolutionary
unfolding of history:

Urge and urge and urge,
Always the procreant urge of the world.

Out of the dimness opposite equals advance, always substance and increase,
    always sex,
Always a knit of identity, always distinction, always a breed of life. (LG, 31)

The experience comes in the form of a direct symbolic sexual union of
body and soul, a union that informs without the intervention of the intellect
of the "talkers," "trippers," and "askers" of the "creeds and schools" or "houses
and rooms" abandoned and held in abeyance for a time. The soul, seizing the
poet by his beard and feet and holding him in a kind of entranced grip, opens
his shirt to the "bosom-bone" and penetrates with the tongue to the "bare-
stript heart." In a kind of spiritual fellatio, the soul plunges tongue to heart,
communing directly and ecstatically with it, where meanings are deeply felt,
short-circuiting the intellect, where meanings are screened and obscured, be-
fogged by the inadequacies of language.

Immediately, the electrifying "peace and knowledge" that lie beyond intellect and argument flow from the soul through the body of the poet. What follows is the poet's groping about with inadequate language, tarnished by the
"trippers" and "askers," to capture the elusive meaning of his ecstatic vision. It
is a knowledge that somehow comprehends God, the brotherhood of men,
the sisterhood of women, the humanhood of all, and the key itself: "a kelson
of the creation is love." But the words fail to match the wonder of intuitive
"truth," and the poet trails off in the end, launching a seemingly meaningless
and incoherent catalog of the minutiae surrounding him in his natural setting—the "limitless" leaves "stiff or drooping in the fields," the "brown ants
in the little wells," the "mossy scabs of the worm fence, heap'd stones, elder,
mullein, and pokeweed." It is as though the poet, overwhelmed by such profound knowledge through his soul-searing experience, must cling to the immediate reality of a visible, touchable world to hold on to sanity.

It is well known that William James cited "Song of Myself," and particularly Section 5, in *The Varieties of Religious Experience* (1902), as an example of
what he called the "sporadic" mystical experience, characterized by the experience's two key elements: a certainty of transcendent knowledge together with
recognition of the ineffability of such knowledge.[11] It has been little noted, on
the other hand, that, writing about the same time, Henry Adams, in *The Education of Henry Adams* (in circulation from 1907, published in 1918), made reference to Whitman in his search for the key to history in the chapter entitled
"The Dynamo and the Virgin." Adams's search led him to reject the sequence
of humans, societies, time, and thought and to focus on the sequence of force.

He came to what he saw as a vital link between the Virgin, who was the source of energy that led to the building of the great cathedrals of the past, and the dynamo, which was symbolic of the source of energy that led to the building of the great skyscrapers of the present.

And the relevance of Whitman? "Adams," the autobiographer wrote of himself, "began to ponder, asking himself whether he knew of any American artist who had ever insisted on the power of sex, as every classic had always done; but he could think only of Walt Whitman."[12] What better lines exemplifying what Adams is referring to here than these sweeping historical lines that lead up to Section 5: "Out of the dimness opposite equals advance, always substance and increase, always sex, / Always a knit of identity, always distinction, always a breed of life." I have often imagined that had William James and Henry Adams ever engaged in a discussion of the meaning of Section 5 of "Song of Myself," they would soon have come to an agreement that the ecstatic union of body and soul portrayed in it served as a perfect illustration in its spiritual dimension for the sporadic mysticism sought by the one and in its sexual dimension for the historical force sought by the other. Just as Whitman repeatedly proclaimed a primal relationship between body and soul, the physical and spiritual, so Adams affirmed sexual energy as the source of the creative power in the construction of the great cathedrals and works of art of the past.

It has been too frequently ignored that Whitman's sexual sympathies flow out of his political themes and that his spiritual intuitions flow from his sexual affirmations in "Song of Myself"—often without any signal to alert the reader that a radical shift in focus is taking place. We may find such a passage beginning in Section 21, in which the poet presses his sexual hug as energetically and indiscriminately as he presses his political embrace:

I am the poet of the Body and I am the poet of the Soul,
The pleasures of heaven are with me and the pains of hell are with me,
The first I graft and increase upon myself, the latter I translate into a new
   tongue. (LG, 48)

Later, in Section 24, he attempts the translation promised here:

I speak the pass-word primeval, I give the sign of democracy,
By God! I will accept nothing which all cannot have their counterpart of on
   the same terms.

Through me many long dumb voices,
Voices of the interminable generations of prisoners and slaves,
Voices of the diseas'd and despairing and of thieves and dwarfs,
Voices of cycles of preparation and accretion,

And of the threads that connect the stars, and of wombs and of the father-
    stuff,
And of the rights of them the others are down upon,
Of the deform'd, trivial, flat, foolish, despised,
Fog in the air, beetles rolling balls of dung.

Through me forbidden voices,
Voices of sexes and lusts, voices veil'd and I remove the veil,
Voices indecent by me clarified and transfigur'd.

I do not press my fingers across my mouth,
I keep as delicate around the bowels as around the head and heart,
Copulation is no more rank to me than death is.

I believe in the flesh and the appetites,
Seeing, hearing, feeling, are miracles, and each part and tag of me is a miracle.

Divine am I inside and out, and I make holy whatever I touch or am touch'd
    from,
The scent of these arm-pits aroma finer than prayer,
This head more than churches, bibles, and all the creeds. (52–53)

This remarkable passage celebrating both sex and lust—clearly linked to
"the pass-word primeval" glossed as "the sign of democracy"—leads into an
even more remarkable celebratory passage that offers a melange of sexual
mixed with nature images, suggesting a great diversity of diffuse sexual feeling.
The lines, exalting and magnifying such feeling, might be read as the clarifica-
tion and transfiguration of those "voices indecent" promised by the poet. It is,
as the first line states, a proclamation of "worship" of the "spread" of the poet's
"own body, or any part of it." We might imagine the poet out in nature alone,
suddenly and almost ecstatically beset by a sudden intense awareness of his
own sexuality, an awareness induced in part by everything in the fecund
natural setting that intermingles inextricably with the overwhelming sense of
sexual identity. The "firm masculine colter" (an iron blade attached to a
plowshare) is clearly the erect phallus, ready for the plowing and sowing in the
act of tilling ("tilth"). The image of "milky stream pale strippings" of the poet's
"life" is clearly suggestive of semen. Metaphors multiply thick and fast in the
catalog of items the poet worships, each line ending with the emphatic "it
shall be you!":

Root of wash'd sweet-flag! timorous pond-snipe! nest of guarded duplicate
    eggs! it shall be you!
Mix'd tussled hay of head, beard, brawn, it shall be you!
Trickling sap of maple, fibre of manly wheat, it shall be you!

Sun so generous it shall be you!
Vapors lighting and shading my face it shall be you!
You sweaty brooks and dews it shall be you!
Winds whose soft-tickling genitals rub against me it shall be you!
Broad muscular fields, branches of live oak, loving lounger in my winding
    paths, it shall be you!
Hands I have taken, face I have kiss'd, mortal I have ever touch'd, it shall be
    you. (LG, 53–54)

What is dramatically presented in these lines is certainly not a sexual experience in the conventional sense, although fragments of previous experiences seem to surge up from the past. It is an imaginative state of sustained ecstasy equaling in intensity an orgasm—a transfiguring realization of one's individual being and sexual identity and an intermingling of that identity with the outside world of nature. The sense of the sexual leads to, becomes inexplicably part of, the sense of the miraculous:

I dote on myself, there is that lot of me and all so luscious,
Each moment and whatever happens thrills me with joy,
I cannot tell how my ankles bend, nor whence the cause of my faintest wish,
Nor the cause of the friendship I emit, nor the cause of the friendship I take
    again.

That I walk up my stoop, I pause to consider if it really be,
A morning-glory at my window satisfies me more than the metaphysics of
    books. (LG, 54)

The poet unconsciously links his generalized and unfocused sexual feeling with feelings of the joy of being, the baffling mysteries of existence, and the obscure "cause" of friendship (the latter linkage an anticipation of Freudian theory, which I have discussed elsewhere). In two climactic lines near the end of Section 24, the poet infuses the entire universe with overwhelming and sexual significance in a kind of transcendent cosmic copulation, dynamically orgasmic: "Something I cannot see puts upward libidinous prongs, / Seas of bright juice suffuse heaven" (54).

It is instructive, in concluding this examination of some of the puzzling dimensions of Whitman's influence on his readers, to review briefly the responses of three women who either wrote about or made important references to him in their work. Leading off is the case of Anne Gilchrist, the British widow of William Blake's biographer, who came to Whitman first through reading William Rossetti's expurgated edition. Whatever she found there led her to seek out a copy of the complete *Leaves of Grass*, where she discovered the missing poem "Song of Myself," as well as the omitted clusters "Children of Adam" and "Calamus." It was these very selections on which she bestowed lavish praise when she came to write "An Englishwoman's Estimate of Walt Whitman," published in a Boston journal, *Radical Review*, in May 1870.[13] Through reading Whitman's book, Gilchrist fell in love with the author. The story of her journey to America with her children and her setting up a household in Philadelphia to be near Whitman has been frequently told. But there has been little speculation of how Whitman's words entangled her deepest emotions so as to affect the fundamental direction of her life. I have always thought that her background in William Blake (she had completed her husband's biography) prepared her to find in Whitman's work certain primal energies which the two poets in quite different ways tapped and celebrated.

The American writer Kate Chopin offers a quite different case, but perhaps no less mysterious than that of Anne Gilchrist. When Chopin published *The Awakening* in 1899, it was severely criticized by reviewers. They found it "unhealthy," even "morbid," demonstrating what a "cruel loathsome monster Passion can be." The moral outrage provoked by the novel in effect cut short Kate Chopin's career by blasting her reputation, and many decades were to pass before her work would be found again and recognized as pioneering and classic. Clearly Walt Whitman was an important influence on Chopin. The depth of her reading in his work may be gauged by her allusion to certain of his lines at key points in her fiction. One example must suffice here. The short story entitled "A Respectable Woman" portrays a developing sexual attachment between a woman and one of her husband's friends, whom the husband persists in inviting to their Louisiana plantation for extended stays. At a signal moment in this budding extramarital relationship, as the two sit outside on a soft southern night, the friend murmurs "half to himself": "Night of south winds—night of the large few stars! Still nodding night—"[14]

Just as we cannot completely comprehend a T. S. Eliot poem without deciphering and understanding his various epigraphs and allusions, so we cannot fully experience Chopin's story without knowing something about the quotation murmured at this point. Here is the full context from Sections 21–22 of "Song of Myself":

Press close bare-bosomed night—press close magnetic nourishing night!
Night of south winds—night of the large few stars!
Still nodding night—mad naked summer night.

Smile O voluptuous cool-breath'd earth!
Earth of the slumbering and liquid trees!
Earth of departed sunset—earth of the mountains misty-topt!
Earth of the vitreous pour of the full moon just tinged with blue!

Earth of shine and dark mottling the tide of the river!
Earth of the limpid gray of clouds brighter and clearer for my sake!
Far-swooping elbow'd earth—rich apple-blossom'd earth!
Smile, for your lover comes.

Prodigal, you have given me love—therefore I to you give love!
O unspeakable passionate love.

You sea, I resign myself to you also—I guess what you mean,
I behold from the beach your crooked inviting fingers,
I believe you refuse to go back without feeling of me,
We must have a turn together, I undress, hurry me out of sight of the land,
Cushion me soft, rock me in billowy drowse,
Dash me with amorous wet, I can repay you. (LG, 49)

Chopin's use of a few words from this passage to suggest the intensity of feeling in the evolving relationship between her "respectable woman" and the
husband's friend is remarkably effective. And such use indicates to me that
Chopin had an instinctive understanding and full appreciation of Whitman's
omnisexual vision.

The American poet Muriel Rukeyser, whose *Collected Poems* appeared
in 1979, published an important essay on Whitman in her *The Life of Poetry* (1949), finding her own way to come to terms with Whitman's sexual
themes.[15] She confronts directly the question of these themes early in her
essay, saying that Whitman's "readers reacted violently from the beginning to
his writing about sex—and of course it is not writing *about* sex, it is that
physical rhythms are the base of every clear line, and that the avowals and the
secrecy are both part of the life of a person who is, himself, a battleground of
forces."[16] In a curious comparison of Whitman with Melville, she highlights
Whitman's achievement in turning his struggle to come to terms with his sexuality into an act of creation. In his poem "After the Pleasure Party," Melville,
she says, expresses "bitter pain at 'The human integral clove asunder,'" and
cries out

> for the power to free sex by setting free the sexless essential man. . . . Whit-
> man, also, used these terms of need; but the "halves" he fought to bring to-
> gether were in himself, and he chose . . . not to allow himself the concept of
> a central sexless man, but to take the other way: to remake himself. It is in
> the remaking of himself that Whitman speaks for the general conflict in our
> culture. For, in the poems, his discovery of himself is a discovery of Amer-
> ica; he is able to give it to anyone who reaches his lines.[17]

If I understand Muriel Rukeyser aright, she is in effect saying that out of
Whitman's struggles—and coming to terms—with his own sexuality, he was

led to his political and spiritual themes, in effect his "discovery of America" through "discovery of himself." Thus, we might find the underlying or root cause for Whitman's intertwining these themes so closely. "It was Whitman's acceptance of his entire nature," Rukeyser says,

> that made the work possible. . . . Whitman as he made himself [is] able to identify at last with both the people in their contradictions and himself in his. Able to identify—and this is his inner achievement—with his own spirit, of which his body, his life, his poems are the language. For Whitman grew to be able to say, out of his own fears, "Be not afraid of my body," and, out of his own scattering, "I am a dance." He remembered his body as other poets of his time remembered English verse. Out of his own body, and its relation to itself and the sea, he drew his basic rhythms. They are not the rhythms, as has been asserted, of work and love-making; but rather of the relation of our breathing to our heartbeat. . . .[18]

As we consider Whitman's influence, I think we could do worse than listen to Muriel Rukeyser's comment on the subject:

> Whitman is a "bad influence"; that is, he cannot be imitated. He can, in hilarious or very dull burlesques, be parodied; but anyone who has come under his rhythms to the extent of trying to use them knows how great a folly is there. He cannot be extended; it is as if his own curse on "poems distill'd from poems" were still effective (as it forever is); but what is always possible is to go deeper into one's own sources, the body and the ancient religious poetry, and go on with the work he began.[19]

Whitman would, I think, agree with Rukeyser; he put it this way: "Not I, not any one else can travel that road for you, / You must travel it for yourself" (LG, 83).

I take the interest of Anne Gilchrist, Kate Chopin, and Muriel Rukeyser in Whitman to be—on some level, in some measure—similar to mine, and I think they might agree to some extent that the critical controversies that have surrounded various lines and passages in Whitman's work appear to substantiate Whitman in his belief that his readers would hardly know who he is or what he means. Their responses to Whitman are curiously at odds, for example, with the responses of Emerson, Thoreau, Lanier, and Swinburne. These women turn to Whitman for the very element that the male writers would suppress. They seem instinctively to understand what Whitman meant when he said in "A Backward Glance": "At last analogy the lines I allude to [embodying sexuality in one form or another], and the spirit in which they are spoken, permeate all 'Leaves of Grass,' and the work must stand or fall with them, as the human body and soul must remain as an entirety." What I have been exploring is what I take to be the genuine "influential Whitman"; the foundation of such an enduring Whitman must be found in the poetry that Rossetti left out of his British edition. Like the "noiseless patient spider" spinning its web "out of itself," Whitman through his book will continue to launch forth filament after filament—"till the bridge . . . be form'd, till the ductile anchor hold." Readers—and among them "poets to come"—will continue to be caught by the "gossamer thread" without knowing precisely how or why.

NOTES

1. Donald Davie, review of *The Freedom of the Poet*, by John Berryman, *New York Times Book Review*, April 25, 1976.

2. Jim Perlman, Ed Folsom, and Dan Campion, eds., *Walt Whitman: The Measure of His Song* (Minneapolis: Holy Cow! Press, 1981), 1.

3. Ralph Waldo Emerson, ed., *Parnassus* (Boston: Osgood, 1874).

4. Perlman, Folsom, and Campion, 2.

5. Edwin Haviland Miller, ed., *A Century of Whitman Criticism* (Bloomington: Indiana University Press, 1969), xxviii.

6. Miller, 70.

7. Perlman, Folsom, and Campion, 5.

8. Miller, 81.

9. Walt Whitman, *Leaves of Grass* (1856), 356.

10. William M. Rossetti, ed., *Poems by Walt Whitman* (London: John Camden Hotten, 1868).

11. William James, *The Varieties of Religious Experience* (1902; rpt., New York: Doubleday, n.d.), 357.

12. Henry Adams, *The Education of Henry Adams*, ed. Ernest Samuels (Boston: Houghton Mifflin, 1973), 385.

13. An abridged version of Anne Gilchrist's "An Englishwoman's Estimate of Walt Whitman" appears in Miller, 33–39.

14. Kate Chopin, "A Respectable Woman," *The Awakening and Selected Stories*, ed. Barbara H. Solomon (New York: New American Library, 1976), 194–197; see Lewis Leary's treatment of the relationship between Whitman and Chopin in *Southern Excursions: Essays on Mark Twain and Others* (Baton Rouge: Louisiana State University Press, 1971), 169–174.

15. Muriel Rukeyser, "Whitman and the Problem of Good," in Perlman, Folsom, and Campion, 102–110.

16. Ibid., 103.

17. Ibid., 103–104.

18. Ibid., 105–106.

19. Ibid., 107.

The Whitman Legacy and the Harlem Renaissance

WHITMAN'S LEGACY to the African American literary tradition remains a largely unexplored topic. We know more today about Walt Whitman among the French, the Russians, the Irish, the Japanese, the Germans, and the Argentineans than about Whitman among the African American modernists. Yet "New Negro" authors enthusiastically embraced Whitman, embraced him with an intimacy that defies the codes typical of interracial relations in the United States and exceeds that of most white American modernists. Ironically, perhaps, they read him as the quintessential "democratic" and antiracist poet, whose legacy could be used to break the racist tradition's control over the limits and possibilities of African American literature. This aspect of the response to Whitman, however, is finally less important than the ways in which *Leaves of Grass* affected black poetics and cultural theory. Inspiring modernist breaks with previous African American as well as Anglo-American literary practices and intellectual traditions, Whitman's writing contributed crucially to some of the most fruitful developments in black writing of the twentieth century. Having discussed Whitman's importance to Kelly Miller and Langston Hughes elsewhere, in this essay I will present a bare outline of his legacy to "New Negro" poetic theory, literary language, cultural nationalist ideology, sexuality, and spirituality by tracing the responses to Whitman of Alain Locke, James Weldon Johnson, and Jean Toomer.

Alain Locke

Strains of unconventional politics and religiosity helped form Alain Locke's personality and made him particularly open to Whitman. His father, Pliny, for example, was raised a Hicksite Quaker and was educated in the Hicksite schools of Germantown, Pennsylvania. But his most intimate intellectual and spiritual guide was his mother, Mary Hawkins Locke, a teacher and "disciple of Felix Adler," who sent Alain to the Philadelphia Ethical Culture school in his early years.[1] While the Ethical Society was identified with racial and educational progressivism, it was also intimately intertwined with "Whitmanism" in Philadelphia and Camden. Virtually the entire Whitman circle was active in the group, particularly Horace Traubel, whose magazine, the *Conservator*, reported regularly upon Ethical Culture meetings and Adler's lectures and appearances, in addition to Whitmaniana. Indeed, members of the Philadelphia Ethical Society had been instrumental in spreading Whitman's reputation as a social and religious prophet, believing that his poetry exemplified the principles of the Ethical movement. It would be surprising if Traubel and Mary Hawkins Locke did not know each other, particularly since Traubel was regarded as a "friend" of the black community of Philadelphia and Camden, as a family friend would explain to Alain after the latter had matriculated at Harvard and joined the Ethical Society of Boston.[2] When Traubel broke with the Ethical Society in 1895, he founded the Walt Whitman Fellowship, International, on which the well-known black educator Kelly Miller would serve as a director from 1904 to 1917.[3] Thus, Whitman was identified with the cause of black equality in the Philadelphia area from Locke's earliest years.

Between 1898 and 1900, when Alain was beginning high school, he and his mother moved from Philadelphia to Camden—in fact, to 417 Stevens Street, one block from Whitman's Mickle Street home and seven doors from the row house where Whitman had lived with his brother from 1873 to 1884.[4] Whitman was still a common topic of neighborhood gossip, having been dead only six or seven years. Moreover, one of Mary's friends had been Whitman's next-door neighbor and had given him the "lap-board" on which he wrote his last letters. A 1904 letter Mary wrote to Alain at Harvard, which praises John Burroughs's *Whitman: A Study* and recounts several neighborhood stories about the poet, reveals an apparently longstanding mutual interest in "Whitman anecdotes" and books on Whitman, as well as a familiarity with sculptures and paintings of him:

> I have read "Walt Whitman" by "Burroughs" and enjoyed it. . . . Miss Button [Whitman's next-door neighbor] told an anecdote of Whitman, when an army nurse in Washington. He asked a young fellow—what he could

get him to eat—(he was almost dying) he said home-made rice pudding—
Whitman had no idea where he could get the article, but he rang several
doorbells, promiscuously, stated his need of the article, till some kindly dis-
posed person made one—he called for it and took it to the poor fellow.
Her mother was sent for, when the artist from England was painting his
picture, to come in every day and sit with W—Miss B says—the Artist did
not like it very well—and when the sculptor made that famous bust, he
made it in the yard and Mrs. B was duly mortified and stood up on some
"soap boxes" and looked over the fence—to see him at his work.[5]

This letter suggests that, even as a first-year student at Harvard, Locke was following the literature on Whitman and that his mother knew he would be interested in personal anecdotes about the famous neighborhood personality.
When she writes "and when the sculptor made that famous bust," we know
that Locke knew what bust she was talking about (Sidney Morse's). He probably knew that the "artist from England" was Herbert Gilchrist. Indeed, it
would be surprising if he had not been hearing anecdotes about Whitman
ever since he moved to Stevens Street, but the evidence no longer exists because it simply was not written down.

By the time Locke entered Harvard in 1904, Whitman had attracted the attention of the scholars who would most influence the aspiring philosopher's
further intellectual development—particularly William James and George
Santayana. Both of these men regarded Whitman as the quintessential American poet—Santayana coming to appreciate Whitman precisely during the
years that Locke was at Harvard.[6] Perhaps even more important for Locke's
personal development, however, were the new readings of Whitman as homosexual, chiefly by his British disciples.

Beginning at least in 1907, when he arrived at Oxford as a Rhodes Scholar,
Locke (who was gay) closely followed the work of writers concerned with "sex
psychology" and particularly homosexuality. Having found a community of
mind and heart among the homosexual intelligentsia of Oxford and London,
Locke came along at a time when this community had redefined Whitman in
line with their own social and sexual preferences. In Edwardian England, as
Eve Kosofsky Sedgwick has pointed out, "*Leaves of Grass* operated . . . as a
conduit from one man to another of feelings that had, in many cases, been
private or inchoate." Indeed, Whitman had a "profound and decisive" influence on the "crystallization" of a new, "broadly-based Anglo-American definition of male homosexuality."[7] Two of the most important contributors to
this redefinition were the Whitman disciples John Addington Symonds and
Edward Carpenter, who combined the exploration of "sex psychology" with

interests in democratic theory and a burgeoning literary "modernism," in the vague sense that term carried before the ascendancy of Ezra Pound and T. S. Eliot.

As Harold Blodgett noted years ago, Carpenter and Symonds believed Whitman's ideas provided a prophecy of a modern transformation in sexual relations, including the liberation and "ennobling" of homosexual desire. Inspired by Whitman, they expected "comradeship" to "regenerate political life and to cement nations." Same-sex friendship, Symonds argued, may become the engine of genuine intercultural communion, world democracy, and reciprocity between peoples—a contention that Locke's training and interests would have made immensely attractive to him. Similarly, Carpenter, known as the "Walt Whitman of England," dreamed of "bringing the Races of the world together," ending inequality between women and men, and restoring humanity to union with nature. Bolder than Symonds in justifying homosexuality, he speculated that the great prophets of the future would be "Uranians" following in Whitman's footsteps and finally realizing his vision. Both Carpenter and Symonds viewed Whitman's "adhesiveness" and religiosity as intimately intertwined, with a spiritualized homosexual love functioning as the herald of a "new social dispensation."[8]

While Locke's published writing never hints of his homosexuality or his view of Whitman's sexuality, his correspondence reveals that he shared Carpenter's *Iolaus* (1902) with Countee Cullen. Significantly, in this work Carpenter presents Whitman as the prophet of an entirely new stage of homosexual self-realization and human liberation, in effect the harbinger of a new stage in universal history. After reading the book Cullen wrote back gushingly: "I steeped myself in its charming and comprehending atmosphere. It opened up for me soul windows which had been closed; it threw a noble and evident light on what I had begun to believe, because of what the world believes, ignoble and unnatural. I laved myself in it, and thanked you a thousand times as many delightful examples appeared, for recommending it to me."[9] Without doubt, Locke's reading of Whitman through Carpenter helped Locke, Countee Cullen, and perhaps other "New Negro" writers (many of whom were gay) redefine their sexual identities. In the 1920s, Langston Hughes would write Locke prior to meeting him in person: "Do you like Walt Whitman's poetry? His 'Song of the Open Road' and the poems in 'Calamus'? I do very much." As Arnold Rampersad points out, Locke could only have interpreted Hughes's query as a way of feeling him out about his sexual orientation.[10]

On the eve of the Harlem Renaissance, Locke regarded Whitman as the first prophet of the modern age and as the only truly "American" artist, whose example all future American writers must take into account. Locke's description of "the American temperament" in his 1911 essay of that title—one of his first publications—in fact reads like a description of the Whitman persona:

> To such a temperament nothing is really trivial, and the points of contact between things are almost infinite. As soon as one examines this trait on an intellectual plane, one sees what curious laws of association govern the American mind. Its superb eclecticism, its voraciousness, its collector's instinct for facts and details, and its joyous disregard for proportion and an artificial order are still in need of adequate exposition. They impose so many handicaps from an artistic point of view that as yet no literary genius except Whitman has found it possible to accept them all.[11]

For Locke, the implied "poetics" of the American self—embodied in Whitman's linguistic eclecticism and apparent disregard for proportion and "artificial" order—has a social correlative.

Deeply impressed by philosophical pragmatism, Locke argued that despite the contradictoriness of the "American temperament," its protean and "contentless" nature, "at present the pragmatic verdict must prevail: it works quickly, effectively as a bond between men and, under the circumstances, seems to them less tyrannous than a convention of forms." The American personality "claims everything and yet refuses to identify itself with anything"— by which Locke means that it refuses to be "pinned down" to a particular social location. Moreover, "the American temperament is histrionic as the healthy child; its naive individuality is unquestionable, and because it is so plastic it knows no self-contradiction." One of the great advantages of this form of individuality is the quickness with which the subject can shift between different group identities. Thus, despite the "startling divergencies and instinctive antipathies" in American society, a corporate feeling has been achieved without the advantages of either "closely knit and socially compact groups" or racial homogeneity. Such traditional bases of national community—and authoritarianism—have been replaced by "an acute responsiveness, an intellectual sensitiveness, that are born of insatiable curiosity and a surplus of individual energy."[12] Clearly, Locke does not describe "the American temperament" as he knows it in daily interaction so much as he describes what he finds exemplary in Whitman. In doing so, he attempts to conceptualize a "cosmopolitan" selfhood consonant with the theory of cultural pluralism, the theory Horace Kallen had formulated in discussions with Locke during their years together at Oxford and that would inform Locke's whole conception of the Harlem Renaissance.[13]

Locke's views about Whitman are further revealed in his essay on Emile Verhaeren published in 1917, which argues for Verhaeren's importance by association with Whitman's. Verhaeren comes across here as Whitman's European successor, joining the American as the prophet of a new epoch. Rather than advancing a merely technical and formal experiment, each poet's style seems "inevitable," "dictated by the idea." (Locke would later use the same terms to valorize classical African art over European modernism.[14]) "This element more than any other, as with Whitman, gives Verhaeren greatness: defying classification, it puts their poetry above that of the schools. . . . The catholic response vibrating to everything, the rhapsodic fling, the cosmic emotion and exultant vitalism in the poetry of each proclaims a striking spiritual kinship between them, which if rightly interpreted establishes their common paternity in the age."[15] Locke goes on to describe these two poet-prophets as the "fathers" of literary modernism.

But what was the nature of this hard-to-define modernism? The answer to this question bears upon Locke's later hopes for the "Negro renaissance," and it differs from the definitions of modernism to which we are accustomed: "Democracy triumphant, the ethics of fervour, the religion of humanity, the cult of cosmicality, emotional pantheism, Dionysian neo-paganism,—all this and more it has been termed without a really satisfying caption. For Whitman and Verhaeren it was all one living creed—but their followers have had to cast lots and part their garments." Locke's concept of modernism is distinctly associated with a sensuous and "pagan" democratic spirituality. Out of the matrix of Whitman's and Verhaeren's prophetic works have sprung the various "isms" of modern literature, "sectarian" cults that fall short of the vision of the seers. "To Whitman belongs the credit of discovery, the sounding of these new notes; to Verhaeren, their linking up and blending into something of a harmony. The modern dithyramb, like the ancient, has a philosophy of life, a religion, back of it: thus there was always in poetry for Verhaeren [and Whitman] an almost religious and paeanizing strain."[16] True to the views of Whitman he had absorbed from many sources over many years, Locke does not differentiate the "political" from the "religious" or "spiritual" poet. Indeed, he regards Whitman's spirituality as indivisible from his social and aesthetic significance.

By the 1920s, Locke believed the unique role of "the Negro" in American civilization to lie in the development of "indigenous" spiritual and cultural possibilities, complementing the more materialistic contributions of Anglo-American culture. African Americans would provide what Whitman had emphatically called for in *Democratic Vistas*.[17] Whereas European Americans had been stunted in their spiritual development by "pioneering" and the pursuit of wealth, African Americans—denied both geographic and social mobility—had developed spiritual compensations and incarnated them in the most "indigenous" cultural products of the New World. They were destined to be America's artists. "The Negro's predisposition toward the artistic, promising to culminate in a control and mastery of the spiritual and mystic as contrasted with the mechanical and practical aspects of life, makes him a spiritually needed and culturally desirable factor in American life."[18] The "Negro" would provide exactly what Whitman had looked for from the future American poet.

It is worthwhile to notice the correspondences between the qualities Locke most revered in what he now called the "folk temperament" and the qualities he had earlier found in Whitman's "American temperament"—"a mysticism that is not ascetic and of the cloister, a realism that is not sordid but shot through with homely, appropriate poetry."[19] Locke admired this temperament for "its irresistibly sensuous, spontaneously emotional, affably democratic and naive spirit"—the true promise of "Negro" art and the project of Whitman's. His approval of the strain of "paganism" or "pantheism" in Countee Cullen's work recalls the "neo-paganism" and "Dionysian" quality he praised in Whitman's and Verhaeren's poetry. And in regard to Langston Hughes, Locke emphasized his "ecstatic sense of kinship with even the most common and lowly folk," the poet's ability to discover "the epic quality of collective strength and beauty" in the masses.[20] Differentiating Hughes from the "dialect school," Locke noted that "Hughes brings to his portrayal of his folk not the ragged provincialism of a minstrel but the descriptive detachment of a Vachel Lindsay and a Sandburg and promises the democratic sweep and universality of a Whitman." Hughes's approach to folk materials, Locke believed, traded on the Whitman legacy at the same time that it grew from and extended African American expressive traditions. This, indeed, is a point that Hughes's own biography and testimony overwhelmingly confirm.[21]

Clearly, many of the qualities Locke most valued and encouraged in black poetry as the "dean" or "midwife" of the Negro Renaissance he had previously meditated upon in relation to Whitman's work as he developed his own orientation to aesthetics and cultural theory generally—well before he had acknowledged anything worthwhile in the black vernacular tradition. Thus, his ideas about and prescriptions for black literature in the years of the Harlem Renaissance often echo the terms of his concept of Whitman. In "Art or Propaganda" (1928), for example, he urges black writers to remain "self-contained," optimistically proclaiming, "I believe we are at that interesting moment when the prophet becomes the poet and when prophecy becomes the expressive song, the chant of fulfillment."[22] The kind of prophecy characterized here is what Locke responded to during his youth while reading Whitman's self-expressive "chants."

James Weldon Johnson

James Weldon Johnson had become increasingly dissatisfied with black "dialect" verse as exemplified by Paul Laurence Dunbar when he came across *Leaves of Grass*. "I was engulfed and submerged by the book, and set floundering," he would write in his autobiography. Whitman made him realize the "artificiality of the conventionalized Negro dialect poetry." Not even Dunbar "had been able to discard [the] stereotyped properties of minstrel-stage dialect." [23] Johnson has been accused unjustly of abandoning "dialect" for "standard English" in a misguided attempt to "elevate the race" in the minds of whites. [24] On the contrary, he accused the dialect poets, unlike the oral "folk" poets, of addressing themselves to an "outside audience" and accepting that audience's discriminations between "levels" of poetic discourse: "The psychological attitude of the poets writing in the dialect and that of the folk artists faced in different directions: because the latter, although working in the dialect, sought only to express themselves to their own group" rather than to cultural "outsiders." [25] Johnson's argument was not with the adequacy of black English vernacular. Rather, as Langston Hughes and Sterling Brown would recognize, he was after an idiomatic vernacular poetics, and he recognized that a modernist break with the "dialect" tradition was the only route to a new, more variously self-expressive, black poetry. Indeed, Johnson's break with Dunbar—who was unimpressed with Whitman—helped make possible the experiments of Langston Hughes and Sterling Brown, who could nonetheless appreciate the importance of Dunbar's achievements.

It is interesting that, like Hughes, Johnson tried his hand at Whitmanesque free verse before returning to the black oral tradition, believing that "the Negro poet in the United States, for poetry which he wishes to give a distinctively racial tone and color, needs now an instrument of greater range than dialect." [26] The traditional form of dialect poetry, after all, had been authorized from "above." The problem was not merely that it was associated with the dehumanizing conventions of the minstrel show but that it depended upon an implicit separation between "high" and "low" speech. Hence the strict distinction between the two-thirds of Dunbar's poems in "literary English"—for which he primarily wanted to be known—and the one-third in "dialect" (both "black" and "white" dialect). Furthermore, the distinction between the formally educated "poet" and the "uneducated" dialect speaker is implicitly emphasized in poems fitting, say, an antebellum sermon into conventional meters and rhymes of the English tradition. Langston Hughes and Sterling Brown may have learned a lot from Dunbar, but on the whole their work derives from a different orientation to the "poetic," an orientation arrived at by a swerve like Johnson's from Dunbar and precipitated by their own encounters with *Leaves of Grass*.

Whitman had not depended on an exoticizing orthography to create a "speakerly text"; instead, he had broken down the boundaries between racy contemporary speech and "literature," boundaries essential to genteel "dialect" poetry—indeed, to Johnson's own poetry before his reading of Whitman. Moreover, Johnson noted that black preachers themselves—among the most powerful wordcrafters and image-makers of the "race"—did not employ "dialect" alone in their sermons but rather a more grandiloquent speech that "was really a fusion of Negro idioms with Bible English." "They were all saturated with the sublime phraseology of the Hebrew prophets and steeped in the idioms of King James English."[27] Readers of Whitman should notice some kinship here.

If a stock element of the minstrel show was a travesty of black oratory, ridiculing precisely the sort of syncretic linguistic feats described by Johnson, Whitman undermines such travesty, syncretically merging the colloquial and the sublime (a practice for which he was, likewise, often ridiculed). This is a strategy to which Johnson, Hughes, Toomer, Hurston, and Brown all caught on. Thus, it is only too appropriate that Johnson's first poems after his transformed view of the vernacular would be inspired by a dominant form of oral black religious expression, the sermon—rendered not in traditional meters and rhymes but in a free verse form with each line corresponding to a breath. As C. Carroll Hollis has shown, Whitman strove mightily to develop an "oral" and "speakerly" style with religious and theatrical, even ritualistic, effects. (Portions of "Song of Myself" have even been compared to Haitian vodun ceremonies.)[28] And among the important influences upon Whitman had been both Old Testament prophets and popular preachers, such as Father Taylor of Boston, who used a vernacular style attuned to their working-class audiences. Whitman wanted, like the black preachers Johnson admired, to move his audience to ecstasy.

Jean Toomer

The linguistic as well as religious and ecstatic or "mystical" side of Whitman would appeal strongly to Jean Toomer, for whom Whitman was a constant point of reference. When, in about 1919, Toomer began seriously to train himself as a writer, he was deeply under the influence of Whitman's example.[29] From Whitman he shortly turned to Goethe's *Wilhelm Meister*, which confirmed his sense of vocation. Then, wrote Toomer, "I returned to Whitman because he was of America, and I felt he had something to give me in terms of the American world. I spent days in the library reading not only all he had written, but all that had been written about him. The rest of my time I practiced writing."[30] Toomer laved himself in *Leaves of Grass*, *Democratic Vistas*, *An American Primer*, and no doubt studies by Burroughs, Bucke, Traubel, and the other early disciples; then he would go home and write his own leaves.

In a manuscript entitled "Whitman, and the Use of Current Popular Idiom," Toomer uses Whitman's *American Primer* and "Slang in America" as "springboards" to an argument about the potential uses of the vernacular in modern literature. He quotes "Slang in America" at length: " 'Slang, profoundly considered, is the lawless germinal element, below all words and sentences, and behind all poetry, and proves a certain perennial rankness and protestantism in speech.' " "Song of Myself," continues Toomer, makes "deeply creative use" of slang, combining it with elements of traditional "high" culture in a way that jars the reader's expectations and throws cultural hierarchies into question. Significantly, he focuses upon the moment in the poem when Whitman "measures" himself against the "elder religions":

> This poem, it will be noted, does something more than use slang for itself. It is, I believe, inevitably used to express the content and contrast contained in this poem. Granted that Whitman wished to bring into relief his own contemporary position as contrasted with the ancient or historical theologies, how better do this than by juxtaposing such words as Kronos and lithographing, buying drafts and Isis? Here then we have Whitman in a profound use of slang. This characteristic has its negative significance in that it will serve to hold in check a superficial use of slang. And, positively, it channels a creative fusion of popular idiom.[31]

Toomer's work exemplifies his own modernist attempt to fuse slang, vernacular, and "standard" diction to bring into relief a new historical, racial, and religious position. He thought of himself as developing a "classic American prose" in the process of serving the nation's "spiritual ripening." Fascinated by the intercultural urban transformation of language, he resisted the romantic enshrinement of so-called authentic black folk speech. Forfeiting the desire for "pure" racial origins, linguistic or otherwise, he built for the future with all the mismatched materials at hand. And in this bricolage he consciously extended the legacy of Whitman. *Cane* was hailed immediately in *Crisis* and *Opportunity* as the harbinger of a new movement in African American letters and has been considered by many ever since as the greatest single achievement of that movement, not least for its linguistic experimentation—despite the fact that Toomer apparently never considered himself a "Negro" author.

Toomer's linguistic experiment followed his commitment to American cultural nationalism, for which, again, Whitman was the central icon. He explicitly mentions Whitman in "Box Seat" in a context suggesting the bard's function as a role model for the protagonist. Dan Moore ponders the experience of a sphinxlike former slave in Washington and seeks in his eyes the imprinted image of America's "wound-dresser"/prophet: "He saw Walt—old man, did you see Walt Whitman? Did you see Walt Whitman! Strange force that drew me to him. And I went up to see. . . . I told him to look into the heavens. He did, and smiled. I asked him if he knew what that rumbling is that comes up from the ground." The "rumbling," we know from an earlier passage, is the sound of "a new-world Christ . . . coming up," born of the "powerful underground races." [32]

Unquestionably, Toomer thought of himself as Whitman's successor in the American prophet/healer's role. He felt in 1923 (the year *Cane* was published) that the revolt against puritanism and materialism had run its course and that great creation must move beyond protest and "inspired propaganda" to that "abundance which includes acceptance. . . . When I have made the path easy and in all ways to be desired, what strength will you show then in taking it." If this passage echoes the early Whitman's exhortations to "shoulder your duds" and take to the American road, another echoes the "later Whitman" in prescribing a literary shift from social critique to a "balance and inclusion. . . . Starting from the premise that an adjustment, adjustment in the sense of an acceptance of, and a healthy functioning from the physical environment, and a stirring towards a desired spiritual fulfillment, are fundamental to the life of any nation." The essay calls for writers to follow Whitman's lead. [33]

The influence of theories of "cosmic consciousness" (which appealed to the Waldo Frank circle because they answered the perceived American need for "spiritual ripening" [34]) began to grow upon Toomer even as he was composing *Cane* and came under the influence of A. R. Orage, a chief sidekick of G. I. Gurdjieff who introduced Gurdjieff's ideas to New York intellectuals in the teens and twenties and then recruited Toomer to proselytize among the Harlem intelligentsia. Wrote one observer, "The 'cosmic consciousness' of Walt Whitman was a great theme of his." [35] P. D. Ouspensky's *Tertium Organum*, which influenced both Toomer and Hart Crane, among others, also borrowed from Bucke's theories and his views of Whitman. [36] Certainly, the more mystical passages of *Cane*, as Rudolph Byrd has argued, are compatible with the theories that would shortly monopolize Toomer's attention. [37]

Toomer apparently never stopped identifying with Whitman. At various points in his unpublished autobiography, "Earth-Being," when an event or remembered scene brings up an association with Whitman or a hint of Toomer's destiny, he connects the two. At other points he launches into clumsy Whit-manesque catalogs, blatantly imitative.[38] Indeed, the inspiring figure of Whitman as role model and American prophet is a crucial connecting link between the various phases of Toomer's disjunctive career. Even after he abandoned the "Gurdjieff work," in the final period of his life he would con-tinue his spiritual seeking in Whitman's natal religious denomination—the Society of Friends.

In conclusion, broadly speaking, the "New Negro" authors who saw them-selves as descendants of Whitman came to believe that African American culture offered precisely the answer to Whitman's prayers, that it filled the void Whitman's white descendants continually decried in their fulminations against the emotionally desiccated, spiritless America of the puritan and the pioneer, against the yawning chasm between the highbrow and the low. Moreover, this position was also typical of the white authors and critics—many of them Whitman disciples—who were most closely allied to the move-ment, who read the manuscripts and reviewed the books of black authors, edited the magazines and anthologies through which their work reached an interracial public, and wrote for the black magazines that showcased the Negro Renaissance. In other words, the early canonization of Whitman in the United States and the rise of black literary modernism were intimately interrelated and complementary developments. Moreover, the very advances for which even its critics credit the "New Negro" movement—generally, for advancing a distinctly African American tradition in literature—are develop-ments in which the impact of Whitman was critical.

Hence, if we accept the validity of recent readings of Whitman's texts as fos-tering a white imperialist self and ideology, complicit with white American hegemony—and I think such readings have merit—then we are left with the paradox that, overall, the effects of his work in the early twentieth century—on African American authors, at least—emphatically contradicted the ideo-logical "message" that recent critics have elucidated. This is as attributable to the interests, needs, and imaginations of his readers and the contexts in which they read him as to the ideological ambiguities of his poetry. James Weldon Johnson recognized the importance of this point when he misquoted Whit-man to conclude a eulogy for Julius Rosenwald at Fisk University in 1932:

> All architecture is what you do to it when you look upon it.
> Did you think it was in the white or gray stone?
> Or in the lines of the arches and cornices?
> All music is what awakes from you when you are reminded by the instruments.
> It is not the violins and the cornets,

It is not the oboe nor the beating drums,
Nor the score of the baritone singer singing his sweet romanza,
Nor that of the men's chorus,
Nor that of the women's chorus,
It is nearer and farther than they.[39]

The power and beauty of the artwork are to be found, Johnson reminds his black collegiate audience, by way of Whitman, in the uses to which one puts it in one's life. To argue for the pervasive impact of Whitman's legacy on the Harlem Renaissance is not, then, to attempt to "save" Whitman from examinations of his racism or to try to contain racial difference within American sameness—but it is to insist on a "mulatto" aspect of American traditions that coexists with and continually revitalizes their multicultural distinctiveness. And it is to demonstrate the need to go beyond ideological interrogation toward diverse historical investigations of the complex, productive, and often ironic or scandalous interrelations between ostensibly separate "racial"/cultural traditions in the United States.

NOTES

1. Michael R. Winston, "Locke, Alain," in Rayford W. Logan and Michael R. Winston, eds., *The Dictionary of American Negro Biography* (New York: Norton, 1982), 398–404; Eugene C. Holmes, "Alain L. Locke and the Adult Education Movement," *Journal of Negro Education* 30 (Winter 1965): 5; Douglas K. Stafford, "Alaine Locke: The Child, the Man, and the People," *Journal of Negro Education* 30 (Winter 1961): 26. Stafford calls Mary Locke "one of the earliest followers of Felix Adler" and notes that, "aside from the Society of Friends [the Ethical Society] was in many ways the most liberal of the respectable organizations open to the Negro, explicitly providing for his participation in all its projects" (26–27). The research for this article was pursued as part of a larger project entitled "American Cultural Nationalism and the Harlem Renaissance," which was funded in 1989–1990 by a National Endowment for the Humanities fellowship.

2. William C. Bolivar to Alain Locke, February 14, 1908, Alain Locke Correspondence Files, Alain Locke Papers, Moorland-Springarn Research Center, Howard University.

3. See the *Walt Whitman Fellowship Papers* for these years. Miller was a member of the organization from its founding in 1895 and addressed its first meeting with his essay "What Walt Whitman Means to the Negro," which I have discussed in "Whitman and the Black Poet: Kelly Miller's Speech to the Walt Whitman Fellowship," *American Literature* 61 (1989): 46–58.

4. Thanks to Tony Gutwein, librarian at the Camden County Historical Society, for tracing these facts for me.

5. Mary Hawkins Locke to Alain Locke, April 12, 1905, Alain Locke–Mary Hawkins Locke Correspondence Files, Box 2, Alain Locke Papers. The Miss Button referred to in the letter was a painter and art teacher who donated the drawing board that Mary Davis (Whitman's housemate and housekeeper) converted into a tray for Whitman to write on during the last weeks of his life (Elizabeth Leavitt Keller, *Walt Whitman in Mickle Street* [New York: Mitchell Kennerley, 1921], 168). The episode with the artists mentioned in the letter took place in the summer of 1887, when Sidney Morse was working on a bust of the poet and Herbert Gilchrist showed up from England at the same time to do Whitman's portrait. The story is vividly told in Keller (76–81).

6. See Kenneth M. Price, "Imagining Whitman at Harvard," *Whitman and Tradition* (New Haven: Yale University Press, 1990).

7. Eve Kosofsky Sedgwick, *Between Men: English Literature and Male Homosocial Desire* (New York: Columbia University Press, 1985), 205, 203.

8. Harold W. Blodgett, *Walt Whitman in England* (Ithaca: Cornell University Press, 1934), 207.

9. Countee Cullen to Alain Locke, March 3, 1923, Alain Locke Correspondence Files, Alain Locke Papers.

10. Langston Hughes to Alain Locke, n.d. (circa May 1923), Alain Locke Correspondence Files, Alain Locke Papers. Locke's sexual pursuit of Hughes, in part provoked by this letter, is discussed in Arnold Rampersad, *The Life of Langston Hughes* (New York: Oxford University Press, 1986), 1:69.

11. Alain Locke, "The American Temperament," in Jeffrey C. Stewart, ed., *The Critical Temper of Alain Locke* (New York: Garland, 1983), 404. The essay was first published in the *North American Review* 194 (August 1911): 262–270.

12. Locke, "The American Temperament," *Critical Temper*, 401, 403.

13. For an account of Kallen's and Locke's interactions vis-à-vis cultural pluralism, see Werner Sollors, "A Critique of Pure Pluralism," in Sacvan Bercovitch, ed., *Reconstructing American Literary History* (Cambridge: Harvard University Press, 1986), 263–273.

14. Locke, "African Art: Classic Style," *Critical Temper*, 151.

15. Locke, "Emile Verhaeren," *Critical Temper*, 37.

16. Ibid.

17. Alain Locke, ed., *The New Negro* (1925; rpt., New York: Atheneum, 1970), 15–16.

18. Locke, "The Negro's Contribution to American Art and Literature" (1928), *Critical Temper*, 448.

19. Locke, "Beauty Instead of Ashes" (1928), *Critical Temper*, 25.

20. Locke, "Color—A Review" (1926), *Critical Temper*, 39–40.

21. Locke, "The Poetry of Negro Life" (1927), *Critical Temper*, 47. George B. Hutchinson, "Langston Hughes and the 'Other' Whitman," in Robert K. Martin, ed., *The Continuing Presence of Walt Whitman: The Life after the Life* (Iowa City: University of Iowa Press, 1992), 16–27.

22. Locke, "Art or Propaganda," *Critical Temper*, 27.

23. James Weldon Johnson, *Along This Way* (New York: Viking, 1933), 158–159. An excellent discussion of the differences between Dunbar and Johnson can be found in Myron Simon, "Dunbar and Dialect Poetry," in Jay Martin, ed., *A Singer in the Dawn: Reinterpretations of Paul Laurence Dunbar* (New York: Dodd, Mead, 1975), 144–154.

24. Perhaps the most influential recent statement of this view is that of Henry Louis Gates Jr., in *Figures in Black: Words, Signs, and the "Racial" Self* (New York: Oxford University Press, 1987), 184.

25. Johnson, *Along This Way*, 158–159.

26. James Weldon Johnson, "Preface," in *God's Trombones: Seven Negro Sermons in Verse* (1927; rpt., New York: Viking, 1942), 8.

27. Johnson, "Preface," 9.

28. C. Carroll Hollis, *Language and Style in Leaves of Grass* (Baton Rouge: Louisiana State University Press, 1983); Robin Magowan, "The Horse of the Gods: Possession in 'Song of Myself,'" *Walt Whitman Review* 15 (1969): 67–76.

29. Just about the time Toomer "discovered" Whitman, his grandfather sold the family home and sent him $600, which Toomer decided to live on, believing he was at a turning point in his life. Toomer quit his job and devoted himself full-time to music and literature. See "Outline of the Story of an Autobiography," 43–44, Box 20, Folder 515, Jean Toomer Papers, Collection of American Literature, Beinecke Rare Book and Manuscript Library, Yale University.

30. Toomer, "Outline," 43–44.

31. Toomer, Typescript, Box 48, Folder 1,009, 1–2, Jean Toomer Papers.

32. Jean Toomer, *Cane*, ed. Darwin T. Turner (New York: Norton, 1988), 68, 65.

33. Ms. fragment, Box 48, Folder 1,010, Jean Toomer Papers. Though the fragment is undated, its emphasis upon the need for fulfillment in American literature and for a movement beyond protest against America indicates that it comes from the period before, during, or immediately after the composition of *Cane*, for Toomer was to abandon interest in such topics by 1924. Moreover, about the time *Cane* came out, he was planning a volume that would follow the lines suggested in the fragment.

34. James Webb, *The Harmonious Circle: The Lives and Work of G. I. Gurdjieff, P. D. Ouspensky, and Their Followers* (New York: Putnam, 1980), 275.

35. Gerald Cumberland, *Set Down in Malice* (New York: Brentano's, 1919), 132.

36. One manuscript reader immediately noticed the similarities between Toomer's ideas and those of Bucke. Anonymous rejection letter, Box 17, Folder 472, Jean Toomer Papers.

37. See Rudolph P. Byrd, *Jean Toomer's Years With Gurdjieff: Portrait of an Artist, 1923–1936* (Athens: University of Georgia Press, 1990).

38. See, for example, "Earth-Being," typescript second draft, Book III, 129, 19–20, Box 12, Folder 386, Jean Toomer Papers. Late in his life, when speculating upon how long it might be before the "American" race would come to fruition, he would write, "May be it will befall my vision as it befell Walt Whitman's in that, just as I today can see no large signs of the country developing along his lines, so an individual one hundred years hence may see no large signs of the country having developed along my lines" (Preface 3 to Book X, 9, Jean Toomer Papers).

39. James Weldon Johnson, *The Shining Life* (n.p., 1932).

Whitman, Dos Passos,
and "Our Storybook Democracy"

OR AMERICAN literary figures, becoming a literary modernist very
often coincided with—and was enabled by—a rejection of the genteel
tradition and a turning toward Walt Whitman as part of a newly usable
past. Studying John Dos Passos's response to Whitman clarifies how one particular writer conceived of himself as an American modernist and committed
himself to the diversity of this culture. Dos Passos's career-long engagement
with Whitman—especially the consistency of this engagement—is intriguing
because of Dos Passos's extreme political shift—from being a fellow traveller
with the Communist party to being a Goldwater Republican.

Dos Passos read Whitman extensively and believed, as he said, that "a great
deal of the . . . slant of my work comes from that vein in the American tradition."[1] Dos Passos's first (commercially) published essay, "Against American
Literature" (1916), sees Whitman as the hope for the nation's literature. The
poet is invoked, echoed, alluded to, quoted at length, or directly discussed in
virtually every one of Dos Passos's significant works, including *Streets of Night,
Manhattan Transfer*, the three volumes of *U.S.A.*, *Midcentury*, and *Century's
Ebb*. Beginning to end, from the Left or from the Right, he maintained his
fascination with *Leaves of Grass* and *Democratic Vistas*.

Dos Passos's interest in Whitman affected the form and techniques of his
most famous work, *U.S.A.*, in the fusion of formal literary categories and in
the mixing of "poetry" and "prose" to create an effective rhythmic impact
conveying a sense of conviction and urgency. More specifically, the Camera
Eye sections draw from Whitman "an emphasis on grammatical and verbal

parallelism as the basic structural device within an unmetrical form,"[2] and the
Biography sections draw from *Leaves* their reliance on the long line movement
with detail building on detail.[3] Rather than pursuing these stylistic affinities, I
want to consider how Whitman helped Dos Passos at a more fundamental
level define himself as a person and as an American writer.

To understand Dos Passos's initial interest in Whitman we should recall
how the poet was routinely characterized in the genteel culture surrounding
Harvard, the culture which nourished Dos Passos. Just before and during Dos
Passos's years at Choate Preparatory School and at Harvard (1907–1916), various New Englanders wrote histories of American literature indicating that
they regarded Whitman's democratic inclusiveness as un-American. For example, one history claimed that the poet was "less American than any other of
our conspicuous writers."[4] Another noted that Whitman's lack of popularity
made it impossible to regard the poet as "representative."[5] Yet another observed that Whitman's "democracy . . . is the least native which has ever found
voice in our country."[6] It is no wonder that Whitman appealed to disaffected
Harvard students such as Dos Passos, because the poet offered hope of freeing
literature from the overrefinement of an elite class and suggested—because
Whitman had been depicted as if he were an unassimilated, slightly suspicious
immigrant—that the literary realm might soon include more than blue-
blooded patricians.

Dos Passos was situated so as to understand all sides of the debate concerning Whitman's "Americanness." His "Against American Literature" praises
Whitman's rejection of gentility and raises the issue of ethnicity explicitly:
"Walt Whitman failed to reach the people he intended to, and aroused only a
confused perturbation and the sort of moral flutter experienced by a primly
dressed old bachelor when a ruddy smiling Italian, smelling of garlic and
sweat, plumps down beside him in the street car."[7] What perspective does Dos
Passos take here—the old bachelor's or the smiling Italian's? Dos Passos was
refined, wealthy, and privileged, and he was a second-generation Portuguese
American. Dos Passos's grandfather was a Portuguese-speaking shoemaker;
Dos Passos's father—a quintessential American success story—rose to be a famous corporate lawyer, a personal friend of President McKinley, a staunch de-
fender of imperialism, and the author of, among other books, *The Anglo-
Saxon Century and the Unification of the English Speaking People.* The oddity
and irony of this book are perhaps exceeded only by a casual remark made by
Dos Passos's mother (and recorded in the autobiographical Camera Eye section 3 of *U.S.A.*): "One night Mother was so frightened on account of all the
rifleshots but it was allright turned out to be nothing but a little shooting
they'd been only shooting a greaser that was all."[8]

Dos Passos had an unusual childhood. Because he was the illegitimate son of John Randolph Dos Passos and Lucy Madison, John Madison (as the boy was known until the age of fourteen) spent much of his time abroad. There his parents could travel openly together. It is possible to see Dos Passos's rebelliousness as expressing hostility toward his father.[9] "I wished I was home but I hadn't any home," he says in *The 42nd Parallel.*[10] Homelessness was at the root of his emotional life and shaped the pattern of his quest for self-identity. As Blanche Gelfant notes, "The passionate attention he gives to the contemporary social scene reveals his search for some group to which he can belong."[11]

For Dos Passos, committing himself to America was a matter of choice, as the title of his novel *Chosen Country* suggests. At Harvard, his foreign accent, swarthy look, and continental mannerisms set him apart from other students—a separation marked even in his nickname, "Frenchy." His early stories show uncertainty in cultural focus: his settings are almost always foreign, though his favorite protagonist was a naive, well-educated Brahmin.[12] Yet ultimately, as he responded to strikes by workers and the onset of World War I, he came to hate Harvard and Brahmin ideals:

> And what are we fit for when they turn us out of Harvard? We're too intelligent to be successful businessmen and we haven't the sand or the energy to be anything else—
>
> Until Widener is blown up and A. Lawrence Lowell assassinated and the Business School destroyed and its site sowed with salt—no good will come out of Cambridge.

On another occasion, thinking back to the circumstances of World War I, he asked why Harvard graduates were such a "milky lot." And why "couldn't one of us have refused to register and gone to jail and made a general ass of himself?" Nobody had guts, he concluded, except the East Side Jews and a "few of the isolated 'foreigners' whose opinions so shock the *New York Times*." These people, so real and alive, show the emptiness of "all the nice young men" turned out by these "stupid colleges of ours," these "instillers of stodginess—every form of bastard culture, middle-class snobbism."[13]

As a youth, Dos Passos had interacted infrequently with "muckers." These few interactions, however, were telling: they introduced him to his opposite or double and offered the possibilities of another social role. As Dos Passos remarked in 1918: "I've always wanted to divest myself of my class and monied background";[14] his interest in Whitman also served this goal. The "mucker" and the vagabond offered Dos Passos a "romanticized and readymade identity" that seemed whole and vital; he dreamed that by adopting external features of the lower class (clothes, speech, habits, vagabondage) he could assume a new identity.[15]

Thus, it is no accident that Dos Passos chose in *U.S.A.* to identify himself with Whitman. In this trilogy, Dos Passos's hostility toward his father and his turn toward Whitman appear at the outset. I believe the opening of *U.S.A.* is a calculated revision of his father's *The Anglo-Saxon Century*. The father, in his opening pages, praises Anglo-Saxon dominance and the glories of British activities in the Boer War and of American efforts in the Philippines; the son opens his trilogy by considering these exact same matters. Yet the opening newsreel of *U.S.A.* marks its difference by insisting on the costs to the soul that such imperial power brings. Dos Passos presents scraps of newspaper stories that speak of America's replacing England as the leading industrial and imperialist nation. In *U.S.A.*, "celebration" of the American century is inseparable from reckoning with the deaths in the Philippines. As America comes to power, it begins to die.

The Camera Eye section of *U.S.A.* that immediately follows deals with a revolutionary moment. Written from a subjective point of view, rendering a memory of Dos Passos's childhood, this section provides more evidence of his debt to Whitman's democratic vision of humanity in the leaf of grass.[16] The boy's first recorded experience is of fleeing with his mother down a street in Belgium from a crowd that mistakenly believes they are British. Dos Passos feels keenly the effects of British imperialism in the Boer War, the effects of unjust persecution; as he flees, he focuses on the fact that "you have to tread on too many grassblades the poor hurt green tongues shrink under your feet."[17] Whitman's "metaphor of the grass," Lois Hughson notes, "expresses his ability to see his self as proxy for all selves which are, at the level of experience he is invoking, identical to his, and so virtually to abolish otherness."[18] The vision of Dos Passos, on the other hand, does not abolish all otherness. To his way of thinking, power inevitably brings gradation, the dominance of one requiring the submission of another.

Throughout the trilogy, Dos Passos establishes a division between political power and the true soul of America, which is seen to reside precisely in those who are powerless. In 1932 Dos Passos wrote, "We have had a proletarian literature for years, and are about the only country that has. It hasn't been a revolutionary literature, exactly, though it seems to me that Walt Whitman's a hell of a lot more revolutionary than any Russian poet I've ever heard of."[19] Yet when Dos Passos links himself with Whitman in Camera Eye 46 of *U.S.A.*, he is overcome by misgivings:

> you suddenly falter ashamed flush red break out in sweat why not tell these
> men stamping in the wind that we stand on a quicksand? that doubt is
> the whetstone of understanding is too hard hurts instead of urging picket

John D. Rockefeller the bastard if the cops knock your blocks off it's all for
the advancement of the human race while I go home after a drink and a hot
meal and read (with some difficulty in the Loeb library trot) the epigrams
of Martial and ponder the course of history and what leverage might pry
the owners loose from power and bring back (I too Walt Whitman) our
storybook democracy.[20]

He feels shame at the futility of what he is asking those lacking his advantages
to do. He is haunted in this passage—too extensive to quote in full—by his
money and by his continuing interest in money. Finally, despite his self-
contempt and the impracticality implied in the epithet "storybook," he re-
dedicates himself to a Whitmanian democracy in which the true Americans
are the poor, the dispossessed, the vagabonds.[21] The true Americans are also
the Isadora Duncans and the Frank Lloyd Wrights of the world. Both are explicitly linked to Whitman, as, for example, when Dos Passos says of the
dancer: "She was an American like Walt Whitman; the murdering rulers of
the world were not her people; . . . artists were not on the side of the ma-
chineguns; she was an American in a Greek tunic; she was for the people."[22]

Behind the rage and the apparent proletarian sympathies of *U.S.A.* is a conservative desire to restore what many contemporary radicals wanted to move beyond.[23] Dos Passos's analysis is ultimately more mythic than historical, resting
on a view of an idyllic golden age reminiscent of Whitman's yearnings for primal purity in "Passage to India." The novelist looked back to the time of the
founders, to a time before America's dominant role in world affairs, and his goal,
like Whitman's, is to return to original innocence and insight, to a "storybook
democracy" of justice and equality, of freedom and opportunity. Such a belief in
a golden age, whatever shortcomings it has as history, contributed to the "fervid
characterization of the world of power that he gives us as well as for the fidelity
to the voice of the submerged groups which is one of the triumphs of *U.S.A.*"[24]

After the execution of Sacco and Vanzetti—so important to the writer's
career and so pivotal in the trilogy—Dos Passos made clear that Vanzetti's
eloquence and intelligence and his being an Italian American immigrant pun-
ished for his beliefs affected him deeply. As Dos Passos saw it, Sacco and
Vanzetti were executed for being "anarchist wops." Dos Passos, too, was an
"anarchist wop."[25] Sacco and Vanzetti were versions of himself—simultaneously stigmatized outsiders and believers in the American dream of a better
life.[26] At the crisis point of the Sacco and Vanzetti ordeal he cries out in anguish over their fate but also in admiration for what they had achieved:

America our nation has been beaten by strangers who have turned our language inside out who have taken the clean words our fathers spoke and
made them slimy and foul

>   their hired men sit on the judge's bench they sit back with their feet on
>   the tables under the dome of the State House they are ignorant of our
>   beliefs they have the dollars the guns the armed forces the powerplants
>   they have built the electricchair and hired the executioner to throw the
>   switch
>   all right we are two nations . . .
>   but do they know that the old words of the immigrants are being renewed
>   in blood and agony tonight do they know that the old American speech of
>   the haters of oppression is new tonight in the mouth of an old woman from
>   Pittsburgh of a husky boilermaker from Frisco who hopped freights clear
>   from the Coast to come here in the mouth of a Back Bay social worker in
>   the mouth of an Italian printer of a hobo from Arkansas   the language
>   of the beaten nation is not forgotten in our ears tonight
>   the men in the deathhouse made the old words new before they died[27]

The strangers, here, are not the immigrants but those who have corrupted
American language, principles, ideals. Through the three volumes of *U.S.A.*,
Dos Passos undergoes a range of experience (recorded in the Camera Eye sections), maturing in insight until he achieves recognition that his role—a role
he shares with Whitman and with Sacco and Vanzetti—is to be a reviver of
democracy.

In the three and a half decades following the final *U.S.A.* volume (*The Big
Money* was published in 1936), Dos Passos, as I have indicated, shifted to the
right. This shift, dramatic enough, to be sure, is often made to seem more
thoroughgoing than it actually was since there was always a conservative core
to Dos Passos's thinking. Clearly, however, Dos Passos did become deeply dis-
illusioned with the Left, stemming in large measure from the betrayal and
murder of his leftist friend José Robles by the Loyalist forces fighting Franco
in the Spanish Civil War.

Dos Passos's final novel, *Century's Ebb*, published posthumously in 1975,
was originally titled *Century's End* in draft, suggesting the mood of this late
work. Dos Passos seems consciously to have made it more upbeat through
revision. Thus, the first segment of the novel, initially titled "Warnings
from Walt Whitman," became "Strike up for a New World." In the course of
writing and in renewed engagement with the sense of promise conveyed by
Whitman's poetry, Dos Passos managed to transform what began as a "last for-
lorn chronicle of despair" into a moving and—despite a few excesses—a be-
lievably mixed account of American life.[28]

The structure of *Century's Ebb* makes Whitman the touchstone of value.
Whitman's views of the American people establish the beginning for the

century discussed in this novel—that is, from roughly the mid-nineteenth to the mid-twentieth century—and in many respects, Whitman's views stand as the apex.[29] Overall, *Century's Ebb* attempts to answer the question, "are we indeed men worthy of the name, Walt Whitman, in these 'years of the modern, years of the unperformed'?"[30] For an answer, Dos Passos juxtaposes glimpses of modern American culture and the lines in which Whitman renders his America a hundred years earlier. In *Century's Ebb*, Dos Passos explores the depths and summits of American life, ranging from the coming of the assassins (accounts of Lee Harvey Oswald and the killing of Malcolm X) to a ringing endorsement of scientific discoveries in hybrid corn and of human courage and mastery of matter in the moon landing.

The entire novel is addressed to Whitman. The opening eight pages are devoted to a thumbnail biography of the poet—the type of biography familiar to readers of *U.S.A.* In the second part of the novel, "Life's Gymnasium," Dos Passos explores the reasons for the changes between Whitman's affirmation of the future and Orwell's *1984*. The title of the section comes from Whitman's plea in *Democratic Vistas* that the country counteract what has happened (already, by 1870) to the promise of young America.[31] In fact, each of the five sections of this work begins from a Whitmanian norm and then proceeds to evaluate modern American life.

The key narrative strand in the work involves Jay Pignatelli. Despite his "deplorable opinions" and his being out of step with his culture, Jay Pignatelli "*is* the American hero toward whom Dos Passos has been working."[32] There is much that is admirable about his optimism, courage, and loyalty to principle. And his similarities to Whitman are worth emphasizing. He has lost more than one position because he followed his own convictions. Moreover, he has another characteristic Dos Passos associated with Whitman: "an offhand down-underneath reverence toward the idiosyncrasy of the divergent, various, incalculable men, women and children who make up the human race."[33] For both men, the most ordinary being might contain the divine spark. It is sometimes argued that, late in his career, Dos Passos produced his harshest satires; yet it is also true that in creating Pignatelli/Dos Passos/Whitman, the novelist found the possibility of a final affirmation, found renewed hope for both self and country.

NOTES

1. John Dos Passos to William H. Bond, March 26, 1938, in Townsend Ludington, ed., *The Fourteenth Chronicle: Letters and Diaries of John Dos Passos* (Boston: Gambit, 1975), 516.

2. Donald Pizer, *Dos Passos' U.S.A.* (Charlottesville: University Press of Virginia, 1988), 58.

3. Linda W. Wagner, *Dos Passos: Artist as American* (Austin: University of Texas Press, 1979), 104.

4. Barrett Wendell, *A Literary History of America* (New York: Charles Scribner's Sons, 1914), 471.

5. George Edward Woodberry, *America in Literature* (London: Harper and Brothers, 1903), 243.

6. Barrett Wendell and Chester Noyes Greenough, *A History of Literature in America*, as quoted in Nina Baym, "Early Histories of American Literature: A Chapter in the Institution of New England," *American Literary History* 1 (Fall 1989): 475.

7. John Dos Passos, *The Major Nonfictional Prose*, ed. Donald Pizer (Detroit: Wayne State University Press, 1988), 37.

8. John Dos Passos, *The 42nd Parallel* (1930; rpt., New York: New American Library, 1969), 50. For a discussion of this passage, see John H. Wrenn, *John Dos Passos* (New York: Twayne, 1961), 22–23.

9. Daniel Aaron, "The Riddle of John Dos Passos," *Harper's* 224 (March 1962): 59.

10. Dos Passos, *The 42nd Parallel*, 240.

11. Blanche Gelfant, "The Search for Identity in the Novels of John Dos Passos," *PMLA* 76 (March 1961): 134.

12. See Wagner, xiii; Charles W. Bernardin, "John Dos Passos' Harvard Years," *New England Quarterly* 27 (1954): 22.

13. All quotations are from Aaron, 56.

14. Ibid., 57.

15. Gelfant, 138.

16. See the discussion in Lois Hughson, "In Search of the True America: Dos Passos' Debt to Whitman in *U.S.A.*," *Modern Fiction Studies* 19 (Summer 1973): 183–184, 190.

17. Dos Passos, *The 42nd Parallel*, 30.

18. Hughson, 191.

19. John Dos Passos, "Whither the American Writer," *Modern Quarterly* (1932), rpt. in Dos Passos, *Nonfictional Prose*, 150.

20. John Dos Passos, *The Big Money* (New York: New American Library, 1969), 167–168.

21. Hughson, 183.

22. Dos Passos, *The Big Money*, 173.

23. John P. Diggins, "Visions of Chaos and Visions of Order: Dos Passos as Historian," *American Literature* 46 (November 1974): 331.

24. Hughson, 192.

25. Dos Passos felt a personal connection: "In college and out I had . . . felt the frustrations that came from being considered a wop or a guinea or a greaser." See John Dos Passos, *The Best Times: An Informal Memoir* (New York: New American Library, 1966), 166.

26. Pizer, 27.

27. Dos Passos, *The Big Money*, 468–469.

28. Quoted in Townsend Ludington, *John Dos Passos: A Twentieth Century Odyssey* (New York: E. P. Dutton, 1980), 505. Occasionally, Dos Passos's latter-day political commitments lead him to make implausible claims: for example, he depicts Joseph McCarthy as a simple farm boy overwhelmed by the complex maneuverings of politicos in Washington.

29. Wagner, 162.

30. John Dos Passos, *Century's Ebb* (Boston: Gambit, 1975), 13.

31. Wagner, 166–167.

32. Ibid., 160.

33. Dos Passos, *The Best Times*, 134.

"Teach Me Your Rhythm"

The Poetics of German Lyrical Responses to Whitman

I N 1971, Gabriele Eckart, then a fourteen-year-old high school student in the German Democratic Republic (GDR) and something like a celebrity as a young poet in her socialist state, wrote the following poem:

TO WALT WHITMAN

searching for meters I met you,
　　　　　Walt Whitman.
I know, if you lived today and here,
you would sing with endless astonishment—
reveal the gigantic themes
　　　　　　in hymns,
you would
　　sing of the surging crowds
　　　　　　　passing the cities,
　　　　rejoicing in the applause of the light facades,
　　sing of the millions of faces,
　　　　flushed with enthusiasm
　　　　high above banners of the blood
　　　　　　　of fallen fighters,
　　sing of the gigantic combines,
　　　　hurrying across the furrows
　　　　　　　like silver birds,
　　sing of the students on the benches
　　　　of the endless chestnut avenue,

> calculating the coming hundred years,
> sing of the lilac, giving shade to the
>   children,
>   they know not Lincoln but build
>   sand castles and rockets that do not
>   remain illusions,
> sing of the breathing of cities,
>   growing into the cosmos,
> sing of the people on their flat roofs
>   up high above, waving to the sun with red scarves,
> sing of the meadows flooded with flowers,
>   carrying the lovers.
> but you are dead, Walt Whitman,
> therefore be my teacher; teach me your meters!
>   I will sing instead of you![1]

Since that time, her poetry has improved radically, and she has become a well-known and respected German writer. In the course of the 1980s, the matured author turned actively against East German–type socialism. Her poetry and prose became highly critical and, after publishing an edition of frank and critical interviews with young GDR workers in West Germany without the permission (and indeed against the will) of the leadership of the Socialist Unity party, Eckart fell into complete disgrace, became a target of persecution by the secret police, and eventually moved to the United States, the land of her early idol.

The poem is a fairly characteristic example of the undefinable yet officially prescribed and sanctioned artistic doctrine of Socialist Realism. The "gigantic theme," the enthusiasm (presumably for socialism) radiating from millions of faces, the development of collectivized agriculture symbolized by the huge combines likened to silver birds, all amount to a celebration of the building of socialism in Whitmanesque language, tone, and diction. If Walt Whitman were alive, the poem claims, he would sing the praises of the new society, "today and here." In fact, it might be possible to identify historical grounds for this optimism. The year 1971, incidentally, was when Erich Honecker came to power in the GDR. It marked the end of the Stalinist period for the GDR and led many to hope for social and political changes, which never truly occurred.

However, when reading GDR literature, one may never stay on the surface. When certain unstated and implicit contexts are considered, the poem also displays interesting, potentially critical dimensions. On the surface, there is a young, fourteen-year-old girl poet looking for a creative writing teacher. All of this seems very innocent until one considers the questions of why is Eckart searching for meters at all and why is she searching for them in American literature. Is there not a proven theory and practice of Socialist Realism; are there not models in the German Marxist literary tradition? And why does she have to search *again* for Whitman's meters and rhythm when so many leftist, Marxist poets had already appropriated Whitman for the international working-class movement?

Possibly the poet is unhappy with the tradition of socialist literature as she inherited it (including the traditional leftist reception of Whitman), and so she is taking a new look at the American author, hoping to gain new ways of expression. In this way, her concern with Whitman's (still) revolutionary poetry would assume a political function. There is a second potentially subversive aspect as well. In spite of the fact that Whitman was canonized among the "progressive writers" of world literature throughout the socialist world, the strong appeal to an *American* writer, regardless of the political orientation attributed to him, was conspicuous in the GDR as it pointed beyond the walls of its closed society. The various lines connected with air, space, and distance ("rockets," "cities growing into the cosmos," "people on . . . roofs . . . waving to the sun," "the endless chestnut avenue") are essentially breaches in the wall, attempts to overcome limiting and inhibiting boundaries. Moreover, a lyrical appeal to Whitman was also breaking barriers because of the difference in language. It was a signal sent across the wall, internationalist, but different from the official internationalism prescribed by the GDR government.

These hidden dimensions of Gabriele Eckart's innocent address to Walt Whitman are characteristic of the lyrical response to Whitman in German-speaking literature in general. In his introduction to *Walt Whitman: The Measure of His Song*, Ed Folsom has referred to the "radical democratic poetics" that have informed some of the most interesting American lyrical responses to Whitman.[2] German responses to Whitman almost uniformly express a point of view critical of German culture and German society. These responses may take the form of political or cultural criticism, but the authors see in Whitman's poetry and particularly in his radical aesthetics a potential solution to their predicament. While Whitman's reception in the German-speaking countries, both critical and creative, has been the object of a series of more or less successful investigations since the early 1900s by both American and European scholars,[3] the revolutionary significance of Whitman's poetics—as expressed through German-language Central European lyrical responses to Whitman, German poets' answers to Whitman—has so far been ignored.

This neglect is unfortunate, because these lyrical responses express in unique ways the German, Austrian, and Swiss literary constructions of Whitman and

Whitman's significance for the poetry of these countries. Research into literary "influence" ("*Einflußforschung*") today is a highly controversial endeavor. It has been criticized as impractical and dilettantish. However, to be influenced by something, especially in literature, often means to give an answer to it. In his keynote lecture at the 1991 annual convention of the German Association of American Studies in Münster, Armin Paul Frank proposed to investigate literary responses rather than to pursue research into influences. Indeed, this would put the stress on dynamic literary dialogues rather than on critical suspicions resting on weak positivistic foundations. Placing the emphasis on "response" also reveals the limitations of Harold Bloom's concept of influence, with its emphasis on the anxious, influence-freeing struggle of individual poets: in his *Anxiety of Influence* (1973), Bloom describes only one type of influence as valuable and excludes all others which are not characterized by this struggle. Lyrical responses, moreover, have the advantage of usually combining—within the poem—poetics with poetic practice in an illuminating way. This does not mean that such poetry is superior or that German lyrical responses to Whitman are uniformly sublime achievements in German poetry but is merely to emphasize that these responses are interesting documents for an understanding of literary dialogue, especially in an intercultural format.

Given a traditional European instinct of cultural and intellectual superiority over America, Whitman's reception in the German-speaking countries (and in Europe at large) is an anomaly. In Eckart's poem, for example, it is Whitman who is the teacher, with the European poet in the role of the apprentice. The variety of addresses found in various lyrical responses to Whitman makes this very obvious: torchbearer, titan, *weltmensch*, prophet, master, glorious man of the world, singer of glowing songs, God's eternal voice, breath of the cosmos, most noble son of Adam, shadow image of a giant. This is just a small selection, but the overall pattern shows Whitman as a model of perfection, the ideal human being. The difference manifests itself in a deficit on the European side.

Although the nineteenth-century revolutionary German poet Ferdinand Freiligrath (1810–1876) did not respond to Whitman lyrically, he is worth quoting here because his is the earliest commentary on what he considered to be Whitman's revolutionary poetics:

> First of all let us open his book. Are these verses? The lines are arranged like
> verses, to be sure, but verses they are not. No metre, no rhyme, no stanzas.
> Rhythmical prose, ductile verses. At first sight rugged, inflexible, formless;
> but yet for a more delicate ear, not devoid of euphony. . . . It is fitting
> that our poets and thinkers should have a closer look at this strange new

comrade, who threatens to overturn our entire *Ars Poetica* and all our theories and canons on the subject of aesthetics.[4]

This surprised but admiring reference to the subject of poetics is linked to a speculation about the sociocultural changes in Germany announcing themselves in the late 1860s:

> Are we really come to the point, when life, even in poetry, calls imperatively for new forms of expression? Has the age so much and such serious matters to say, that the old vessels no longer suffice for the new contents? Are we standing before a poetry of the ages to come, just as some years ago a music of the ages to come was announced to us? And is Walt Whitman greater than Richard Wagner?[5]

Do the ages to come require a new ars poetica, or do the poetics ring in a new age?

The revolutionary impetus associated with Whitman's poetics is again revealed in an innocuous piece of correspondence regarding the first book-length German translation of *Leaves of Grass*. This translation of 1889 was the result of a collaboration by a German American, Karl Knortz (1841–1918), and a Germanophile Irishman, Thomas William Rolleston (1857–1920). In a letter to Whitman's friend Richard Maurice Bucke, Rolleston complains about Knortz's attempts to "mainstream" Whitman's poetry in German translation:

> But I greatly fear that his [Knortz's] revision would extend beyond the meaning of that term and that he would alter the whole plan of my translation. . . . My aim was not to make him acceptable, but simply to make the German translation for a German reader as far as possible what the English original is for an English reader. . . . A German translation of W. which should never startle the "ordinary reader" or seem ridiculous or coarse to him, would not be Whitman at all.[6]

Thus, Rolleston develops an aesthetic program out of Whitman's poetry designed to provoke the German bourgeois readers when he, in a letter to Whitman, describes Germans to be "suffering under an unprecedented plague of mediocrity—in all branches of imaginative art. Dry bones everywhere. . . . Wagner is the only man that is really alive among them."[7]

Whitman's most energetic "hot little prophet," Germany's version of Horace Traubel, was the naturalist writer Johannes Schlaf (1862–1941). In a Whitman necrology in 1892, he describes his reaction to a reading of the first section of "Starting from Paumanok":

> It is as if everything existing miles away in a fabulous distance all of a sudden becomes alive in its fresh beauty, everything we feel to be in *contrast* to

our life here, which we know, yet do not understand. In free verses, it appears before us with all of its miracles. With unheard-of sounds and rhythms which seem like the fresh roaring of the wind, like the sea waves approaching with their vast rolling splendor. Unfamiliar, totally separate from the refinements of our aged and wizened art.[8]

This is German cultural criticism turned Whitmanesque at its most characteristic, an implicit critique of the ills brought about by the newly emerged industrial society combined with an almost tangible albeit literary utopia. However, Schlaf is not as naive a Whitman admirer as these sentences may suggest. His Whitmanesque utopia has a strongly regressive quality:

> We are forced to stop. Astonished. This is a child's stammering. Helpless, unwieldy, unarticulate, ridiculous to our well-trained thinking and feeling. But we understand: it is . . . the surprised jubilant cry with which a child liberates itself from its sweet burden, joyfully, verifying the data it perceives. . . . The naïveté of a child perceiving a new object and calling its name ten, twenty, a hundred times in succession without becoming tired, with equal delight over the same activity of its vocal chords and over the properties of the object thus designated. . . . [Reading Whitman] we have overcome isolation and separation which has confused us and made us afraid. Misery and happiness, poverty and wealth, all the incomprehensible oppositions which tortured us in our narrow life: they can no longer harm us or obscure the connectedness of all things.[9]

Schlaf addresses in Whitman a healer of a special sort: the ills of modern society will not be solved through intellectual exercises but through regressive surrender. Liberation through naïveté, regression through the material-physical foundation of human speech: the vocal chords are going to bring about deliverance from isolation, confusion, and separation—in short, from alienation. True democracy—for Schlaf and Whitman—would never exist on the level of hierarchical intellect. "All men are *created* equal"—and if they are to stay that way, they must either remain children or regress to that station of life. In Whitman, Schlaf admired not so much a political message but the epistemological egalitarianism transported by Whitman's poetry.

Arthur Drey's poem "Walt Whitman," written in 1911, is the earliest *direct* lyrical response to Whitman in German. The poem demonstrates the expressionist's exaggerated adoration of Whitman as a poet and as a God-like giant. It is characterized by an extreme pathos in the German meaning of the word, the yearning for a lost totality. The address to Whitman as torchbearer and titan suggests the degree to which the human individual is dwarfed by modern industrialized society dominated by an ever-present war machinery.

WALT WHITMAN

Swinger of the torch! Blazing titan of virgin primeval forest!
Your eyes kiss the world, and dream-caressing
The white sun of your hair flows over the sea—
Universal man!

Your heart is love between the struggling blocks
In the torn-open breast of bleeding brotherhood—
Children kneel down eye-tired before your youthful soul—
Dream!

From out of your pale tears warm peace gleams,
And to your dear lips flowers are words—
Which we drink, healing spring—
Miracle!

Your ancient edifice grows, wild gold . . .
Pious lands spread out their gray hands
For the capture—Lonely, you stand on the brink of the world—
Prophet![10]

The powerful (or, to many readers, ridiculous) rhetoric of this poem may
overshadow Whitmanesque poetics, but the poem is remarkable because it
follows Whitman's famous line, "Camerado, this is no book, / Who touches
this touches a man." The poem translates Whitman, the man, into poetry
(just as Whitman himself had attempted to "textualize" his body), thereby en-
compassing the whole world and achieving a new totality, a new wholeness.
His "eyes kiss the world," his white hair extends across the oceans, and his
heart radiates love between the two warring factions (a line foreshadowing
World War I). Whitman is described as a healer: from his "pale tears" emerges
"warm peace," and the words from his "dear lips" are "flowers" which the readers drink, a "healing spring," a "miracle." Although "pious" countries are
preparing for war, the poet remains on the edge of the world. Aggressive an-
thropomorphization of the object world, investing machines and other lifeless
things with human qualities, is almost a trademark of the expressionist movement in German poetry. In this poem, the identification of a textualized
Whitman with the world as a whole is carried to a hysterical extreme amount-
ing to both hope and desperation.

Johannes R. Becher (1891–1958) was another expressionist writer with an
early interest in Whitman. To him, the American poet is a fighter against
bourgeois decadence. In his call to support a "Socialist army" (in 1917, the
year of the Bolshevik revolution), he enlists Whitman as well: "Let's organize,
once and for all: o most splendid, most glorious of all deeds, let us willingly

discipline ourselves. En masse: what magic! What magic! What a flow, what a word: en masse! . . . Let's join!"[11] Becher's poetry shows that Whitman was a significant source of the Marxist "mass" rhetoric in Germany during the 1920s and 1930s. Becher reads Whitman's catalogs as direct lyrical expressions of an emerging socialist culture of the masses, referring to Whitman's "steaming mass of armies of lines." And, anticipating Gabriele Eckart's fantasy, he announces: "In this century, I am taking over your command."[12]

In the course of his development toward more dogmatic Marxist positions, however, Becher became increasingly critical of Whitman, although he retained his fascination for the poet. During World War II, already a well-known leader among German exiles living in the USSR, he wrote a sonnet to Whitman, starting with the following quatrain (rhymed in German):

> In the high-flung bridges of his rhythms
> —The expanses of the sentences drawn out like prairies—
> He was the enraptured hymn of freedom,
> Lincoln's spirit breathed freely through him.[13]

The past tense and the classical genre of the sonnet suggest that Becher had moved far away from Whitman, who is no longer a living presence, no longer in a dialogue with the author. The one long line, "—The expanses of the sentences drawn out like prairies—," seems almost ironical. Nonetheless, Becher stayed true to Whitman in other ways. He later became the first minister of culture of the GDR and ensured continued availability of Whitman texts in that country.

Literary satires, of course, are the other side of the coin. As we know from *Walt Whitman: The Measure of His Song*, satirical treatments of Whitman were common in the United States very early on. It was the unconventionality of Whitman's poetry that provoked these American satires. However, a satirical treatment such as the one by Christian Morgenstern (1871–1914), one of Germany's most interesting poets, pertains as much to the uninspired imitators of Whitman's formal innovations as to Whitman's poetry itself. Morgenstern liked and admired Whitman and, in a poem devoted to the American poet, he takes up Whitman's global theme very earnestly. The following poem, published in the early 1920s after Morgenstern's death, is not part of a literary dialogue but is a response to Whitman nevertheless:

THE DEMOCRATIC SONG OF MY ROOM

> I sing the song of my room.
> I sing the song of my wallpaper, my ceiling, my floor, my doors, my windows, my around-rooms, under- and over-rooms.

I sing the stove in the corner, wide, protruding, its decoration on its chest.

I sing the three other corners, empty or filled with cabinets, busts, shelves,
   perpendicular running to the left or to the right.

I sing the rug, the table and the chairs. Horizontally it lies on the floor.
   Vertically they rest their legs on it.

I sing the pictures and maps on the wall. Each in its own way.

I sing the pictures and mirrors on the other wall. Each in its way.

I sing the desk and its books, leaves, springs, frames . . .

Enter, my friends!

This is my room!

Oxygen, neutrogen, light, warmth, air pressure (but only as much as needed),
   soft pillows or a divan (because you may have become tired), an apple, a
   pear, both from Borsdorf sent in a crate, straw, paper wrapped around by
   considerate hands.

What if you wanted wine?

Enters the grocer, from two floors below. He looks around. Politely he lifts his
   hat. He asks with a loud voice.

He names his wines . . .

Choose, my friends. Let him bring what he has got. My room is large enough.

My room is not just my room. My room is the world, *die Welt, orbis pictus.*

Hear me, habitans of rooms in all five continents,

Great room comradeship of democracy!

Camerados!

Sing with me the song of the room, millionfold!

Sing with me the democratic chant of the room![14]

This poem represents more of a satire of banal Whitmanesque writing in German than of Whitman's poetry itself. It satirizes Whitmanesque writing in the context of the German predilection for their own four walls, the stuffiness of German society. From this point of view, Morgenstern would question the effectiveness of Whitmanesque writing in Germany: Whitman's aesthetic innovations cannot apply to Central European bourgeois society.

One final example of German responses to Whitman is indeed highly critical of Whitman. Jürgen Wellbrock's "I Can't Sing Your Self" is the most radical example of "talking back" to Whitman. Curiously enough, given the long-standing leftist interest in Whitman, Wellbrock (b. 1949), a writer based in Berlin, attacks Whitman from the left. In a commentary on the poem, he notes his ambivalent attitude toward Whitman. He admires the rhetoric relating to freedom and democracy but severely criticizes Whitman's pathos, especially the glorification of muscular strength and body.

I CAN'T SING YOUR SELF
(*For Walt Whitman*)

You sing yourself, you singer and perfect soldier, and your song, carrying no
    address, meets a corpse.
       Sounds that are caught
in your frailest leaves,
knotted not in the old knot of contrariety,
which you, chewing prairie-grass, have knotted from haste and bones.

WRITING mocks the technique of your wrist:
you never sang the divine average.
Whoever touches you these days, touches a book,
moving in the hands of busy corpses.

The word "Democratic" I utter, if you will, calmly,
but my physiology has no boot-soles.
    Instead I am shooting again,
and the resulting crack is the song
to the curvature of your writing-finger
    (o how it's flattering me).

The same old laughter.

Do not announce what comes after you:
your own finale drowned in the chords.
To know what it is to be evil
does not make us better.[15]

This 1976 poem is a clever montage of Whitman quotations famous in Germany, each of which is refuted. Whitman's rhetoric is said to be hollow and without substance. The poem is a characteristic product of a younger, postwar, discourse-conscious West German writer who is extremely critical of ideologies hidden in any literature or text. The lyrical presentation of everyday life, the dialogue and meeting between author and reader in the poem, the physiological presence of the writer throughout the printed book, the visionary pose of the bard—all of which served, as we have seen, progressive, if not revolutionary, ends—have suddenly become targets of suspicion.

Wellbrock's poem shows that a decided turn in the creative reception of Whitman is taking place. What Wellbrock is critiquing is not so much Whitman himself but the somewhat monotonous German construction of Whitman as savior and healer since Schlaf's 1892 essay. This rhetoric has become pathetic to the ears of the very nation that has created it. The future reception of Whitman in the German-speaking countries, then, including lyrical responses to Whitman, will have to be less serious, more ironic and playful. The question is whether Whitman's poetry will thereby retain its revolutionary aesthetics or whether irony will reveal itself as incompatible with Whitman's art. I suspect there is no such incompatibility: a less serious reception of his poetry may open up interesting new potentials of a poetry which will continue to have a revolutionary impact in a changing Europe.

NOTES

1. Gabriele Eckart, "An Walt Whitman," in Bernd Jentzsch, ed., *Ich nenn euch mein Problem: Gedichte der Nachgeborenen* (Wuppertal: Hammer, 1971), 154ff. All translations, unless otherwise indicated, are my own.

An Walt Whitman

auf der suche nach metren bin ich dir
                              begegnet, Walt Whitman.
ich weiß, lebtest du heute und hier,
du würdest singen in endloser erstaunung—
die gigantischen themen in hymen
                              erschließen,
du würdest
    singen von den wogenden zügen, die die
                              städte durchschreiten,
        jubelnd im beifall der hellen fassaden,
    singen von den millionen gesichtern,
gerötet von begeisterung
hoch darüber fahnen vom blute
                              gefallener Kämpfer,
    singen von den riesigen kombines, die wie
                              silbervögel
        über die ackerfurchen eilen,
    singen von den studenten auf den banken
        der endlosen kastanienallee,
        die nächsten hundert jahre berechnend,
    singen vom lila flieder, der die kinder
                              beschattet,
        sie kennen nicht Lincoln, doch bauen
                              im sande
        raketen und schlösser, die keine
                              illusionen bleiben,
    singen vom atmen der städte,
        die ins all hineinwachsen,

singen von den menschen auf ihren flachen dächern
   hoch oben, die der sonne winken mit roten tüchern,
singen von den blumenüberfluteten wiesen,
   die die liebenden tragen.
doch du bist tot, Walt Whitman,
deshalb sei mein Lehrer; lehr mich deine rhythmen!
ich singe statt deiner!

2. Ed Folsom, "Talking Back to Walt Whitman: An Introduction," in Jim Perlman, Ed Folsom, and Dan Campion, eds., *Walt Whitman: The Measure of His Song* (Minneapolis: Holy Cow! Press, 1981), lii.

3. For a survey, see Walter Grünzweig, *Walt Whitmann: Die deutschsprachige Rezeption als interkulturelles Phänomen* (München: Fink, 1991), 11–27.

4. Ferdinand Freiligrath, "Walt Whitman," *Augsburger Allgemeine Zeitung* (Wochenausgabe) 17 (April 24, 1868): 257–259, translated in *Eclectic Magazine* (Baltimore) 2 (July 1868): 325–329.

5. Ibid.

6. Thomas William Rolleston to Richard Maurice Bucke, January 8, 1885, Container 53, Charles E. Feinberg Collection, R. M. Bucke Papers, Library of Congress.

7. Thomas William Rolleston to Walt Whitman, February 14, 1882, in Horst Frenz, ed., *Whitman and Rolleston: A Correspondence* (Bloomington: Indiana University Press, 1951), 57.

8. Johannes Schlaf, "Walt Whitman," *Freie Bühne für den Entwickelungskampf der Zeit* 3 (1892): 980.

9. Ibid., 981.

10. Arthur Drey, "Walt Whitman," *Die Aktion* 1 (1911): Col. 907, trans. John M. Gogol, in *Walt Whitman Review* 20 (September 1974): 105 (translation slightly corrected).

Fackelschwinger! Lodernder Titan des keuschen Urwalds!
Deine Augen küssen die Welt, und traumschmeichelnd
Fließt die weiße Sonne deiner Haare über das Meer—
Weltmensch!

Dein Herz ist zwischen den streitenden Blöcken Liebe
In aufgerissener Brust blutenden Brudergefühls—
Kinder knien augenmüde vor deiner Jünglingsseele—
Traum!

Aus deinen bleichen Tränen blinkt warmer Friede,
Und Blumen sind deiner lieben Lippen Worte—
Die wir trinken, heilenden Quell—
Wunder!

Dein Urgebäude wächst, wilderndes Gold . . .
Es breiten fromme Länder ihre grauen Hände
Zum Fang—Einsam stehst du am Saume der Welt—
Prophet!

11. Johannes R. Becher, *Das Neue Gedicht* (Leipzig: Insel, 1918), 117, 135.

12. Ibid., 135.

13. Becher, *Sonett-Werk: 1913–1955* (Berlin: Aufbau, 1956), 307.

In seiner Rhythmen hochgespannten Brücken
—Satzweiten dehnten sich wie die Prärien—
War er der Freiheit hymnisches Entzücken,
Der Atem Lincolns strömte frei durch ihn.

14. Christian Morgenstern, "Der Zimmergesang der Demokratie," in *Die Schallmühle: Grotesken und Parodien* (München: Piper, 1928), 66.

Der Zimmergesang der Demokratie

Ich singe den Gesang meines Zimmers.
Ich singe den Gesang meiner Tapete, meines Plafonds, meines Fußbodens,
    meiner Türen, meiner Fenster, meiner Umzimmer, Unter-und Überzimmer.
Ich singe den Ofen in der Ecke, breitspurig, hervortretend, seine Verzierung
    auf der Brust.
Ich singe die drei andern Ecken leer order gefüllt mit Schränken, Büsten,
    Wandbrettern, rechtwinklig laufend nach rechts oder links.
Ich singe den Teppich, den Tisch und die Stühle. Waagrecht liegt er am
    Boden. Senkrecht setzen sie ihre Beine auf seine Fläche.
Ich singe die Bilder und Karten an der einen Wand. Jedes nach seiner Weise.
Ich singe die Bilder und Spiegel an der andern Wand. Ein jedes auf seine
    Weise.
Den Schreibtisch besinge ich und seine Bücher, Blätter, Federn, Gestelle . . .
Tretet herein, Freunde!
Hier ist mein Zimmer!
Sauerstoff, Stickstoff, Licht, Wärme, Luftdruck (doch nur so viel, wie gerade
    recht), weiche Kissen oder ein Divan (denn ihr könntet müde geworden
    sein), ein Apfel, eine Birne, beides aus Borsdorf, in einer Kiste geschickt,
    Stroh, Papier herum von fürsorglichen Händen.
Oder wenn ihr Wein wollt?
Herein tritt der Kaufmann, zwei Stock tiefer. Er sieht sich um. Höflich zieht
    er den Hut. Er fragt mit lauter Stimme.
Er nennt uns seine Weine . . .
Wählt meine Freunde. Laßt ihn bringen, was er hat. Mein Zimmer ist groß
    genug dazu.

Mein Zimmer ist nicht nur mein Zimmer. Mein Zimmer ist die Welt, the
world, orbis pictus.
Hört mich an, Ihr Zimmerbewohner aller fünf Weltteile!
Große Zimmergenossenschaft der Demokratie!
Camerados!
Singt mit mir den Zimmergesang, den millionenhaften!
Singt mit mir den Zimmergesang der Demokratie!

15. Jürgen Wellbrock, "Dein Selbst kann ich nicht singen," in Hermann Peter
Piwit and Peter Rühmkorf, eds., *Literaturmagazin 5. Das Vergehen von Hören und
Sehen. Aspekte der Kulturvernichtung* (Reinbek: Rowohlt, 1976), 136.

DEIN SELBST KANN ICH NICHT SINGEN
(*Für Walt Whitman*)

Du singst das Selbst, du Sänger und vollkommner Krieger,
und dein Gesang, unadressiert, trifft einen Toten.
        Töne, die sich verfangen
in deinen zartesten Halmen,
verknoten sich nicht im alten Widerspruch,
den du, Präriegras kauend, geknüpft hast
aus Eile und Gebein.
SCHREIBEN spottet der Technik deines Handgelenks:
im Goldenen Schnitt hast du nie gesungen.
Wer dich heut herührt, berührt ein Buch,
das sich bewegt in den Händen rühriger Leichen.

"Demokratisch" spreche ich, wenn du willst, gelassen aus,
aber meine Physiologie hat keine Sohle.
        Statt dessen schieße ich schon wieder,
und der Knall, der entsteht, ist der Gesang
auf die Krümmung deines schreibenden Fingers
        (o wie er mir schmeichelt).
Dasselbe alte Lachen.

Verkünde nicht, was nach dir kommt:
dein eignes Finale ertrank in den Akkorden.
Wissen, was es heißt, schlecht zu sein,
macht uns nicht besser.

Sänger, du hast Blasen an den Lippen!

Whitman Criticism in the Light of Indian Poetics

INDIAN STUDENTS of Whitman have long dwelt upon his mysticism and appropriated him to their own philosophical tradition. They have sought to spiritualize his sexuality—which is apparently at odds with his mysticism—either by interpreting it symbolically in terms of Yogic experience or by relating it to the sexual mysticism of the Tantric cult. Whitman's nationalism and his democratic faith, too, they sought to derive from his unitive consciousness. In any case, of course, the aim of all these studies has been to provide the best vindication possible of the poet and to find a place for him among the great visionaries of world literature.

But aside from the philosophical tradition, there is another critical tradition in India which stays largely clear of the metaphysical schools and approaches literature purely as art and as a mode of communication and explores its formal as well as psychological dimensions. It has established a body of critical principles (comparable in some respects to the classical system in the West), more specifically, a theory of poetic emotions and a theory of meaning and interpretation to go with it. It is this other tradition that I want to draw upon for my approach to Whitman to see how useful it will prove in settling some of the major critical issues pertaining to the study of *Leaves of Grass*. Whitman, like a magnet, has attracted a great variety of methods and approaches, based on competing paradigms or explanatory categories. But my object is to examine whether the Indian theory can provide a framework for mediating between the divergent approaches.

The theory of poetic emotions—called *Rasa* in Sanskrit (meaning, literally, "gustation")—conceives of the end of poetry not as the mere conveying of ideas or knowledge for its information value but as the presentation or evocation of emotions, such as erotic love, heroic enthusiasm, pathos, wonder, comic laughter, fear, disgust, wrath, and serenity (which are the basic stereotypes) and a host of other, minor emotions, like joy, pride, eagerness, agitation, jealousy, anxiety, doubt, and shame, which merge with the major emotions as transitory states. The experience of these emotions is felt variously as an expansion, contraction, melting, or distraction of the mind.

Emotions are expressed in poetry, as in life, through their objects (which may be a situation or thought, which produces them) and through their behavioral manifestations. A poem of some length is usually an orchestration of several feeling tones, in which a major emotional theme develops into a dominant tone by subordinating various minor feelings, which become dissolved into a dominant impression. Aesthetic unity is achieved through the tension of diverse impulses. This unity may be traced by studying the system of prominences that every poem establishes for itself through image and statement and by its conclusion as well, for the conclusion can reverse the tone of a whole series of previous statements and set up a new tone. In a short poem—such as an imagist poem or haiku—it is possible to present a single emotional theme, without variations. But, in any case, every poetic presentation, to be worth the name, must contain an explicit or implicit emotional attitude, perception, or reflective thought. There can be no pure objectivist poem, divested of all lyrical, emotive content. Ideas, ideals, facts, and so forth are no doubt an important part of all human discourse, but in poetry they exist only as objects of emotions (they occasion feelings in the speaker), not as mere objects of knowledge.

Single images or statements cannot, by themselves, dictate the structure of the poem; it is rather the whole collocation of images and thought elements and emotional strands of varying strength or prominence that establishes its dominant tone. This tone alone will be the point or presentational force of the poem—its aesthetic character. Since the emotions of a poem operate within a well-defined context of situation, the focus of attention should be the single poem rather than the entire oeuvre of a writer, which, in most cases, cannot sustain a unified emotional theme.

Another important tenet of the *Rasa* theory is that emotions, once they get expressed in poetry, become de-particularized or depersonalized—they become separated from their originating contexts/landscapes—and take on a universal character. Thus, the "Americanism" of Walt Whitman, unique as it may be in its own form, gets translated into every reader's experience as an emotion that he or she can relate to. The particularities of time, place, and person are transcended. This is called generalization (*sādhāraṇīkarana*)— which has its parallels in Western theory, too, since Aristotle. Poetic experience is ahistorical/atemporal, impersonal, and gender-neutral (that is to say, the deictics relating to gender, either of the poem or of the author or reader, do not figure in the contemplation of the presented experience).

To fix the emotional tone of a poem, one must, of course, first interpret the drift of its words, their purport or final expressive force. The ancient tradition of Vedic exegesis, grammar, and logic also developed a theory of language and a hermeneutics. This theory argued vigorously against the deconstructive logic of the Buddhist and upheld the referentiality, objectivity, and determinacy of verbal meaning. It looked upon the text—and not the author or the reader—as the only source of its meaning, although meanings have often to be construed by the reader from the linguistic data of the text and various other, "contextual" factors. Another important rule of this kind of interpretation is that the directly stated meaning of a text is more authoritative than meaning deduced metaphorically or imported from outside the text. Where a literal reading yields a consistent meaning, no attempt should be made to read occult or hidden meanings into the text, even for the purpose of enriching it.

An application of the general theory of poetry and meaning outlined above may be seen to have an important bearing on our study of *Leaves of Grass*. First, viewed in the light of *Rasa*, the poems will be valued not for the ideas they express concerning self, identity, democracy, the American Union, the body, sexual relations, and so on, but for the feelings or emotional attitudes such ideas occasion in the poet. Whitman was, unquestionably, committed to certain ideas all his life and projected them quite insistently in his poems and prose works. But these ideas were not for him conceptual notions merely but emotional experiences of precise kinds: joy, pleasure, pain, anxiety, despair, fervor, and so forth, and it is of these that his poems—at least the more successful ones—are composed. Most recent criticism of Whitman has stressed the ideological aspect of his poetry to the neglect of the role of emotions in his life. In this criticism, Whitman is seen primarily as a metaphysician of the self or as a poet responding to the socioeconomic or political crises of his nation or to the sexual-textual politics of his day.

Of course, poetry is always a response to some objective or subjective situation; it does not come out of nothing. Democracy, camaraderie, identity, sex, the national crisis, the future promise—all were grist to the poet's emotions and occasioned his poetic expression. Surely, it was the facts and circumstances of the latter half of the nineteenth-century America that spurred his imagination. But these material facts do not wholly account for the power of his poetry. His lyrical emotion far exceeds the ideas and ideals that inspired it or in which it had its roots. "Song of Myself" is not merely a "democratic performance"[1] confined to the affairs of the human polity but also an ecstatic celebration of a certain vision of things, and, in this sense, it may be called "mystical" or "transcendental" (terms that have fallen out of favor today). M. Wynn Thomas, however, does recognize that the social facts in Whitman's poetry are transmuted into a visionary cosmos. Whitman "spiritualizes" circumstance.[2] And this is precisely the point. "Spirituality," understood not as an abstract metaphysical perception but as an emotional state of a special kind, an ecstasy engendered by that perception, is the aesthetic center of that poem and of other poems of that order—poems of joy, of celebration, of the "visionary compact," of illumination and fulfillment. Such a mood is also the essence of mystical experience—at least of a certain kind or of a certain phase of it.

It must be granted, too, that Whitman's physical self—the body beautiful—is the vital center of his poems, not an illness or a pathological symptom, as the psychoanalysts would have it. As Robert K. Martin insists, we also should not eliminate the specifics of that experience, namely, the homosexuality, by mysticizing it.[3] We may also grant Michael Moon's contention that gender politics dictated Whitman's homosexual disguises and some of the revisions that he effected in order to make his proscribed meanings more acceptable to the public.[4] In addition, it may be conceded that at least one of his aims was to subvert the discourse of male sexuality and power relations in his day. In terms of the *Rasa* theory, one does not have to apologize for the eroticism or even try to spiritualize it (as the mystical and religious critics have tended to do). Not everything that Whitman wrote is readily translatable into spiritual terms. Evidently, some of the sexual poems or passages have no connection with god-love or divine eroticism (despite David Kuebrich's claims).[5] They are plain sex, plain body language, sometimes arousing guilty feelings in the poet and at other times ecstasy and release. But we can look at them for what they are—as expressions of certain emotions—and value them for their presentational power. After all, eroticism (whether directed on a male or female partner is immaterial) accounts for a large portion of our psychic heritage. However, in a great number of Whitman's poems of sex and body—whatever their origins and affinities—the feeling is one of release and ecstasy or "mystic deliria": "What is it that frees me so in storms?" says Whitman ("One Hour to Madness and Joy," LG, 105). As both Harold Aspiz and Martin recognize, "the sexual urge and the urge to transcend" coexist in Whitman,[6] or sexuality becomes the means to a "mystic penetration of the universe."[7] In any case, the resultant ecstasy is what matters for poetry. The lines beginning "Swiftly arose around me" or "landscapes projected masculine" and the ubiquitous visions of omnipotence, health, and unity are great poetry whether their roots are in the "complexities of blood or mire" or in the planes of Yogic consciousness and whether they are a form of sublimation[8] or regressive narcissistic fantasy, defensive illusion, or "psychological catharsis."[9] All poetry, all art may be fantasy, for that matter, and there is no need to dig beneath the surface for buried motives, no need to expose the dark underside. Moreover, although the subversive intention is implied in Whitman's sexual poems, it would be an exaggeration to say that that alone is their focal point. The celebratory, ecstatic treatment of bodily experience is what determines their aesthetic character. Nor is it true that even the celebration of the body beautiful is the sole purpose of *Leaves of Grass* or that all of Whitman's imagination is "spermatic" in nature. Sex or the body is the subject matter of a few poems or passages only.

This brings us to the question of the unity of *Leaves of Grass*. An oft-debated question is whether the book should be read as a single long poem or as a collection of lyrics. We know that Whitman himself claimed that the poems constituted a "totality" centering round certain controlling themes and warned his readers not to judge his work "piecemeal" (HT, 2:116). Whitman's wishes have been respected to a large extent by successive generations of critics, and the unity of *Leaves of Grass* has been described in a variety of ways, largely in the terms provided by Whitman himself—such as a central unity of purpose, a consistent worldview, the continuity of the mind behind the poems, and the search for identity or selfhood. Apart from the studies concerning the structure of *Leaves of Grass* in its final shape, one overriding interest of recent criticism has been the personality or poetic mind of Whitman and the image of the self emerging from the poems in their totality. Thus, Whitman has been pictured, among other things, as a mystic, a shaman, a Christian prophet, a poet of angst, a social-sexual rebel, and an American spokesman. Not all of these images are mutually exclusive, but critics have tended to take the single image as representative of the whole.

There is, no doubt, ample justification for constructing such a total image of the poet when we consider Whitman's own metonymic identification of himself with his book: "Who touches this touches a man." The modern concept of the long poem as a growing corpus or as a continuing series of emanations from the poet—based on the examples of Pound, Olson, Zukofsky, and others—lends support to this approach, especially since *Leaves of Grass* grew like rings around a tree. The phenomenological critic, too, would try to reconstruct the mind behind the work, assuming the unity of the entire oeuvre, and all this is no doubt a legitimate scholarly interest.

But there are also dangers in viewing *Leaves of Grass* as a totality: it does not do justice to the great diversity in tone and style of the poems in the book, and it also tends to misrepresent the character of the individual poems themselves. Such a misrepresentation is nowhere more evident than in the attempt to give a consistent account of Whitman's self. It is recognized, of course, that the image of the self changes from poem to poem and over the years, even as the historical Whitman did.[10] But a composite image of it is constructed to reveal it to be problematic and riddled with uncertainties. Or the impression of poems of one order is interpolated into those of another order, and an image of the poet is painted as a "hollow man," a "fractured personality" who betrays a sense of desperation and emptiness not only in his more obviously elegiac poems but underneath the élan of his celebratory poems as well.[11] Thus, "Song of Myself" is contrasted to "Calamus" or "As I Ebb'd" to show the hollowness of the poet's godlike pose, the cosmic persona. Or the contradictions within a single poem ("Song of Myself," "The Sleepers," or "Crossing Brooklyn Ferry") are interpreted as signs of weakness and incoherence in the poet's vision.

Harold Bloom remarks on the shifting images of Whitman's self and concludes that his "real Me" always eluded him.[12] Bernard Duffey argues that Whitman's poetic self is not a positive principle but a vacuum into which the images of a "wholly material cosmos" are fed.[13] Another critic finds two distinct voices or speakers in Whitman's poems—"one, timid, gentle, frequently disconsolate, the other large, all-inclusive, affirming"—Whitman's "I" shuttling between the two poles.[14] In their own typical pseudological ways, the deconstructive critics (Paul Bové, Joseph Kronick), too, have argued that Whitman had no fixed notion of the self and that his poetic self is radically ungrounded and centerless. In any case, several approaches to Whitman—biographical, psychoanalytical, existentialist, Buberian, deconstructive—have converged to show that Whitman's many selves are disintegrative and thus to project a unitary image of him as a divided human spirit, as a dialectical and tensional self.

But, granting the problematics of Whitman's identity, the search for an authentic self is not only a "hopeless quest" but may even be a mistake. For although all of Whitman's poems are about himself—both about his inner self and his responses to the world around him—the only identity that we can construct of him is that of a lyrical personality recording its shifting moods over a period of some thirty years, the quality and form of this personality changing according to the content of its experience.

The approach in the light of *Rasa* would therefore prefer to study the single poem or a homogeneous group of poems concentrating on a single emotion or mood, for aesthetic unity can be found only in a well-integrated piece of work, not in a collection. Moreover, any generalized impression of the collection as a whole would be apt to ignore important distinctions between one poem and another poem and between kinds of poems, each conveying a different aesthetic value. Aesthetically speaking, the distinction in emotional tone between "Song of Myself" and "As I Ebb'd" and the "Calamus" poems is more significant than any generalized conception of selfhood that may be deduced from these poems put together.

In terms of their emotional tone, Whitman's poems fall into six broad categories:

1. There are poems that convey enthusiasm, dilation, afflatus (of the heroic kind), transport and amazement, or the pride and joy of the soul—in which the poet is saying generally: "What a wonderful world! How lucky to be alive!" Of this order are "Song of Myself," "Song of the Open Road," "Crossing Brooklyn Ferry," "A Song of the Rolling Earth," "A Song of Joys," "A Song for Occupations," "Broad-Axe," "Starting from Paumanok," "Salut au Monde!," "Children of Adam," "I Hear America Singing," "Our Old Feuillage." The point of these poems, in terms of *Rasa*, is not merely any metaphysic of the self—on the Vedantic, Buberian, or deconstructive models—but the emotions produced in the speaker by his various encounters with himself in relation to the objects and states of affairs he is contemplating. The self in these poems is no doubt the protagonist of all actions and enactments, but it is there, not as a concept merely, but as the vessel of an emotion—the cosmic emotion, if you like. The sources of this emotion are: the feeling of health and physical well-being, the body beautiful, the sensation of living, the transmission of energy currents from person to person and from nature to humans; the vision of the American sublime (landscape, national power, the vision of a New Eden and plenitude of materials); and unrestricted faith in the cosmic scheme and immortality and the sense that the self stands "imperturbe," "aplomb in the midst of irrational things," and hence the feeling of transcendence coexisting with a Dionysian frenzy and deep stirrings, the released self playing the cosmic drama of identification in a bid to outstrip the universe.

2. There are poems that express the sexual emotion—both the pleasures and pains of the erotic urge or relationship. "Calamus" is a collection of sentimental love lyrics, oscillating between one mood and another—between restless yearning and the repose of fulfillment. But both these moods are natural to the erotic passion, and so the dominant emotion of these poems is still erotic. "Children of Adam," too, contains some tender love lyrics.

3. There are the elegiac poems expressing a sense of crisis, tension, doubt, or tragic despair and helplessness of one sort or another—of which the

outstanding examples are "As I Ebb'd," "Tears," "Yet, Yet, Ye Downcast Hours," "The City Dead-House," "A Hand-Mirror" (which expresses self-loathing), and "To the Man-of-War Bird" (with its wistfully elegiac tone). "Out of the Cradle," in which the poet awakens to his destiny as a poet of the tragedy of love and death, makes no final affirmation of any principle of transcendence. The Lincoln elegy ends on a note of reassurance. But in it, although the grief of the poet finds relief in the thought of the ever-returning spring and a momentary burst of joy, the grief is not completely transcended. Both image and statement confirm the pervasive impression of grief. The tragic emotion has a certain morbid quality to it, such that it tends to dominate the mind unless there occurs a complete reversal of thought. In this case, the joyful thoughts, although they provide outlets for the poet's overwhelming sense of loss, are not powerful enough to subdue that feeling but are themselves subdued by it. Thus, the final impression is that of a man trying in vain to overcome his grief. The wailing does not cease.

4. In some of the war poems (especially "First O Songs for a Prelude," "Eighteen Sixty-one," "Beat! Beat! Drums!," "Rise O Days from Your Fathomless Deeps," "The Centenarian's Story," "Give Me the Silent Splendid Sun," "An Army Corps on the March"), Whitman exploits the sentiment of heroic zeal, although the "Drum-Taps" cluster itself covers a range of other emotions as well, including pathos ("By the Bivouac's Fitful Flame," "Come Up from the Fields Father," "Vigil Strange I Kept on the Field One Night," "A Sight in Camp in the Daybreak," "The Wound Dresser") and wonder ("Cavalry Crossing a Ford," "Bivouac on a Mountain Side"). "The Return of the Heroes" ("Autumn Rivulets") expresses joy, thankfulness, and praise.

5. There are the purely descriptive poems, including some in "Drum-Taps," which attempt to render a scene or an object for its own intrinsic interest, without any generalizing statement or sentimental reflections. But even these bare descriptive sketches imply a point of view, an emotional attitude which, in instances like "After the Sea-Ship," "Sparkles from the Wheel," "The Dalliance of the Eagles," and "The Runner," is the sense of wonder. "Sparkles from the Wheel" is primarily focused on an objective scene which "seize[s] and affect[s]" the viewer with a sense of wonder. The viewer also reflects on his own relation to the scene (a "phantom" at once absorbed in the scene and contemplating his own detachment from it). But this does not deflect from the scene itself as the object of his wonder. "A Farm Picture" is strongly suggestive of peace and serenity. In some poems, on the other hand, the descriptive terms are so loaded as to present the object or scene in an explicit emotional light. In "Patroling Barnegat," the scene of the turbulent

ocean is rendered in an objective manner. But the whole description is evocative of the terror of the ocean's destructive force and the pathos of the human forms struggling against it.

6. Finally, there are the poems, mostly of old age, that register a state of relative restfulness and serene joy, consequent on the poet's achieving acceptance and reconciliation, such as "Passage to India," "Proud Music of the Storm," and shorter pieces: "Thou Orb Aloft Full-Dazzling," "Joy, Shipmate, Joy!," "Thanks in Old Age," "Soon Shall the Winter's Foil Be Here," "A Prairie Sunset," "Twilight," "An Evening Lull," "Old Age's Lambent Peaks," "To the Sun-Set Breeze," "Death's Valley," "Halcyon Days," and "Youth, Day, Old Age and Night."

The above classification is by no means exhaustive, but it serves to show that Whitman's poems traverse a wide spectrum of moods, according to changing psychological circumstances and pressures. However, the emotions of wrath, the comic spirit, and disgust do not have a place in his poetry, although there is an outburst of satiric anger in the rejected poem "Respondez!" If one must make a generalization about *Leaves of Grass* as a whole, then, one can describe the emotional curve of Whitman's poetry, even as the poet saw it himself, as a movement from "moods of towering pride and joy" (1876 "Preface," PW, 2:464, 466–467) through "crises of anguish" ("Long, Too Long, America," "Drum-Taps") to serene reflections on the spiritual world. Nonetheless, there is no strict consistency within this movement, for moods of all kinds—reassuring thoughts as well as pensive reflections—keep intervening at any given point of the curve or during any given period in the poet's life.

Another important contribution of the *Rasa* theory to poetic aesthetics is its concept of the dominant emotion and the subordination of secondary emotions to it within the structure of a single composition. Emotions or images of all sorts may get mixed up within a poem, but they must, through interanimation, necessarily become fused with and take on the coloration of one dominant emotion, which will be the dominant tone of the poem. This concept will help us to explain the inconsistencies/alternations of moods which give the look of incoherence to some of Whitman's poems. John Snyder is perceptive enough to notice these shifts in the poet's moods between passages of what he calls "lyrical" and "tragic" communion. But for him, tragic communion alone, in which the poet recognizes and respects the existential conditions of time and space (human limitations, in other words), is the genuine mode, and the lyrical affirmations of identity and transcendence are empty rhetoric and bluff.[15]

Other critics, too, for whom Whitman is primarily a poet of uncertainties, longing, and despair, point to the internal contradictions within the joyful

poems in support of their argument. These poems, no doubt, contain a mixture of images and reflections—joyful, erotic, and pensive: the suicide sprawl-
ing on the floor, the muted anguish of the woman watching the bathers, the
crises of erotic sensation, and the tragic episodes of Sections 34 and 36 of
"Song of Myself"; the "dark patches" of "Crossing Brooklyn Ferry"; the image
of the other self in "Open Road," "skulking and hiding" beneath appearances,
with "death under the breast-bones, hell under the skull-bones"; the tragic
episodes in "The Sleepers" of the beautiful gigantic swimmer, of the ship-
wreck, the defeat at Brooklyn, and the sad anecdote of the "red squaw"; the
dark questionings and feverishness of Section 5 of "Passage to India"; and the
"fierce enigmas" and "strangling problems" of Section 9. But the moods of
these passages are quickly swallowed up by the preponderant affirmations of
lyrical joy and by the concluding statements as well, so that this emotion
alone emerges as the dominant tone. A close analysis of these poems will reveal that the unhappy images/reflections are no more than transient episodes
in the flow of the dominant emotion and do not betray any weakness in the
poet's lyrical stance. For instance, the Blakean vision of the early sections of
"The Sleepers"—of human degradation, death, and violence—is dispelled by
the "dramatic change of mood"[16] in the later parts, to one of tranquil restoration. There is a dramatic reversal after the fifth section of "To Think of
Time," and the final assertion of conviction completely nullifies the previous
statements.

The foregoing outline of the approach in the light of the poetic emotions
will obviate the need to discover a procrustean mold into which Whitman's
many selves and the diversity of moods that his poetry exhibits must be neatly
fitted. In terms of *Rasa*, there is no stake in arguing either for Whitman's mys-
ticism/transcendentalism or for a unitary or divided self; no need to gloss over
the conflicts/crises to project a triumphantly emerging poetic self or to de-
emphasize the ecstatic elements to paint a self that is inwardly torn; no need to
ignore or explain away the physical/sexual passages or to suppress the expressions of transcendence and read in them underlying motives, needs, and fantasies. Whitman contains multitudes and resists anything better than his own
diversity. Each expression should be appreciated for what it is, without pronouncing a value judgment on the experience itself.

This approach avoids the epistemological and other mystifications (so common in our day) and focuses on the concrete, experiential content of the
poems—which can be shared by people of all ages and climes, rather than
limiting their significance to particular historical periods, ideological stances,
or cultural attitudes. Whitman's poetry should be valued, not for the ideas
merely, ennobling as they may be, but for its "gusto" (as Hazlitt termed it), for

its power of communicating experiences which can be lived and relived and contemplated over and over again.

NOTES

1. Betsy Erkkila, *Whitman the Political Poet* (New York: Oxford University Press, 1989), 103.

2. M. Wynn Thomas, *The Lunar Light of Whitman's Poetry* (Cambridge: Harvard University Press, 1987), 116.

3. Robert K. Martin, *The Homosexual Tradition in American Poetry* (Austin: University of Texas Press, 1979), 5.

4. Michael Moon, *Disseminating Whitman: Revision and Corporeality in Leaves of Grass* (Cambridge: Harvard University Press, 1991), 3–4.

5. David Kuebrich, *Minor Prophecy: Walt Whitman's New American Religion* (Bloomington: Indiana University Press, 1989).

6. Harold Aspiz, "Sexuality and the Language of Transcendence," *Walt Whitman Quarterly Review* 5 (Fall 1987): 1.

7. Martin, xvii.

8. Edwin Haviland Miller, *Walt Whitman's Poetry: A Psychological Journey* (Boston: Houghton Mifflin, 1968).

9. Stephen A. Black, *Whitman's Journeys into Chaos: A Psychoanalytical Study of the Poetic Process* (Princeton: University Press of Princeton, 1975), 46–47.

10. E. Fred Carlisle, *The Uncertain Self: Whitman's Drama of Identity* (East Lansing: Michigan State University Press, 1973), 41.

11. Graham Clarke, *Walt Whitman: The Poem as Private History* (New York: Vision Press, 1991), 7.

12. Harold Bloom, ed., *Modern Critical Views: Walt Whitman* (New York: Clark House, 1985), 2–3.

13. Bernard Duffey, *Poetry in America: Expression and Its Values in the Times of Bryant, Whitman, and Pound* (Durham: Duke University Press, 1978), 110 and passim.

14. Mitchell R. Breitweiser, "Who Speaks in Whitman's Poems?" in Peter C. Carafiol, ed., *American Renaissance: New Dimensions* (Lewisburg, Penn.: Bucknell University Press, 1983), 121.

15. John Snyder, *The Dear Love of Man: Tragic and Lyric Communion in Walt Whitman* (The Hague: Mouton, 1975).

16. R. W. French, "Whitman's Dream Vision: A Reading of 'The Sleepers,'" *Walt Whitman Quarterly Review* 8 (Summer 1990): 6.

Notes on Contributors

GAY WILSON ALLEN is professor emeritus of English at New York University. He is the general editor of *The Collected Writings of Walt Whitman* and the author or editor of over fifteen books on American poetry and American writers, including *The Solitary Singer: A Critical Biography of Walt Whitman* (1955, rev. 1985), *Walt Whitman Abroad* (1955), and *The New Walt Whitman Handbook* (1975, rev. 1986).

HAROLD ASPIZ is professor emeritus at California State University, Long Beach, and the author of *Walt Whitman and the Body Beautiful* (1980).

ROGER ASSELINEAU is professor emeritus at the University of Paris-Sorbonne, where he was chair of the English Department and director of the Center for Research in American Literature and Civilization. The co-editor of *Études Anglaises*, he is the author or editor of many books on American literature, including *The Evolution of Walt Whitman: The Creation of a Personality* (1960), *The Evolution of Walt Whitman: The Creation of a Book* (1962), and *The Transcendentalist Constant in American Literature* (1980); his 1972 translation of *Leaves of Grass* is the standard French version of Whitman's text.

V. K. CHARI is professor of English at Carleton University, Ottawa. He is the author of *Whitman in the Light of Vedantic Mysticism* (1964) and *Sanskrit Criticism* (1990).

BETSY ERKKILA is professor of English at the University of Pennsylvania and the author of *Walt Whitman among the French* (1980), *Whitman the Political Poet* (1988), and *The Wicked Sisters: Women Poets, Literary History, and Discord* (1991).

ED FOLSOM is professor and chair of English at the University of Iowa, where he edits the *Walt Whitman Quarterly Review* and directs the Walt Whitman Centennial Project. He is the author of *Walt Whitman's Native Representations* (1994) and the co-editor of *Walt Whitman: The Measure of His Song* (1981). He is currently co-editing, with Gay Wilson Allen, *Walt Whitman and the World.*

ARTHUR GOLDEN is professor emeritus of English at the City University of New York, City College. One of the editors of *Leaves of Grass: A Textual Variorum of the Printed Poems* (1980), he has also edited *Walt Whitman's Blue Book* (1968).

WALTER GRÜNZWEIG is professor and chair of American Studies at the University of Dresden. He is the author of books and articles on the relationship between German and American literature, including *Walt Whitmann: Die deutschsprachige Rezeption als interkulturelles Phänomen* (1990).

C. CARROLL HOLLIS is professor emeritus at the University of North Carolina, Chapel Hill. Among his many publications on Whitman is *Language and Style in Leaves of Grass* (1983).

GEORGE B. HUTCHINSON is associate professor of English and chair of the American Studies Program at the University of Tennessee, Knoxville. He is the author of many articles on American literature and of *The Ecstatic Whitman: Literary Shamanism and the Crisis of the Union* (1986); he is currently completing a book on American cultural nationalism and the Harlem Renaissance.

M. JIMMIE KILLINGSWORTH is associate professor of English and director of the Writing Programs at Texas A&M University. Among his many publications on Whitman are *Whitman's Poetry of the Body: Sexuality, Politics, and the Text* (1989) and *The Growth of Leaves of Grass: The Organic Tradition in Whitman Studies* (1993).

JEROME LOVING is professor of English at Texas A&M University and the author of *Walt Whitman's Champion: William Douglas O'Connor* (1978), *Emerson, Whitman, and the American Muse* (1984), and *Lost in the Customhouse:*

Authorship in the American Renaissance (1993). He has also edited *Leaves of Grass* and was the editor of *Civil War Letters of George Washington Whitman* (1975). He is currently at work on a biography of Whitman.

ROBERT K. MARTIN is professor and chair of English at the University of Montreal. He is the author of many publications on American literature, including *The Homosexual Tradition in American Poetry* (1979) and *Hero, Captain, and Stranger: Male Friendship, Social Critique, and Literary Form in the Sea Novels of Herman Melville* (1986); he also edited *The Continuing Presence of Walt Whitman: The Life after the Life* (1992).

JAMES E. MILLER, JR., is the Helen A. Regenstein Professor of Literature at the University of Chicago and the author or editor of over twenty books on American literature, including *A Critical Guide to Leaves of Grass* (1957), *Walt Whitman* (1962, rev. 1990), and *The American Quest for a Supreme Fiction: Whitman's Legacy in the Personal Epic* (1979).

JOEL MYERSON is professor of English at the University of South Carolina, where he edits *Studies in the American Renaissance*. Among his many editions, bibliographies, and critical collections are *Whitman in His Own Time* (1991), *The Walt Whitman Archive: A Facsimile of the Poet's Manuscripts* (1993), and *Walt Whitman: A Descriptive Bibliography* (1993).

VIVIAN R. POLLAK is professor of English at the University of Washington and the author of *Emily Dickinson: The Anxiety of Gender* (1986); she is currently at work on a gender analysis of Whitman's erotic experience.

KENNETH M. PRICE is professor of English at Texas A&M University, where he edits the *South Central Review*. He is the co-editor of *Dear Brother Walt: The Letters of Thomas Jefferson Whitman* (1984) and the author of *Whitman and Tradition: The Poet in His Century* (1990). He is currently working on a book about Whitman's role in American fiction.

M. WYNN THOMAS is senior lecturer at the University of Wales, College at Swansea. He is the author of numerous books on Welsh literature and *The Lunar Light of Whitman's Poetry* (1987); he edited a special edition of Whitman's *Drum-Taps* published by Gregynog Press in Wales (1992).

ALAN TRACHTENBERG is professor of English and American Studies at Yale University and the author of *Brooklyn Bridge: Fact and Symbol* (1965), *The*

Incorporation of America: Culture and Society in the Gilded Age (1982), and *Reading American Photographs: Images as History, Mathew Brady to Walker Evans* (1989).

JAMES PERRIN WARREN is associate professor of English at Washington and Lee University and the author of *Walt Whitman's Language Experiment* (1990).

Index of Names

Index of Whitman Works

Gramley Library
Salem College
Winston-Salem, NC 27108